A TREATISE ON MONEY

VOLUME II
THE APPLIED THEORY OF MONEY

MACMILLAN AND CO., Limited
LONDON · BOMBAY · CALCUTTA · MADRAS
MELBOURNE

A TREATISE ON MONEY

BY

JOHN MAYNARD KEYNES

FELLOW OF KING'S COLLEGE, CAMBRIDGE

IN TWO VOLUMES

VOLUME II

THE APPLIED THEORY OF MONEY

NEW YORK

HARCOURT, BRACE AND COMPANY

First published 1930

PRINTED IN GREAT BRITAIN
BY R. & R. CLARK, LIMITED, EDINBURGH

CONTENTS

VOLUME II

THE APPLIED THEORY OF MONEY

BOOK V

MONETARY FACTORS AND THEIR FLUCTUATIONS

CHAPTER 22

CHAPTER 23

CHAPTER 24

CHAPTER 25

CHAPTER 30

BOOK VII

THE MANAGEMENT OF MONEY

CHAPTER 31

CHAPTER 32

CHAPTER 33

CHAPTER 34

CHAPTER 35

CHAPTER 36

CHAPTER 37

CHAPTER 38

BOOK V

MONETARY FACTORS AND THEIR FLUCTUATIONS

CHAPTER 22

THE APPLIED THEORY OF MONEY

WE now pass from the Pure Theory of Money and a qualitative study of the characteristics of a System of Representative Money to the Applied Theory and a quantitative study of the facts as they exist in the leading Monetary Systems of to-day, chiefly in Great Britain and in the United States.

The plan of this volume is as follows.

In Book V. we shall treat of the Monetary Factors and their statistical fluctuations, such as the proportions in which the aggregate of Bank-money is divided between Savings-deposits and Cash-deposits, the Velocity of Circulation of Bank-money, and the causes which make this aggregate of Bank-money to be what it is. The somewhat detailed character of these chapters is essential to enable us to judge of the relative quantitative importance of different factors. For, when the aggregate of Bank-money has been determined, the statistics of the Savings-deposits are the most important indication as to how much of this aggregate is being employed in the Financial Circulation and how much is left for the Industrial Circulation ; and given the volume of the Industrial Circulation, the Velocities of Circulation determine, broadly speaking, what level of output and incomes this is capable of supporting.

In Book VI. we turn aside from what might be called " influences on the side of money " to " in-

fluences on the side of investment ", examining the
causes of fluctuations in the rate of investment and
illustrating the argument of this and the preceding
Books by analysing what happened on several typical
occasions in recent history.

In Book VII. we reach for the first time the norma-
tive side of our subject—namely, the question of what
ideal objectives ought to be aimed at by the Currency
Authorities of National Monetary Systems and also of
the world as a whole, of the obstacles in the way of
the attainment of these objectives, of the dilemmas
which sometimes present themselves, and of the best
means of solution.

In Book V. I may appear to the reader to be
reverting to the old-fashioned " quantity of money "
approach to the problem of price-determination, inasmuch as I shall be concentrating on the *supply* of
monetary facilities, or rather on the amount of them
available for the Industrial Circulation. It may be
well, therefore, that I should say a precautionary word
as to the relationship, as I conceive it, between the
quantity of money and the price-level.

If habits and methods in the receipt and disposal
of incomes are assumed unchanged, if the level of incomes and the volume of output are given, and if there
is no change in the velocity of circulation of the
business-deposits A, the amount of monetary facilities
needed in the Industrial Circulation is uniquely determined. If less than this is *available* after providing
for the requirements of the Financial Circulation, it
will be impossible to maintain the existing volume of
incomes. Furthermore, in equilibrium, when all the
factors of production are employed and Savings are
equal to Investment, not only does the volume of the
Industrial Circulation determine the volume of incomes, but it also determines the level of prices and,
subject to correction for fluctuations in the volume of
output and employment, the rate of earnings. That

is to say, *when the price-level is in equilibrium with the cost of production* the quantity of money available for the Industrial Circulation *does* (if habits and methods are unchanged) rule the situation; and the only modification which we need introduce into the traditional formula is the addition of the words " available for the Industrial Circulation ". The significance of the changes in the accepted theory which we have developed in Books III. and IV. lie in their application to the *modus operandi* of price-determination when equilibrium is disturbed, by reason of inequality between Savings and Investment, and during the transition from one position of equilibrium to another.

This change is, of course, formally compatible with the traditional Quantity Theory ;—indeed it must be, since the latter is an identity, a truism. But it is not brought out by the traditional theory in an instructive and intelligible form, and lies covered up, along with other factors, under the omnibus conception " velocity of circulation ".

Let us write our Quantity Equation as follows :

$$M' . V' = \Pi . O$$

where M' is the volume of the Industrial Circulation, O the volume of output, and Π the price-level of output ; then—so we have claimed—V' is a complex notion not identified with V, the Velocity of Circulation. It is compounded of two elements ;—one of them dependent on habits and methods of banking, business and industry, which is of a similar character to the traditional velocities of circulation, and the other dependent on the balance between Saving and Investment, being greater than unity when investment is in excess, equal to unity when investment and saving are equal, and less than unity when saving is in excess.

Now Book V. of this Treatise consists, in the main,

of a statistical study of the monetary elements on the left-hand side of this Equation, as distinguished from what we have called the investment elements; and these purely monetary elements are the same as, or similar to, those of which the traditional Quantity Equation takes account.

CHAPTER 23

THE PROPORTION OF SAVINGS-DEPOSITS TO CASH-DEPOSITS

THE meanings of Savings-deposits and of Cash-deposits have been defined in Chapter 3, and their relationships to the Financial Circulation and the Industrial Circulation in Chapter 15. Since the two together make up the total deposits, it follows that a fluctuation in the proportion of the Savings-deposits to the total deposits is liable to react on the volume of the Cash-deposits, and in particular on that of the Income-deposits, unless it is deliberately counteracted by a corresponding fluctuation in the volume of the total deposits. In this chapter we shall consider, on the basis of the statistical evidence, the extent to which the proportion of the Savings-deposits fluctuates in actual experience, so as to be in a position to consider the magnitude of the reaction of these fluctuations on the general monetary situation.

We saw in Chapter 3 that Deposit Accounts in England and Time Deposits in the United States roughly correspond to the Savings-deposits, whilst Current Accounts in England and Demand Deposits in the United States roughly correspond to the Cash-deposits. In the United States the law requires that the amounts of Time Deposits and Demand Deposits respectively shall be separately published, so that there is no difficulty in obtaining statistical *data*— provided we can regard fluctuations in Time Deposits as approximately representative of the Savings-

7

deposits. But in England it has been impossible hitherto to obtain any reliable indications, except by the courtesy of the banks themselves.

1. *England.*—As a result, however, of inquiries, which, though not exhaustive, represent a fair sample, I have obtained indications which are very interesting indeed and will serve to illustrate the practical, as well as the theoretical, importance under the present British banking system of transferences backwards and forwards between the deposit and the current accounts. At the same time we must remember, what has been pointed out in Chapter 3, that in England the dividing line between deposit and current accounts is decidedly blurred. The bulk of the deposits are held at quite short notice—seven to fourteen days— and as a matter of actual practice are often repaid on demand, a few days' interest being deducted in lieu of notice. The deposits definitely fixed for longer periods are said to be not above a quarter to a third of the total deposit accounts.

In pre-war days the normal percentage of fixed deposit to total deposits in England was generally assumed to have approached 50 per cent.[1] During the war deposit accounts were (relatively to the increase of deposits generally) very greatly depleted, and by 1919 they seem to have stood at not much more than one-third of the total deposits instead of one-half. On the basis of such information as I have been able to obtain from bankers,[2] the annual percentages of deposit and current accounts to total deposits seem to have moved as follows :

[1] Annual averages have been given by Lloyds Bank back to 1902. The percentages of fixed to total deposits were 41·8 in 1902, about 44 from 1903 to 1905, 46·4 in 1906, and about 48·5 from 1907 to 1914. This is very similar to post-war experience. The fixed deposits seem to have been depleted by the Boer War, to have recovered steadily thereafter towards 50 per cent, and to have had this recovery sharply stimulated by the collapse of " bull " markets in 1906–7.

[2] The figures given are the average of indications supplied to me by three of the " Big Five ". More recently two of these have published their figures.

PERCENTAGE OF DEPOSIT ACCOUNTS AND CURRENT ACCOUNTS
TO TOTAL DEPOSITS IN ENGLAND

	Deposit Accounts.	Current Accounts.
	Per Cent.	Per Cent.
1913	48	52
1919	34	66
1920	38	62
1921	44	56
1922	44	56
1923	43	57
1924	44	56
1925	45	55
1926	46	54
1927	46	54
1928	47	53
1929	48	52

Thus there has been a progressive restoration in the proportion of deposit accounts towards the pre-war figure almost uninterruptedly from 1919 to 1929.

Since the Midland Bank and Lloyds Bank now publish their percentage figures month by month—examples which will, I hope, be followed by the other banks—it will be useful to quote these figures alongside the more comprehensive estimate given above :

PERCENTAGE OF DEPOSIT ACCOUNTS TO TOTAL DEPOSITS

	Midland Bank.	Lloyds Bank.
	Per Cent.	Per Cent.
1919	28·6	39·3
1920	33·8	43·3
1921	39·7	49·3
1922	40·0	50·3
1923	40·2	48·5
1924	41·5	49·0
1925	42·7	50·4
1926	43·7	51·4
1927	44·3	52·6
1928	44·7	53·6
1929	46·8	54·8
1930 (6 mos.)	48·3	55·5

These figures show that the changes in the relative proportions of deposit and current accounts have been sufficiently large to cause the movements in total deposits to be a very misleading guide to the movements in current accounts—as is clearly brought out by the following table :

	Average Total Deposits of Nine Clearing Banks. 1924 = 100.	Assumed Proportion of Current Accounts to Total Deposits.	Calculated Total of Current Accounts. 1924 = 100.
1919	90 *	66	106
1920	100 *	62	111
1921	108	56	108
1922	106	56	106
1923	100	57	102
1924	100	56	100
1925	99	55	97
1926	100	54	96
1927	103	54	99
1928	106	53	100
1929	108	52	100

* Estimated figures.   The actual figures have never been published.

Thus, if these estimates are correct,[1] whilst total deposits may have been no higher in 1920 than in 1926, current accounts were 16 per cent higher. The continual transference from current to deposit account, brought about by the gradual recovery of the deposit accounts after their war depletion to their normal pre-war proportion, was, in fact, operating as a concealed measure of deflation, sufficient— assuming that it affected the Business-deposits and the Income-deposits equally—to explain a drop in the price-level of about 20 per cent without the

[1] If they are not, I hope that the bankers who are in a position to know will correct them.

help of any change in the volume of the total deposits.

These figures are particularly helpful towards explaining the magnitude of the fall of price-levels between 1920 and 1923, which was quite out of proportion to the fall, if any, in the total deposits, and also their subsequent history between 1923 and 1926. Between 1923 and 1926 the total Bank Deposits, as published, were unchanged, whilst the Consumption Index was also almost unchanged. The Total of Current Accounts, however, as is shown by the above table, fell from 102 to 96. Since the Volume of Output was almost certainly less in 1926 than in 1923, the decrease of Current Accounts during this period supplies an important missing part of the explanation of the course of monetary events.

The most striking contribution to the explanation of the course of monetary events which is supplied by the separation of the figures of Current Accounts from Total Deposits in England relates, however, to the War Period. It will be remembered that after the failure of the first War Loan in 1914, which had to be largely subscribed by the Bank of England and other Banks, there was an intensive campaign of propaganda to secure subscriptions to subsequent War Loans from the public. It was argued that subscriptions by the Banks were inflationary, whereas subscriptions from the public were not ; and this argument was held to cover even the case where members of the public took money off deposit-account to pay for their subscriptions to War Loans—indeed the Banks made special " patriotic " arrangements to facilitate this course. I do not think that it was noticed at the time by anyone that this procedure was capable of becoming a potent instrument of inflation. Actually such subscriptions had the same effect as if the Banks had subscribed directly themselves and had increased their current accounts by the full amount of these subscriptions. The transference of money held on deposit-account by the public, where it was not functioning as cash at all, to the current account of the Government by whom it was expended, thus swelling other current accounts, increased the quantity of active money quite out of proportion to any observable movement in the total deposits of the banks. Some of the deposit accounts thus disturbed were probably amongst the oldest standing and most reliable accounts of this kind which the banks held. If we were to suppose that no more than one-third of the pre-war deposit accounts were invested in War Loans under the influence of patriotic propaganda, then (supposing deposit accounts to have accounted for half the total deposits before the war) current accounts would be swollen by 33 per cent and would be sufficient to support price-levels this much higher than before. The character of the Government expenditure was, in fact, such that by far the greater part of it found its way rapidly into the Income-deposits, with the result that the transferences from Savings-deposits had their full effect in diminishing the purchasing power of money. The course of monetary events in Great Britain in 1915 and 1916 is, indeed, almost a perfect illustration of the manner in which such transferences can affect prices.

It is probable, therefore, that this unobserved factor of transferences backwards and forwards between deposit and current accounts played a con- siderable part both in the rise of British prices between 1914 and 1920 and in their fall between 1920 and 1926. We should, however, be able to judge of this more precisely as regards the past, and also to adjust our policy in the future, so as to take account of this factor, if all the Banks would agree to publish separately the figures of their deposit and of their current accounts, both retrospectively and henceforward.

There is, moreover, a reform of banking practice, as well as of banking publicity, which is indicated as desirable. The present practice of the British banks is to keep the same proportion of reserves against their deposit accounts as against their current accounts. In the United States, on the other hand, this is not so. The Member Banks of the Federal Reserve System are required by law to keep a reserve of only 3 per cent against their time deposits as compared with figures of from 7 to 13 per cent against their demand deposits. This greatly mitigates the inflationary or deflationary influence on the Industrial Circulation of fluctuations in that part of the Financial Circulation which is represented by the Savings-deposits. It would tend to a smoother working of the British Banking System in its effects on industry if the banks were to work to a very low reserve percentage against deposit accounts instead of to the same percentage as against current accounts.[1]

If, indeed, we could be assured that deposit accounts accurately corresponded to the Savings-deposits, it would be justifiable from some points of view to maintain no reserves at all against them—which would ensure that changes in the volume of the Savings-deposits need involve no changes in the aggregate of Cash-deposits. The practical argument against this course, and even against allowing a lower reserve ratio for deposit accounts than for current accounts, is the risk of encouraging banks to make private arrangements with, and concessions to, their customers, by which what were really Cash-deposits would masquerade as Savings-deposits, and so avoid

[1] The Royal Commission on Indian Currency (1926) has recommended (§ 161) the American arrangement for the proposed new Central Bank for India. Indian Banks are to keep 10 per cent of their demand liabilities and 3 per cent of their time liabilities with the Central Bank. Moreover, this arrangement has been in force in South Africa since 1923.

the necessity of providing a reserve. It is stated (see p. 17 below) that this evasion has in fact occurred to a certain extent in the United States. If this objection is held to be a good one on practical grounds, much the same result could be reached by the Central Bank having regard to the proportion of the Member Banks' deposits held on deposit- and on current-account respectively in deciding the appropriate level at which the aggregate of the reserves of the Member Banks might be allowed to stand. At present in Great Britain it is probable that the Bank of England does not even know the proportion, and much more probable that it does not appreciate its relevance.

Granted that it is often desirable that the Central Bank should pay attention to the volume of the Financial Circulation with a view to avoiding Capital Inflations or Deflations, which are liable to react sooner or later on the volume of Investment, nevertheless any change is desirable which would make it easier for the Central Bank to consider and deal separately with the Industrial and the Financial Circulations.

2. *The United States.*—This brings us to a study of the same phenomenon in the United States—though for the reason given above it cannot be as disturbing a factor there as it is in Great Britain. Nevertheless it is significant to notice that it was the growth of time deposits in the Federal Reserve System between 1925 and 1929 which made possible the great increase in the loans and investments of the Member Banks without a corresponding increase in their reserve requirements and, at the same time, without an increase in commodity prices.

The statistics of the Federal Reserve System is a separate study in itself, upon which I am not qualified to embark. The following table, however, of Demand and Time Deposits respectively will serve to illustrate the significance of fluctuations, in the United States

equally with Great Britain, of the ratio between
Savings-deposits and Cash-deposits :

PERCENTAGE TO TOTAL DEPOSITS [1]

	Time Deposits.	Demand Deposits.
1918	23	77
1919	24	76
1920	28	72
1921	32	68
1922	32	68
1923	35	65
1924	36	64
1925	37	63
1926	38	62
1927	40	60
1928	42	58

Thus the upward tendency of the ratio of time
to demand deposits has been more or less the same
in direction and in amount in the United States
as in Great Britain. Owing to the much lower
percentage of reserves required against Time Deposits, this movement has permitted a substantially greater growth of available Bank Credit on
a given basis of Reserves than could have existed
otherwise. Moreover, if there had not been so great
a growth of Time Deposits, there could not have been
so great an extension of Bank Credit without raising
prices. This has been a healthy development. But
if the same reserve practices had been observed as in
Great Britain, this growth of Time Deposits would
have exercised a severe deflationary influence. Even

---

[1] These figures are based on the average of the amounts held on the
" call " dates (3 to 5 a year) ; see *Thirteenth Annual Report of the Federal
Reserve Board* (1926), p. 142. The Time Deposits include postal-savings
deposits. Very slightly different figures would result from taking " net
demand deposits " instead of " demand deposits ".

as it is (with the requirement of a 3 per cent reserve), it has been an influence towards lower price-levels on a given basis of reserves than those reserves would have supported otherwise.

The different effects of the British and American banking practices respectively as regards the percentage reserves held against Time Deposits can be illustrated by the following calculation. Taking the average reserves held in America against Demand Deposits at 11 per cent and against Time Deposits at 3 per cent, and the reserves held in Great Britain against Total Deposits at 11 per cent; then if 10 per cent of the total deposits are transferred from demand account to time account, so that time deposits increase from 30 per cent to 40 per cent of total deposits, the effect on price-levels in the United States is to bring about, other influences apart, a tendency towards a fall of 4 per cent, whilst a similar transference in Great Britain would produce a tendency for price-levels to fall 14 per cent.

In fact the great growth of Time Deposits in the United States, which doubled between 1920 and 1929, allowed the Financial Circulation to increase during those years to an extent which, with British reserve usages, would have involved either a severe fall of prices resulting from the contraction of the Industrial Circulation or a proportionate increase in reserves. The British system in its anxiety to prevent the possibility of inflationary activities on the part of the banks as purveyors of money for industrial purposes allows them no elasticity in the performance of their other function, namely, of meeting the far more fluctuating requirements of the Financial Circulation. The American system, on the other hand, puts only a slight break on the expansion of the Financial Circulation.

For preserving industrial stability the American system functions with the greater wisdom and effectiveness. It can be objected on the other side that this system may be capable, for this very reason, of allowing Capital Inflation to proceed to lengths which would be impossible on the British system. But if the maintenance of industrial stability and the optimum output is to be—as, on the whole, I think it ought to be—our main objective, then the American system is, nevertheless, preferable.

I should add that the American statistics must be read, quantitatively speaking, with caution. The increase in Time Deposits, according to the *Report of the Federal Reserve Board* (1926), p. 8, " to some extent represents merely a transfer from demand to time deposits caused by the lower percentages of reserves required against time deposits and the greater efforts made by member banks to encourage savings accounts ".[1] This is balanced, however, by the stringent character of the provision which reckons all funds held at less than thirty days' notice in the demand category—an excellent provision in itself, since a system is to be welcomed which encourages as strict a segregation as possible between savings deposits and cash deposits.

Further, the rate of growth of Time Deposits in the United States since the war is partly due to the greater efforts now made by the Member Banks, under the stimulus of the low reserve proportion required to be held against them, to secure this business at the expense of the Mutual Savings Banks. The following table, given by Mr. W. R. Burgess (*The Reserve Banks and the Money Market*, p. 38), shows the result of combining the two classes of Savings-deposits :

[1] This is confirmed by Professor Parker Willis, " Great Changes in American Banking " (*The Banker*, May 1927, p. 385), where he attributes the growth of time deposits to excessive competition between the banks, which leads them, not only to offer high rates of interest, but also to encourage customers to shift over into the time category funds which would normally have been held on demand.

(In millions of dollars)

Year.	Savings Deposits.			Total Individual Deposits.	Per cent of Savings and Time Deposits to Total.
	Mutual Savings Banks.	Time Deposits in Commercial Banks.	Total.		
1911	3,459	4,504	7,963	15,604	51
1914	3,910	4,802	8,712	18,891	46
1916	4,102	5,357	9,459	22,065	43
1918	4,382	7,153	11,535	24,518	47
1920	5,058	10,256	15,314	32,361	47
1922	5,818	11,761	17,579	36,336	48
1924	6,693	14,496	21,189	41,064	51
1926	7,525	17,171	24,696	47,472	52

This table is chiefly interesting, perhaps, for the remarkable stability of social practices in changing circumstances which it shows ; and also for the remarkable proximity between the corresponding American and British figures,—for if, to make them more nearly comparable with the above, we were to include in the case of Great Britain the Post Office Savings Bank deposits, the British pre-war and post-war percentages corresponding to the last column above would both be about 54,[1] as compared with 51 and 52 for the United States.

3. *Elsewhere.*—It is evident that the normal percentage of Savings-deposits to total bank-deposits will vary widely from country to country in accordance with the varying customs and traditions of the banking public. I do not venture to quote figures for European countries with any confidence, since banking statistics are apt to mean different things in different countries. Some comprehensive figures are available, however, for Germany. On March 31, 1928,

[1] The inclusion of the Trustee Savings Banks would raise the figure by 1 or 2 per cent.

83 credit banks (including the 6 principal Berlin banks) 22 State and provincial banks, and 17 Giro-zentralen, having altogether deposits of £688,000,000 (exclusive of cheques in transit), held 39 per cent of these at call within seven days, 50 per cent at more than seven days' and less than three months' notice, and 11 per cent at more than three months' notice. In the case of Australia the fixed deposits at interest, many of them fixed for one or two years, were estimated in 1927 at 60 per cent of the total deposits of £285,000,000.

CHAPTER 24

THE VELOCITIES OF CIRCULATION

(i.) THE CONCEPTION OF "VELOCITY" AS APPLIED TO BANK MONEY

THE expression " velocity (or rapidity) of circulation " first came into use before the development of the cheque system, when the currency was mainly composed of coins and bank-notes. The " velocity " measured the average frequency with which a coin (or a bank-note) changed hands, and thus indicated the " efficiency " of the currency for the transaction of business.[1] This was a definite and unambiguous idea. But it was necessary for its clarity that it should be applied only to the coins and notes which were being actually used *as money*, and not to hoards. For, otherwise, an increase (or decrease) in the amount of the hoards would appear as causing a decrease (or increase) in the velocity of the money, whereas what they were really causing was a decrease (or increase) in the supply, or *quantity*, of effective money. Thus it has been usual to limit the " velocity of circulation ", so far as practicable, to the effective money

---

[1] There is also, however, a very ancient tradition in favour of regarding " velocity " as connected with the ratio between a country's annual income and its stock of cash. I return to this in the next section of this chapter. For a most interesting historical summary of the development of the conception of velocity, bearing on this and other matters, see Holtrop's " Theories of the Velocity of Circulation of Money in Earlier Economic Literature " (*Economic Journal History Supplement*, Jan. 1929).

or money in active circulation, and not to stultify the conception by watering down the velocity of the money in circulation by including money which was not in circulation at all, but was being used as a " store of value " and therefore had *no* velocity ; changes in the amount of hoards being allowed for by regarding these as involving changes in the supply or quantity of circulating money rather than as changes in its velocity. For example, in estimating the velocity of circulation of money in India, it has been the practice to exclude hoarded rupees as far as possible ; and even in the days of open mints, it was not usual to include in the stock of circulating money the hoarded ingots and ornaments held as a store of value by the nobles and the people of the country. A reduction of these hoards, as a result of famine for example, is more conveniently described as increasing the quantity of circulating money than as increasing the velocity of circulation.

When we extend the conception to Bank-Money, an analogous question arises whether we should take the total deposits or the cash deposits as representing the volume of money. It has been not uncommon to treat the whole of the deposits as belonging to the active circulation for this purpose,[1] defining the velocity of circulation, when applied to Bank-Money, as being measured by the ratio of the total volume of cheque transactions per unit of time to the total volume of the Bank Deposits. In England, where we have no separate statistics of the deposit-accounts and the current-accounts, this is tantamount to treating " hoards " as cash for the purpose of computing the velocity. For we are treating as current money what is really a " store of value "—with the result that variations in the amount of this store

---

[1] *E.g.* Professor Pigou takes this course (*Industrial Fluctuations*, chap. xv.), but not Professor Irving Fisher, who limits the application of " velocity " to the demand deposits.

appear in the misleading guise of variations in the velocity of circulation. For reasons which we have made clear in Chapter 23 this inconvenient terminology is liable to stand in the way of drawing the right conclusions.

To avoid this difficulty, I propose to employ two terms, namely *Velocity* (V) and *Efficiency* (E) ;[1] of which the latter represents the ratio of the Bank Clearings to the Total Deposits. This leaves us free to use the expression " velocity of circulation " to denote unambiguously the velocity or rate of turnover of what is truly serving the purposes of cash, namely the Cash Deposits. It follows that $E = Vw$, where w is the proportion of the Cash-deposits to the total deposits. It is not inappropriate to call the expression E the *Efficiency* or *Cash-Efficiency* of Bank-Money. For the greater this fraction becomes, the greater is the volume of cash-turnover which corresponds to a given volume of Bank-Money ;—a growth of savings-deposits decreasing, and a falling away increasing, the " efficiency " of Bank-Money for cash purposes.

(ii.) The Velocity of the Income-deposits and of the Business-deposits distinguished

Even more important, however, than the distinction between the Velocity (V) of the Cash-deposits and the Efficiency (E) of the total deposits, is the distinction between V_1, the Velocity of the Income-deposits, and V_2, the Velocity of the Business-deposits. The expression V is an average of two quite different things, and in a sense is not a true velocity at all. V is capable of changing, even though there is no change in either V_1 or V_2, as a result of a change in the propor-

---

[1] In an earlier chapter I have used the letter E to stand for " Earnings ". I hope that this duplication of the symbol will not lead to confusion.

tions of the Cash-deposits which represent Income-deposits and Business-deposits respectively ; just as the velocity of transport of London passengers by tram and train might increase without there being any change in the velocities of trams or trains, because of an increase in the proportion of passengers travelling by trains.

Thus if, as before, M_1, M_2, M_3 and M represent the Income-deposits, the Business-deposits, the Savings-deposits and the total deposits, the velocities of M_1, M_2 and M_3 are V_1, V_2 and zero, the average weighted velocity of M_1 and M_2 is V, and the average weighted velocity, or, as I have called it, the efficiency of M_1, M_2 and M_3, *i.e.* of M, is E ; so that, if B is the total volume of cash-transactions or money-turnover, we have

$$B = M_1V_1 + M_2V_2 = V(M_1 + M_2) = E(M_1 + M_2 + M_3) = EM.$$

It is obvious from this that E and V may vary, even though V_1 and V_2 are constant, as a result of variations in the ratios of M_1, M_2 and M_3 to M. We have, therefore, to distinguish between changes in the composites V and E due to changes in the true velocities V_1 and V_2, and those due to changes in $\dfrac{M_1}{M}$, $\dfrac{M_2}{M}$ and $\dfrac{M_3}{M}$.

This distinction will enable us, I think, to clear up a very ancient confusion. From the earliest literature on the subject, as Dr. Holtrop has shown,[1] monetary theorists have oscillated between an inclination to regard Velocity (or Rapidity) as a relation between the national stock of money and the national income, and an inclination to regard it as a relation between the stock of money and the total volume of transactions. The earlier writers were mainly influenced by the former conception, but during the nineteenth century the latter has gained ground, until

[1] *Op. cit., passim.*   Also his *De Omloopssnelheid van het Geld.*

it has now become somewhat firmly established,
especially in contemporary American literature, by
the writings of Professor Irving Fisher. Nevertheless
clear traces of the former are still to be found not only
in John Stuart Mill, but also—as we shall see—in the
writings of Professor Schumpeter and Professor Pigou.

The element of confusion is this. If we are to
interest ourselves in the relationship between the
average stock of money and the national income, we
must mean by the former the average stock held by
the members of the public as enjoyers of income, *i.e.*
the income-deposits, and not the total stock of money
including the business-deposits. The relationship
between the total annual receipts of income-receivers
and the average stock of money held by them is one
thing, which we call the velocity of the income-
deposits ; and the relationship between the total flow
of transactions for all purposes and the average stock
of money held for all purposes is another thing, which
we call the velocity of the cash-deposits. But the
relationship between the total annual receipts of
income-receivers and the average stock of money
held for all purposes is a hybrid conception having
no particular significance. Yet it is something of
this kind which turns up in economic literature over
and over again. For example, Professor Pigou, in
a recent discussion round this problem (*Industrial
Fluctuations*, chap. xv.), distinguishes three kinds of
" Velocity ". Velocity in his first sense (*op. cit.* p.
152)—the one for which he has, I think, a preference
—is measured by the ratio of the *money income* of
the community to the total stock of money ; his
second by the ratio of the money value of the quantity of *income goods turned over for cash* to the total
stock of money ; and the third by the money value
of the quantity of *all kinds of things turned over for
cash* to the total stock of money. The third of these
is, in my terminology, the velocity (V) of the Cash-

deposits, or, if Professor Pigou includes the Savings-deposits in " money ", it is the efficiency (E) of Bank-money. But the first of them $= \dfrac{M_1}{M} V_1$ in my notation, and is, therefore, the product of two quite different things. It is as though he were to divide the passenger-miles travelled in an hour by passengers in trams by the aggregate number of passengers in trams and trains and to call the result a " velocity ". Professor Schumpeter, also, has employed the term in what is, I think, nearly the same way.[1]

(iii.) THE VELOCITY OF THE INCOME-DEPOSITS

Since we do not at present possess for any country even an estimate of the amount of the Income-deposits separately from the Business-deposits, it is impracticable to calculate their velocity directly by comparing their amount with the National Income. It is possible, however, to arrive at some estimate of the approximate limits within which this velocity is likely to lie by general considerations based on what we know of the habits of the community.

The velocity of the Income-deposits is a function of the community's habits in regard to the intervals between wages and salary payments, whether weekly, monthly or quarterly,[2] and so forth, as to whether

---

[1] Whether the expression " circuit velocity of money " used by Messrs. Foster and Catchings (in *Profits*) is intended in my sense or in that of Professors Pigou and Schumpeter, I am not quite sure.

[2] This point was quite clearly apprehended by Sir William Petty in his *Verbum Sapienti* (1664), quoted by Dr. Holtrop (*op. cit.*), in a passage where he is considering the adequacy of the money in circulation : " The expense being 40 millions, if the revolutions were in such short Circles, viz., weekly, as happens among poorer artisans and labourers, who receive and pay every Saturday, then 40/52 parts of 1 million would answer these ends. But if the Circles be quarterly, according to our custom of paying rent and gathering taxes, then 10 millions were requisite. Wherefore supposing payments in general to be a mixed Circle between one week and thirteen, then add 10 millions to 40/52, the half of the which will be 5¼, so as if we have 5½ millions we have enough."

they disburse their income regularly or irregularly between income-dates, and as to what proportion of their incomes they carry forward from one income-date over the next. More precisely :

Let R = the annual income in question,

x = the number of times incomes are paid annually (*e.g.* $x = 52$ if incomes are paid weekly).

Let us assume that incomes are spent at a regular level rate between one income-date and the next, and that fluctuations are concentrated on the amount carried forward at the end of each income-period, *i.e.* on the amount of income-deposits in hand just before an income-date (this assumption is really no more than a matter of arithmetical convenience) ; and let the average amount so carried forward be $\dfrac{R}{y}$.

It follows from this that the average level of the income-deposits is $\left(\dfrac{1}{2x} + \dfrac{1}{y}\right)R$, and, therefore, that their velocity $V_1 = \dfrac{2xy}{2x + y}$.

The numerical value of V_1 on various hypotheses is easily calculated. If incomes are paid weekly, *i.e.* $x = 52$, and $\dfrac{R}{y}$ is three weeks' income, $V_1 = 15$ approx. ; whilst if $\dfrac{R}{y}$ is one week's income, $V_1 = 35$. If incomes are paid monthly, *i.e.* $x = 12$, and $\dfrac{R}{y}$ is a fortnight's income, $V_1 = 12$. If incomes are paid quarterly, *i.e.* $x = 4$, and $\dfrac{R}{y}$ is one month's income, $V_1 = 5$ approx. The reader is free to make any other hypothesis which seems to him to be plausible. It is evident that the shorter the intervals at which incomes are paid, the larger will be the sum carried forward on the average in proportion to the amount of each income-payment, because for given incomes the more numerous will be the disbursements which fall at longer intervals than income-payments—*e.g.* holiday expenses.

It would not be difficult by means of a sampling inquiry to ascertain what proportion of their annual incomes typical members of typical classes hold on the average in cash or on current account. Failing this, I venture to guess, including in the definition of income-deposits both notes and bank-balances, that in England at the present time the value of V_1 may be somewhere in the neighbourhood of 12 per annum, being perhaps 17 for weekly wage-earners and about 10 for those paid monthly and quarterly, etc. This means that *on the average* a weekly wage-earner would hold cash equal to about 3 weeks' income, whilst the rest of the community would hold cash and current bank-balances equal to about 5 weeks' income, the average for the community as a whole working out at nearly a month's income.[1] These figures are for the balances held on the average of the year and are compatible with substantially higher balances at quarter-days, etc.

These figures are, of course, in the absence of statistical evidence, no better than guesses intended to indicate the probable order of magnitude of the quantities involved and to stimulate the production of better statistics in future. Nevertheless the figures given would tally reasonably well with the known facts. For if we take the incomes of the weekly wage-earners without banking accounts at £1,700,000,000 per annum and those of others at £3,000,000,000 per annum,[2] it would follow from the

---

[1] Perhaps this is much too high for weekly wage-earners and somewhat too low for others. If so, notes held for business purposes must be in excess of my estimate.

[2] These two figures add up to more than the net income of the country, because it is the gross income (before deduction of the interest on the National Debt, etc.) which is relevant to the present calculation.

above that the average quantity of Notes held as income-cash by the former class would be £100,000,000, and the average quantity of Notes and Income-deposits held by the latter would be £300,000,000, of which, let us say, £275,000,000 would be Bank-deposits and £25,000,000 Notes. Since the active Note Circulation (*i.e.* notes in circulation not held by the banks) is probably about £250,000,000, the above assumption would leave £125,000,000 of Notes held otherwise, of which (say) £100,000,000 might be Business-cash and £25,000,000 Savings-cash (*i.e.* hoards held by those with no bank-accounts) ; and since bank balances on current account are probably about £1,075,000,000 (on the average of the year), it would leave £800,000,000 to cover the Business-deposits and disguised Savings-deposits. All these figures seem quite plausible. For if we raise the velocity for the salaried classes to 15, this would diminish the Bank Income-deposits to £175,000,000 (which seems much too low) and raise the Business-deposits, etc., to £900,000,000. On the other hand, a reduction of the velocity for weekly wage-earners seems scarcely compatible with the known facts of the volume of note issue ; whilst any material reduction of the velocity for the salaried classes would raise the Bank Income-deposits to what would appear to be an improbably high figure in relation to the Business-deposits. If any amendment is necessary it is likely to be in the direction of increasing the estimated velocity for wage-earners. This would change the average distribution of notes in active circulation as between earners and business, but would not affect the above general conclusions relating to bank-money.

In defining the Savings-deposits and the Income-deposits in Chapter 3, we pointed out that the line between the two is not quite precise. A man who has Savings-deposits, upon which he can fall back if necessary, may regard this as a reason for economis-

ing in the amount of his income-deposits. Some
statistics relating to the amount of the Savings-
deposits will, therefore, be in place here. In 1926
the deposit-accounts in Great Britain amounted,
according to our estimate below (p. 31), to about
£850,000,000, not the whole of which, however, would
be held for the account of private individuals. The
Savings - deposits in the Post Office and Trustee
Savings Banks, which broadly speaking are the
corresponding thing for weekly wage-earners who
have no bank-account, were in that year about
£370,000,000 (including Ireland). Thus the total
Savings-deposits of private individuals may have
been somewhere about £1,000,000,000, which is equal
to about a quarter of a year's income. If, therefore,
our estimates are correct, the Income-deposits, including Income-cash, are between one-tenth and one-
twelfth of a year's income, and the Savings-deposits
about a quarter of a year's income.

The fact of some important disbursements, against
which income has to be accumulated, being made at
longer intervals than those between the date at
which the majority of wages and salaries are paid,
is clearly responsible for reducing the velocity of
circulation below what it would otherwise be. The
most important of these are probably quarterly rents,
half-yearly rates and income-tax, annual payments
of insurance premiums, holidays and Christmas
extravagance (according to Mr. Burgess, *op. cit.* p. 75,
department stores in New York and other cities
usually do about one-seventh of their year's business
in the month of December alone). The payment of
salaries at such long intervals as quarterly, harvest
receipts to agriculturalists at annual intervals, and
the payment of interest and dividends usually (in
Great Britain) at half-yearly intervals also operate
in the direction of reducing the velocity of circulation.
As has been pointed out already, the more nearly

the receipts and disbursements of ordinary individuals
synchronise in date the less will be the average cash-
requirements in proportion to income, and the greater,
therefore, the velocity of circulation. Thus the velocity of circulation is to a great extent a function of
social habits and practices.

For this reason one would expect the velocity of
the Income-deposits to be relatively stable from one
year to the next, although it might show a definite
trend over a longer period due to a progressive change
of custom. But this conclusion is subject to one
important qualification. Many individuals are unable
or unwilling to adjust their expenditure quickly to
a change in their incomes, especially downwards.
Thus at a time when money-incomes are changing,
the sums carried forward from one income-date over
the next may also tend to change in the same direction.
That is to say, the first brunt of falling incomes will
be borne by income-balances, and also the first
advantage of rising incomes. For example, if Unemployment and bad times were to reduce the
working-class average holdings of cash from three and
a half weeks' income to two and a half weeks', and the
middle-class holdings from five weeks' to four weeks',
the result would be to increase the corresponding
velocities of circulation from 15 to 20 and from 10
to 13, and the average from 12 to 15 ; and similarly
in good times the velocity of circulation might be
diminished below the normal. But there is no reason
to expect that the abnormal figures would be lasting.

(iv.) The Velocity of the Business-deposits

In the case of the Business-deposits we have no
secure *data* on which to base our guesses, corresponding
to the probable amount of balances in proportion to
income held by individual consumers. On the other
hand, if our guesses about the volume of the Income-

deposits and of the Savings-deposits can be regarded as reliable, we can deduce the volume and velocity of the Business-deposits from the statistics available for the total deposits and the total clearings.

There are many pitfalls and a wide margin for error in our figures; but here again it should be possible to make a fair shot at the order of magnitude of the quantities involved, which is all we require in order to make progress in our general argument.

1. *Great Britain*

We will begin by attempting to calculate the velocity of the Cash-deposits, *i.e.* the weighted average of V_1 and V_2, the velocities of the Income-deposits and the Business-deposits respectively. The following table applies to England and Wales : [1]

(£ Million)

	(1) Total Clearings.*	(2) Total Deposits on Dec. 31.	(3) Current accounts.		(4) Crude Velocity (Ratio of 1 to 3).
			% of Total.	Amount.	
1909	14,215	711	52	370	38
1913	17,336	836	52	435	40
1920	42,151	2012	62	1247	34
1921	36,717	2023	56	1133	32
1922	38,958	1885	56	1056	37
1923	38,429	1856	57	1058	36
1924	41,414	1843	56	1032	40
1925	42,302	1835	55	1009	42
1926	41,453	1878	54	1014	41
1927	43,261	1923	54	1038	42
1928	45,878	1982	53	1050	44
1929	46,495	1940	52	1009	46

* Including Provincial Clearings.

[1] The figures for Great Britain, including Scotland, would probably be about 10 per cent greater.

These figures are of value for the purpose of indicating the variability of the velocity of the Cash-deposits, and therefore, assuming that the velocity of the Income-deposits is approximately constant, of the variability of the velocity of the Business-deposits. But before we can reach an estimate of the absolute value of this velocity certain corrections are necessary. In the first place, the total clearings, as already explained, do not cover the total cheque-transactions, since they do not include internal clearings between a bank's own customers or local clearings between banks where there is no official clearing-house. Now that the bulk of the business is done by so small a number of banks as five, this must involve a serious error. To reach the aggregate of the total cheque-transactions, we must probably increase the total clearings by at least 35 [1] per cent, making the total for England and Wales £58,725 million on the average of the years 1926–28. In the second place, the total Deposits, as published on Dec. 31 of each year, certainly overstate the average figure for the year, probably by as much as 6 per cent and perhaps by as much as 10 per cent. If, therefore, we raise column (1) in the above table by 35 per cent and reduce columns (2) and (3) by 6 per cent, the crude velocity given in column (4) will be increased by 43 per cent. Thus our best estimate of the average velocity of the Cash-deposits from 1924–29 is raised to about 60 per annum.

These estimates for the English banking system as a whole may be compared with some more exact figures with which I have been supplied by the courtesy of Barclays Bank. This Bank compiles annual aggregates of the *total* debits passed through its books, *i.e.* of the

---

[1] Even in the United States, where there are innumerable banks, it is estimated that only about two-thirds of the cheques drawn pass through the clearings (*vide* J. S. Lawrence, " Borrowed Reserves and Bank Expansion ", *Quarterly Journal of Economics*, 1928, p. 614).

total volume of cheque-transactions, and not merely of those passed through the clearings, and these aggregates can be divided by the actual average amounts held on current account. The results are as follows :

VELOCITY OF CURRENT ACCOUNTS IN ENGLAND

	Barclays Bank (actual figures).	The Banks as a whole * (estimated).
1924	49	57
1925	51	60
1926	55	59
1927	58	60
1928	58	63

* This column is the " crude " velocity, as calculated above, increased by 43 per cent. As these pages are being passed through the press, it is announced that the banks as a whole have decided to publish the figures of total debits.

It is evident that the velocity for any particular bank will be influenced by the extent to which it is the bank's practice to require its customers to keep a minimum balance on current account as a means of remunerating the bank, in preference to other methods of remuneration ; and also, in a large degree, by the extent to which it participates in high-velocity business such as Stock Exchange and other financial transactions.

From the above and from our previous estimates relating to the Income-deposits we can deduce an estimate of the velocity of the Business-deposits. Our previous arguments indicate the following approximate figures in round numbers for Great Britain (1926–28):[1]

Total Cheque-transactions	.	.	.	. £Mn.64,500
Total Current Accounts .	.	.	.	. £Mn.1,075
Velocity of Bank Cash-deposits	.	.	.	60

[1] The figures for clearings and for Cash-deposits just given, which relate to England and Wales, are increased by 10 per cent to allow for Scotland.

Bank Income-deposits	£Mn.275
Velocity of Bank Income-deposits . . .	11 [1]
Cheque-transactions against Income-deposits .	£Mn.3000
Business-deposits	£Mn.800
Cheque-transactions against Business-deposits .	£Mn.61,500
∴ Velocity of Business-deposits . . .	77

To sum up, the best guesses we can make on the basis of existing statistics are that in England the volumes of the Bank Income-deposits, Business-deposits and Savings-deposits are roughly in the proportions 1 to 3 to 4 ($M_3 = 4M_1$, $M_2 = 3M_1$), whilst their velocities are (V_1) 11, (V_2) 70-80, and zero.[2] But these guesses at the normal proportions between the different types of deposit must not lead the reader to forget what is an essential part of our analysis, namely, that these proportions are within limits *variable*, with the result that changes in E $\left(= \dfrac{M_1V_1 + M_2V_2}{M_1 + M_2 + M_3} \right)$ or in V $\left(= \dfrac{M_1V_1 + M_2V_2}{M_1 + M_2} \right)$ may be due not only to changes in V_1 and V_2, but to changes in the ratios between M_1, M_2 and M_3. Indeed I lean to the view that the velocity of Bank-deposits held for a given purpose does not readily change to any great extent except over long periods, and that the observed sharp short-period fluctuations in the efficiency (E) of the currency or in the velocity (V) of the Cash-deposits taken as a whole may often be due mainly to variations in the proportions of the deposits held for different purposes. We shall return to this matter in Section (v.) of this chapter.

---

[1] This is consistent with our previous estimate of a velocity of 10 for income-cash, if we include the encashment of cheques " to self " for notes as cheque-transactions against income-deposits, but exclude such changes of one kind of money for another in our previous calculation.

[2] Adam Smith concluded in a well-known passage (*Wealth of Nations*, Bk. II. chap. ii.) that the velocity of circulation of business-cash was *less* than that of income-cash. But the argument by which he supports this, namely that the individual transactions are smaller in the latter case and that " small sums circulate much faster than large ones ", is not impressive, and was probably invalid even in his own day.

I should remind the reader that we have been dealing above with the velocity of " current accounts " in the sense of this term ordinarily adopted by British banks, and that the velocity of the " cash facilities " (see Chapter 3) would therefore differ from this. For we have had to include in "current accounts" the fixed minimum deposits retained by customers by agreement with their banks to remunerate the latter, but on the other hand have made no allowance for unused overdraft facilities. Perhaps these two sources of error may be regarded as roughly cancelling one another out.

2. *The United States*

The corresponding figures for the United States rest on a more secure statistical basis than the above. The pioneer work, in this case as in so many others relating to monetary statistics, was done by Professor Irving Fisher.[1] Subsequently Dr. Burgess [2] made a careful statistical examination for the period Jan. 1919 to Feb. 1923. Over such a period as this the figures naturally showed, not only an important seasonal fluctuation, but a wide cyclical fluctuation (seasonal range between maximum and minimum about 20 per cent and cyclical range at least 30 per cent). But as regards the average velocity during this period, Dr. Burgess concluded that for the whole country it was between 25 and 35 times a year, and probably under rather than over 30. This average figure concealed, however, wide variations for different parts of the country ranging from 74 for New York and 46 for Chicago to 20 for Buffalo and Rochester and 10 for Syracuse.

More recently Mr. Snyder has made further

---

[1] Professor Fisher's guesses have turned out too high. Since my guesses for England are not much better based than were his for the United States twenty-five years ago, they also may suffer from the same defect.

[2] " Velocity of Bank Deposits ", *Journal of the American Statistical Association*, June 1923.

investigations, which add three years to the period
dealt with by Dr. Burgess and cover 1919–1926.
Mr. Snyder's figures, for which he claims that the
error does not exceed 5 per cent, broadly confirm
Dr. Burgess's. But they bring out even more clearly
the wide divergences of the average for different
parts of the country, as the following table [1] shows :

CASH-DEPOSITS IN U.S.A.

	Velocity.			Whole Country.	
	New York City.	141 Cities including New York.	Whole Country.	Volume of cheque payments. Billions of dollars.	Volume of Cash-deposits. Billions of dollars.
1919	75·2	42·3	28·8	546·8	18·99
1920	74·1	41·9	27·9	587·7	21·08
1921	68·3	38·5	24·7	484·0	19·63
1922	75·8	40·5	26·1	533·9	20·47
1923	79·1	41·4	25·8	570·3	22·11
1924	79·6	40·9	25·5	600·1	23·53
1925	87·7	44·2	25·1	653·4	25·98
1926	..	..	27·2	695·3	25·57
Average 1919–25	77·1	41·4	26·3	..	..

It will be noticed that the average figure for New
York, which is dominated by the Business-deposits,
namely 77·1, is very near my figure, namely 77,[2] for

[1] The figures for New York and the 141 Cities are taken from Snyder's
Business Cycles and Measurements, p. 294 ; those for the whole country
from Wesley Mitchell's *Business Cycles*, p. 126. I understand that the
former have been computed for each year separately, whereas the latter
are primarily based on a single computation made in 1922 for 240 cities
holding more than four-fifths of the total deposits. Subsequently (*Review
of Economic Statistics*, Feb. 1928) Mr. Snyder has estimated the cheque-
transactions in 1927 at 766 billions and the average velocity for the whole
country in that year at about 30.

[2] The extreme closeness of these two figures is a chance coincidence.
I had forgotten what the American figure was, and did not look it up, so as
to avoid being influenced, until after I had worked out my English figure.

the velocity of the Business-deposits in Great Britain. Cheques drawn on New York City banks make up, moreover, between 40 and 50 per cent of all cheques drawn in the United States.[1]

As an example of the variability of the velocity according to the type of deposit in question, Dr. Burgess shows [2] that, in the case of the balances of the Treasury Department, the velocity is in the neighbourhood of 300 times a year.

Let us next make a very rough attempt (in the hope of stimulating something better) to estimate separately the Income-deposits and the Business-deposits in the United States in 1923. The coin and notes in active circulation amounted to about 3·7 billion dollars, of which we might perhaps assume that 2 billion dollars would be held on the average as income-cash (*i.e.* held by the public as current cash apart from their hoards). If the velocity were about the same as that assumed for England, namely 15, the total income expended in this way would be 30 billions.[3] The net income was 70 billions, so that allowing an increase for gross income and for sundry duplications in payments, this would leave (say) 55 billions of income-transactions to be transacted by means of cheques.[4] If we were to assume the same velocity as in England, namely 10,

---

[1] Snyder, *Review of Economic Statistics*, Feb. 1928, p. 41.

[2] *The Reserve Banks and the Money Market*, p. 91.

[3] This agrees reasonably with Wesley Mitchell's estimate of 26 for the velocity of the cash in all uses, since every payment from income-cash to business-cash will be balanced by an equal payment from business-cash to income-cash, so that the above would account altogether for 60 billions turnover out of Mitchell's estimated total of 94. In any case 30 billions seems a fully high proportion to be expended in this way.

[4] Since making the above quite independent guess, I find that this figure is confirmed by Wesley Mitchell, who puts what I call the income-transactions at about 10 per cent of the total, which in 1923 would be 57 billions. The whole of the passage in which he makes this estimate is interesting and deserves quotation (Wesley Mitchell, *Business Cycles*, p. 149): " Retail sales account for not much more than $\frac{1}{20}$th of the aggregate volume of payments, and the payment of money incomes to individuals for about $\frac{1}{10}$th. Even the round flow of money incomes to individuals and from

this would give a total of 5·5 billions of income-deposits out of the total of 22, which is nearly the same proportion as in England. Further, we should be left with 16·5 billions of Business-deposits and 515 billions of cheques drawn against them, which yields a velocity of 31 [1]—much lower than the English figure of 77. It is, however, evident on a broad survey of the figures and without making detailed hypotheses that the average velocity of the business-deposits in England must be much greater than in the United States. Conceivably this might be due partly to the greater use of the overdraft in England, but more probably to the greater distances in the United States which means a much greater loss of monetary efficiency through the delays of cheques in the post.[2] In this case the use of air-mails might revolutionise the average volume of balances required to transact a given volume of business.

If we were to confine our attention to the 141 cities, then assuming that one-quarter of the cash-deposits are income-deposits with a velocity of 10, the velocity of the business-deposits works out at 55—which is much nearer to the English figure.

It is interesting to notice that our guesses for the total income-deposits (cash and bank-balances together) for Great Britain is £400 millions against a net income of £4000 millions or 10 per cent, whilst the total for the United States (in 1923) is $7·5 billions against a net income of $70 billions or 11 per cent. The reasonable agreement of these figures is some

---

individuals seems to make only ⅛th of the aggregate payments in average business years. While these rather precise ratios may be faulty, it seems certain that the payments arising from other business transactions are several times the volume of payments involved in receiving and spending personal incomes."

[1] If we lowered the velocity of income-deposits to 6, we should on the above hypotheses raise that of the business-deposits to 40.

[2] As soon as I have posted a cheque, I treat this as out of my balance; but you do not treat it as in yours until the cheque has been received by your bank.

slight confirmation that the *order of magnitude* of these guesses may be fairly accurate—which is all I claim for them.

(v.) THE VARIABILITY OF THE VELOCITY OF THE BUSINESS-DEPOSITS

We have endeavoured above to estimate the order of magnitude of the velocity (V_2) of the Business-deposits. But we have no direct evidence of its *variability*, except as an inference from the observed variability of the Cash-deposits taken as a whole.

We must begin, therefore, by considering the variability of the velocity of the Cash-deposits as shown by the English statistics. The best we can do with the existing statistics is to take an index of the total Bank Clearings and divide them by an index of the volume of Current Accounts [1] (based on the estimated proportion of Current to Total Accounts given on page above) ; or alternatively to take an index of the Country and Provincial Clearings and—since no separate statistics are available of Provincial Current Accounts—divide them by the same figure. The first set of figures will give us an index of the variability of the velocity of *total* Business-deposits, but, being overshadowed by the financial transactions of the City, will not be a satisfactory index of the velocity of the industrial Business-deposits or Business-deposits A, as we have called them above (Vol. i. p. 244) ; whilst the second set, which is better calculated to indicate the velocity of Business-deposits A, will be vitiated by the assumption that the Provincial Current Accounts have varied in the same degree as the aggregate of Current Accounts. The result, for what it is worth, is as follows :

---

[1] This index, based on the monthly average of the nine clearing banks, differs slightly, but not materially, from the index, given on p. 31, based on the end-year figures of all the banks.

ENGLAND AND WALES (1924 = 100)

	Total Bank Clearings.	Country and Provincial Bank Clearings.*	Computed Level of Cash-deposits.	Velocity of Cash-deposits based on	
				Total Clearings.	Country and Pro-vincial Clearings.
1920	102	152	111	91	137
1921	88	101	108	81·5	93
1922	93	96	106	87	91
1923	92	96	102	90	94
1924	100	100	100	100	100
1925	102	101	97	105	104
1926	101	93	96	105	97
1927	105	98	99	106	99
1928	111	98	100	111	98
1929	112	98	100	112	98

* The Provincial Clearings are based on five towns up to 1921 and eleven towns subsequently.

The velocities in this table, based on the Country and Provincial Clearings, probably supply as good an estimate as we can get of the variability of the velocity of the Industrial Circulation ; whilst those based on the Total Clearings indicate the effect of the varying proportions in which the latter are made up of trans-actions relating to the Financial Circulation and to the Industrial Circulation respectively.

The general direction of the changes shown by the velocity based on the Country and Provincial Clearings is a satisfactory corroboration of the conclusions of Books III. and IV. that we should expect velocity to be higher when business profits are being enjoyed than when losses are being suffered. The extent to which the Country Cheque Clearings are relatively free from the influence of large financial transactions is shown by the average value of the cheques passing, as calculated on two selected test days in 1928, namely as follows :

	January 3,* 1928.		August 24,† 1928.	
	No. of Items.	Average Value.	No. of Items.	Average Value.
Town clearing .	322,000	£538	116,000	£911
Metropolitan clearing	234,000	35	129,000	34
Country clearing .	488,000	31	297,000	25

* Selected as a typically heavy day.   † Selected as a typically light day.

This is confirmed, subject to a qualification, by Mr. Holland-Martin, the Secretary of the Clearing House, who said in his Report on the year 1928 :

> I should like to warn you that the town figures day by day become more swollen by the growing habit, for easier accounting, of using cheques for each transaction, and not for the balances of transactions, so that they are little guide to trade movements. The figures of the Country Clearing and those of the Provincial Clearings are a more reliable guide, but these also tend to be upset if, as happened in one district at the end of last year, the figures were swollen by large cheques passing between firms as the result of sales and purchases of businesses.

Now comes the question—are the observed changes in the velocity of the Cash-deposits really a reflection of changes in the velocities of the Business-deposits ? Or are they a reflection of changes in the proportionate amounts of the Business-deposits and of the Income-deposits, or of different categories of the Business-deposits ? The statistics themselves cannot answer this question. But we can calculate, first, what changes in the proportionate amounts of the Business-deposits and of the Income-deposits would produce the observed results, given constancy in their respective velocities ; and, secondly, what changes in the velocity of the Business-deposits are implied, assuming a constant proportion between the two types of deposits and a constant velocity for the Income-deposits.

For the first of these two calculations, let us assume that the normal relation between the Income-deposits and the Business-deposits is that the quantity of the latter is 3 times that of the former, and its velocity 7 times that of the former (these velocities being both constant at 77 and 11 respectively). Then, since

$$V = \frac{M_1V_1 + M_2V_2}{M_1 + M_2}, \quad V = \frac{11 \ (M_1 + 7M_2)}{M_1 + M_2} \ ; \quad \text{from which it}$$

follows that a downward fluctuation of V from 60 to 55 implies a change in $\frac{M_2}{M_1}$ from about 3 to 2, whilst an upward fluctuation of V from 60 to 64 implies a change in $\frac{M_2}{M_1}$ from 3 to 4 approximately.

Next, let us assume that the relative amounts of the Income-deposits and the Business-deposits are constant. Then, taking the Business-deposits (M_2) at 3 times the Income-deposits (M_1) and the velocity of the latter (V_1) as 11, since $V_2 = \frac{1}{M_2} \left\{ (M_1 + M_2)V - M_1V_1 \right\}$, it

follows that $V_2 = \frac{1}{3} \ (4V - 11)$. Consequently, if the velocity of the Cash-deposits (V) fluctuates from 60 to 55, we can infer on these assumptions that the velocity of the Business-deposits (V_2) moves from 76 to 70 ; whilst if V moves from 60 to 64, V_2 moves from 76 to 82.

Furthermore, just as the Cash-deposits can be analysed into Income-deposits and Business-deposits with different velocities, so the Business-deposits in their turn can be analysed into Industrial-deposits and Financial-deposits having different velocities, which in Vol. i. I have called Business-deposits A and Business-deposits B respectively, the former belonging to the Industrial Circulation and the latter to the Financial Circulation ; so that observed fluctuations in the velocity of the Business-deposits may be due to fluctuations in the proportionate amounts of the Financial-deposits and the Industrial-deposits without any change in the velocities appropriate to these different types of deposit. Since it is probable that the velocity of the Financial-deposits is much greater than that of the Industrial-deposits, this may be important.

The available statistics do not allow us to carry our inductive illustrations any further. But enough has been said to show that the observed facts do not necessarily require for their explanation a substantial fluctuation in true velocities ;—for they can also be explained by fluctuations in the proportions of deposits employed in different uses. Thus the observed increase in the velocity of the Cash-deposits during booms and its observed decrease during slumps may be only partly due to changes in true velocities ;—part of the change may be regarded as due to an increase of transactions relating to Business-deposits B, and part as a corroboration of our previous expectation that the value of transactions relating to the Industrial Circulation will increase relatively to the Income-deposits during profit-periods and decrease relatively during loss-periods.

(vi.) FACTORS DETERMINING TRUE VELOCITIES

It is important, therefore, to distinguish between the "average" velocity of money in a variety of uses and the "true" velocity of money in a particular use,—meaning by the latter the ratio of the volume of a particular type of transactions to the quantity of money employed in them ; for fluctuations in "average" velocities may be due, not to fluctuations in "true" velocities, but to fluctuations in the relative importance of different types of transactions. But we must now consider a little further the factors capable of causing fluctuations in the true velocities.

In deciding what amount of balances to hold in proportion to the prospective volume of transactions (both measured in money), a depositor is influenced partly by what amount is requisite for the transaction of business with a given degree of *convenience*, and partly by the degree of *sacrifice* involved in locking up that amount of resources in that way. Thus the level of balances held for a given type of transaction, proportionately to the volume of transactions, *i.e.* the true velocity in that use, is determined by a balance at the margin between the conveniencies gained and the sacrifices involved. The degrees both of convenience and of sacrifice vary. But the variability of the latter is probably much greater than that of the former. Experience shows that the business world can get on, when the sacrifice is great, with a volume of balances which is only a fraction of what they hold at a time when the sacrifice is so slight that they can afford to indulge their convenience.

The considerations of convenience are chiefly governed by slowly-changing social and business habits. But there is also a less sluggish short-period influence—namely that, when business is brisk, the business world can carry through a greater volume of transactions by means of the same quantity of cash facilities without any loss of convenience.

Nevertheless the observed correlation between brisker business and increased velocity, in so far as this is due to an increase in " true " velocities, is probably also to be explained by the fact that when business is brisk it means a greater *sacrifice* to lock up in the shape of cash a command over real resources which might be converted into working capital. We must turn, therefore, to possible causes of variability in the degree of sacrifice involved in holding balances

as compared with using this command over resources
in some other way. In particular, we have to consider
the influence of (a) changes in the demand for working capital and in the rate of discount, and (b) expectations as to the future course of prices.

There is an element of sacrifice under heading (a)
because the holding of balances locks up, so far as
the individual depositor is concerned, a command of
resources which but for this could be used in other
ways—on fixed deposit, in investment, or in the
expansion of business. When business is dull and
investment unattractive, the cost of holding cash-
deposits is merely the sacrifice of interest involved in
holding them thus rather than as savings-deposits or
bills or other liquid short-dated investments. If, at
the same time, the rate of discount and the deposit
rate of interest are low, considerations of convenience
in determining the amount of balances proportionately
to business done can be allowed to have their way.
When, on the other hand, business is active and
expanding, so that the whole of the resources of a
firm or an individual are required as active working capital, when its borrowing powers are already
strained towards their limit, and when the interest
payable and obtainable on loans is high, then there
will be a powerful motive to restrict balances to as
low a level as is in any way practicable, even if this
involves taking some risk in the provision made
against contingencies. Thus more transactions will be
carried through with the same real balances as before,
or higher-priced transactions with the same money-
balances as before, *i.e.* with diminished money-
balances proportionately to the money-volume of
business.

When demand for working capital is keen and is
tending to outstrip the supply, the pressure of these
motives to economise balances may have a very
important influence on prices. Obviously this state

of affairs may be associated with a simultaneous increase in the volume of transactions ; but on the other hand there is no necessary connection. This is part of the reason why those who seek to find an exact relationship between the variability of V and that of T, the volume of transactions, are able to discover a statistical verification of what they expect when they direct their inquiries to some periods, yet fail to do so at some other period. For example, in the boom of 1920 in the United States the increase in the volume of transactions was accompanied by a stringency in the supply of working capital, with the result that V and T appeared to move together. In the recovery, however, which followed the slump of 1921–22 the volume of transactions reacted back to its former high level, but this time without any accompanying stringency in the supply of loanable funds, with the result that the supposed correlation between V and T, which the earlier period had appeared to substantiate, no longer held good. In other words, it is stringent conditions of credit which tend to increase velocity.

Thus the amount of sacrifice under heading (a) depends on the degree of the competition from other opportunities of employing resources. The amount of sacrifice under heading (b), however, depends on whether there is an expectation or a fear of depreciation in the real value of the balances—i.e. on the possibility of rising price-levels.

The downward movement of real balances resulting from this cause has, of course, reached its extreme limit in the European post - war experiences of distrust of the currency resulting in a so-called " flight " from the currency. But the same pheno- menon is present when depositors generally are inclined to make purchases in excess of their im- mediate or normal needs, because they fear that, if they put them off to the usual time, the price will have moved against them in the meantime.   To a certain extent this shades off into the increased demand for working capital discussed under (a) above ; but the two influences can be distinguished according as the additional demand for goods is due to brisker trade rendering a larger supply necessary or to the expectation of higher prices leading to the purchase of more goods than are genuinely required at the moment.   Obviously the two phenomena may often tend to exist together.

I am not clear that this cause is an important one in its direct influence on prices through increasing (or decreasing) velocity, except in the extreme cases where the fear of the depreciation of money is acute. It only operates where people take delivery of more goods than they require for the time being for their normal operations and hoard the goods, so to speak, *in specie*.   This rarely occurs on a large scale.   For it must not be confused with speculation or anticipatory purchases or sales of goods on the forward markets.

In extreme cases, however, where the expectation of a rising price-level is universal, so that private individuals begin turning their cash balances into goods or securities as soon as possible after receiving them for fear lest they depreciate in value on their hands, the effect of this influence towards diminishing real balances (and increasing velocity) and thus raising prices may be catastrophic.   Recent examples of this are so familiar that the point scarcely needs to be expanded.[1]   As soon as alarm has been awakened, price-levels tend to rise faster than the rate of monetary inflation ; and when alarm has become universal they tend to rise much faster.   When this stage has been reached, even the restriction of further issues of currency will be of little avail in retarding the rise of prices, unless and until it has the effect of restoring popular confidence.   Measures of

---

[1] I have dealt with it myself in my *Tract on Monetary Reform*, chap. ii.

deflation, of high bank-rate, of exchange control, of price control, etc., have to be judged by reference primarily to their probable effects in influencing the public to restore their real balances to a normal level, rather than by their reactions on the other monetary elements.

In a country such as France, where the efficiency of the currency is normally rather low—mainly on account of the readiness to hoard notes—the value of money is especially susceptible to sentiments of distrust, inasmuch as efficiency can be greatly increased without anyone being put to any real inconvenience.

CHAPTER 25

THE RATIO OF BANK MONEY TO RESERVE MONEY

THE crude Quantity Theory of old days—though it protected itself with the words *other things being equal* —was liable to suggest that the total quantity of money (M) was the main, if not the exclusive, determinant of the supply of cash-facilities. Experience, under war finance and during the post-war monetary inflations, of price fluctuations which did not closely correspond with the changes in the ratio of the total quantity of money to the volume of output, has led almost everyone to-day to lay a more equal stress on the relative importance of the other monetary factors. Nevertheless the total quantity of money remains, if not an overruling factor, at least in the long run a dominant one—and of exceptional practical significance because it is the most *controllable* factor.

Let us, therefore, now proceed to a determination of the causes governing the total quantity of money. We shall move by two stages in this and a later chapter, considering, first of all, how the quantity of Bank-money is related to the quantity of Reserve-money, and then (in Book VII. Chapter 32) what governs the quantity of Reserve-money.

We have seen in Chapter 2 that the aggregate volume of the deposits of the member banks of a modern banking system depends on the reserve-ratio (*i.e.* the proportion of reserves to deposits) which the member banks aim at keeping, and the amount of these reserves (in the shape of cash and deposits at the Central Bank). For if any bank finds itself in the possession of an amount of reserves which exceeds this ratio, it proceeds to " create " additional deposits, as described in Chapter 2, by lending and investing more freely ; which has the effect of increasing the reserves of the other banks and so causing them to create additional deposits ; and so on, until the normal reserve-ratio has been restored for the system as a whole. Thus, although the first bank will not be able to create additional deposits which are the full multiple (measured by the inverse of the reserve-ratio) of the surplus reserve with which it finds itself, since, as soon as it begins to lend more freely, it will lose a part of this additional reserve to other banks, nevertheless the existence of the surplus reserve in the banking system as a whole will set up a reverberation which will end in the aggregate deposits being increased in the same proportion as the aggregate reserves have been increased (after deducting from the initial increment of the latter any loss of cash out of the reserves into the active circulation consequent on the higher level of deposits) —for until this situation is reached *some* bank will find itself with more than a normal reserve-ratio. Thus the additional reserves and the increase of lending and of deposits will, in the end, be shared in appropriate proportions by all the banks of the system, and it will be of no consequence which particular bank started the ball rolling. Some bankers have been inclined to dispute these propositions. But their objection usually turns out to amount to the contention that any given bank finding itself with surplus reserves cannot then increase its own lending by ten times (or whatever multiple corresponds to the normal reserve-ratio) the amount of this surplus —which is, of course, true.

The precise quantitative effect of the injection of

additional reserve resources into a banking system
partly depends on what increment of cash in active
circulation corresponds to a given increment in the
volume of bank-money, as well as on the ratio of the
reserves to the volume of bank-money. For example
—to take the simplest possible numerical illustration
—if cash in circulation increases by 10 per cent of the
increment in the volume of bank-money and if bank-
reserves are normally 10 per cent of bank-money, an
injection of additional resources will lead ultimately
to an increase in deposits of five times their amount,
since these additional resources will be eventually
half added to the cash in circulation and half left as
reserves, which latter half will lead to an increase in
deposits of ten times their amount.

In the United States attempts have been made
to estimate the actual statistical ratios relevant to
this calculation. Governor Strong in his evidence
before the U.S. Congress Committee on stabilisation,
estimated that the increment of cash in circulation is,
in the United States, about 20 per cent of the increment in demand-deposits and the reserves 10 per cent
of the demand-deposits. If these figures are correct,
an injection of additional resources (in cash or Central-
Bank money) will lead to an ultimate increase in
demand-deposits equal to 3·3 times the amount of
the additional resources.[1]

But whilst the amount of income-cash in circulation
might be expected to bear a fairly stable relation to
the amount of the income-deposits, it is not at all
to be expected that the total amount of cash in circulation will bear any stable relation to the total
amount of cash-deposits—at any rate over short
periods or without an appreciable time-lag. Nor is

---

[1] Professor J. S. Lawrence, in an interesting article in the *Quarterly
Journal of Economics*, 1928, " Borrowed Reserves and Bank Expansion ",
pp. 593-626, arrives by a complicated argument, which I have not been
able clearly to follow, at 4·97 as his " coefficient of ultimate expansion ".

the trend of change necessarily the same. For example, from 1921 to 1929 the amount of cash in circulation in the United States remained almost stationary, whereas during the same period the cash-deposits increased by more than 40 per cent. Indeed, one of the causes of disequilibrium in any period of change is sometimes the fact that, when reserves are first increased, bank-money can expand in a greater degree than can be sustained in the long run after there has been time for a corresponding increase in money-incomes and in that part of the income-deposits which consist of cash. It is a tiresome—and indeed a dangerous—feature of existing systems that different amounts of reserves have to be kept against income-deposits in the shape of cash from those which have to be kept against cash-deposits in the shape of bank-money, so that a change-over between the one and the other possesses a practical significance which it ought not, perhaps, to have.

The quantity of Bank-Money, *i.e.* of Bank-deposits, depends, therefore, on the amount of the reserves of the member banks and on the reserve-ratios at which the member banks are aiming either in conformity with law or convention or to suit their own convenience. In this chapter I propose to assume the amount of the member banks' reserves as given and to consider the amount of deposits which they will create on this reserve basis. In Chapter 32 of Book VII. we shall proceed to the further problem of the factors which determine the amount of the member banks' reserves, and in particular to the question how far, in different monetary systems, the member banks are able themselves to influence the amount of these reserves, and how far the amount is determined for them either by the Central Bank or by external circumstances over which they have no control.

(i.) THE STABILITY OF RESERVE-RATIOS

It has sometimes been suggested that the banks vary their reserve-ratios in accordance with the state of trade. For example, Professor Pigou (*Industrial Fluctuations*, p. 259) says that " this proportion is not rigid but elastic. In booms the joint-stock banks, feeling optimistic like everybody else, may be willing to cut down their proportion, and in depressions, being pessimistic, may wish to expand it." The only evidence which Professor Pigou quotes in support of this conclusion relates to more than a hundred years ago. As we shall see below, modern statistics do not bear this out, so far as concerns Great Britain and the United States. We shall find that the ratio varies with different types of bank, and that it has been changed, for various reasons, from time to time. But at any given time banks stick closely to their established ratio, and, as the figures to be given below will show, such fluctuations as there are exhibit no correlation with the state of trade. This result is what one would expect. To let the ratio fall below the figure which has been fixed upon as that which is recommended by considerations of prudence and of reputation would be a sign of weakness or, at least, of weak-mindedness; whilst to let it rise above would be to forgo quite unnecessarily a source of profit, since surplus reserves can always be employed in the purchase of bills or of investments.

Accordingly, the statistics (to be quoted below) show that, save in exceptional circumstances, all banks use their reserves up to the hilt; that is to say, they seldom or never maintain idle reserves in excess of what is their conventional or legal proportion for the time being. Indeed, why should they, so long as a perfectly liquid asset can be purchased which yields a rate of interest? The problem

before a bank is not how much to lend—the answer
to that question, namely the appropriate multiple
of its reserves, can be furnished by simple arithmetic
—but what proportion of its loans can be safely
made in the relatively less liquid forms. Thus, in
practice, the Member Banks exercise no effective
control whatever over the aggregate of their deposits
—unless they are in a position to control the aggregate of their Reserves, to which possibility I will return in Book VII.

The conclusion that banks lend up to the hilt, in
the sense that they never maintain idle reserves in
excess of their normal ratio, depends, nevertheless,
upon two conditions being satisfied :

(i.) It must be the case that interest-yielding assets
are available, the liquidity of which is beyond question. Otherwise, a bank may sometimes have to
keep excess reserves as the only means of avoiding
a deficiency at some subsequent date. If a situation
was to arise, such as has happened before now
in Italy, where the Treasury could not be relied
on to pay its Treasury Bills in cash at their maturity
and where the Central Bank was not making new
advances to the market against them, or if there was
a fear that such a situation might arise, then this
condition would not be satisfied. But with Central
Banking on modern lines such a situation, or even the
fear of it, is abnormal. In the United States the
Federal Reserve Banks virtually undertake to discount bills of certain specified types ; and in Great
Britain the Bank of England does so by long un-
broken custom. The obligation of modern Central
Banks to buy for cash certain specified types of
interest-bearing documents is almost as absolute as
their obligation to give legal-tender for their notes
(if their notes are not themselves legal-tender). The
Bank Bill, therefore, is as good as gold—and better,
because it earns interest. There is no reason, there-

fore, why a bank should sacrifice the interest thus obtainable (directly, or indirectly by call loans to the market) by holding cash in excess of what is required by the written, or the unwritten, law.

(ii.) It must also be the case that the cash reserves which a bank habitually keeps, in virtue of law or of binding custom, are in excess of the maximum which it requires for the convenient transaction of business. In former times this was not always the case. It is not the case everywhere to-day. But the diminished use of cash, as compared with cheques, the greater rapidity of the means of transport from head-quarters, and the improbability of a serious " run " by the depositors of the banks (at any rate in England in the case of the " Big Five ") to turn their deposits into cash, have combined to reduce the amount of cash in proportion to their deposits which the banks strictly need as till-money. In addition to their till-money the Banks require a balance at the Central Bank to meet the contingency of an adverse balance at the " clearing ". But beyond these requirements the Banks, provided they have a sufficient amount of abso-lutely liquid interest-bearing assets to meet all reason-able contingencies, have no need to hold any cash re-serves at all—if it were not for law or binding custom.

Let us now test these generalisations by reference to the actual facts in England and in the United States.

1. *England.*—In England there is no law governing the proportion of cash which must be held by the member banks against their deposits. The figure is determined by custom and convention ; though, once the figure is determined, it would be bad for the prestige of a bank to lower its own ratio of reserves below the prevailing level. But there are two pecu-liarities about the English custom in this matter.

In the first place, since there is no law governing the question, it is more important to satisfy the custom on the dates for which the figures are published than on those for which they are not published. Formerly they were only published half-yearly ; now they are published monthly. Partly, perhaps, as a survival from the days when these were the only published figures, the banks are still accustomed to work to a much higher customary figure in their annual accounts at the end of the calendar year than in their monthly accounts, publishing indeed in their annual accounts a total of cash in hand and at the Bank of England as much as 50 per cent higher than they normally carry except on the annual balance-sheet day—which seems a stupid practice, whether or not it is intended to deceive. It is also the case —but to what extent no details are available—that the figures published in their monthly accounts, being averages of four days in the month, namely, of the day in each week on which their weekly balance-sheets are made up, are higher than their true daily average.[1] Nor is this all : the " Big Five " Banks which follow this practice, being four in number (excluding the Midland Bank), can and do choose different days of the week for their little manœuvre. That is to say, each takes it in turn to call from the money market a certain quantity of resources which will swell their balance at the Bank of England on the day of the week sacred to the particular Bank which is calling. In this way a certain part of the published reserves of the " Big Five " is a stage army which appears four times over. When Bank A's sacred day has passed, it lends to the Money Market that part of its Bank of England balance which is no longer required for publication purposes, for the Money Market to pass on as promptly as possible to Bank B whose sacred day has arrived, so that a Bank of England balance which

---

[1] Except, I think, in the case of the Midland Bank. It is of course essential to the smooth working of the system that a stable average should be compatible with sharp daily fluctuations for individual banks above or below this figure.

belonged to Bank A's reserve at dawn has put in a
public appearance before sunset as part of Bank B's;
and so on day by day.   In short, as Dr. Leaf, when
chairman of the Westminster Bank, frankly expressed
it, the published reserves are " to a certain extent
fictitious ".[1]   In this way the traditional "strength"
of the British Joint-Stock Banks is safely preserved
and handed on for the admiration of posterity.

In the second place, the banks do not all work to
an identical figure for their proportion of reserves.
These differences of practice may be due to differences
in the class of business transacted or to differences
in the amounts held of the next most liquid asset.
But they may also be mere survivals from past conditions, which no longer have any distinct meaning,
or they may represent different estimates of the
advertisement or prestige value of working to a
proportion higher than the average.[2]   In spite of
these differences, each bank—the figures show—is,
generally speaking, steadfast to its own figure, with
the result that the proportion for the average of the
banks as a whole is—allowing for the half-yearly
movements upwards—remarkably stable also.

Apart from the higher proportions for the half-
yearly balance-sheets, particularly in December, these
figures represent for the period 1921 to 1926 something
as near absolute stability as one can expect to find.
Over these troubled and changing years the figures
exhibit no correlation whatever with the state of trade
or with the bank-rate or with the fluctuating proportions of the advances (given below, p. 68), or with any
such influences ; and for the average of each year from
1921 to 1926 the reserves bore a ratio to the deposits
stable to within one thousandth part of the latter. The
drop in the average since 1927 was mainly due to a

[1] *Banking*, p. 133.
[2] This probably explains the high figure to which the Midland Bank
worked up to 1927—a figure which dates back to Sir Edward Holden's day,
who introduced it and made much of it.

change in the practice of the Midland Bank, which will be referred to later, and to a decrease in "window-dressing" at the end of each half-year.

PERCENTAGE OF THE AMOUNT OF CASH IN HAND AND AT THE BANK OF ENGLAND TO THE AMOUNT OF DEPOSITS HELD BY THE NINE [1] CLEARING BANKS

	1921.*	1922.	1923.	1924.	1925.	1926.	1927.	1928.	1929.
Jan.	11·3	11·4	12·0	11·7	11·9	11·7	11·6	11·3	10·9
Feb.	11·0	11·5	11·5	11·6	11·8	11·7	11·6	11·0	10·5
Mar.	11·1	11·6	11·7	11·6	11·6	11·7	11·5	11·1	10·6
April	11·7	11·7	12·0	11·6	11·8	11·7	11·7	11·1	10·8
May	11·7	11·9	11·8	11·5	11·6	11·8	11·6	11·1	10·9
June†	12·3	11·8	11·9	11·9	12·2	12·1	11·8	11·2	10·9
July	11·7	11·5	11·8	11·5	11·9	11·8	11·5	11·0	10·7
Aug.	11·7	11·7	11·8	11·6	11·9	11·8	11·5	11·1	10·7
Sept.	11·8	11·7	11·9	11·7	11·8	11·7	11·5	11·2	10·9
Oct.	12·0	11·6	11·7	11·6	11·6	11·7	11·4	11·0	10·7
Nov.	11·3	11·6	11·6	11·6	11·6	11·6	11·3	11·0	10·6
Dec.†	12·4	12·1	12·2	12·4	12·1	12·0	11·7	11·3	11·3
Aver.	11·7	11·7	11·8	11·7	11·8	11·8	11·6	11·1	10·8

* The relatively low figures for the first quarter of 1921 are probably to be explained by the fact that this was the beginning of the post-war publication of monthly figures, so that the conventional ratios of the different banks had not yet had time to settle down.

† It will be noticed that the outburst of display at the end of the year has the effect of raising somewhat the weekly average for December, and that, until recently, the same thing has also occurred on a smaller scale in June. The figures since 1927, however, suggest that this practice is disappearing.

As between the different banks there are, however, appreciable differences of practice. Of the ten Clearing Banks which publish monthly figures, the Midland Bank used to maintain a reserve ratio much higher than the others, namely from 14·5 to 15 per cent, but now in the neighbourhood of 11 per cent —which may be relatively higher than appears, since it is believed that the Midland Bank's monthly figures are not "window dressed"; [2] Lloyds Bank and

[1] The National Bank, which is now included in the Clearing House figures, is excluded from this table so as to secure continuity of record.

[2] It is possible that the true daily averages of the other banks, apart from "window-dressing", might not work out at much above 9 per cent.

Williams Deacon's Bank, publish reserves of 11 to
11·5 per cent; then five others from 10 to 11 per
cent; and finally Coutts' Bank, the business of which
is rather different from that of the others, with 8 to
9 per cent. On the other hand the Midland Bank
partly balances its high cash reserves by holding less
"cash at call and short notice" than the average,
and Coutts' Bank by holding more.

If we turn to pre-war statistics, we find a tendency
for the reserve-ratio to change slowly; but changes
were very gradual and in no way correlated with
bank-rate or the state of trade. The publication of
monthly figures was first made by thirteen banks in
1891 at Goschen's suggestion.[1] The proportion of the
reserves then amounted to 13 per cent. By 1898 the
proportion had risen to 14 per cent, and by 1908 to
15 or 16 per cent, which was still the figure in 1914
before the outbreak of war. The pre-war figures,
however, included in the reserves " Balances with and
Cheques in course of Collection on other Banks in the
United Kingdom ", as well as cash in hand and
Deposits at the Bank of England. If these were to
be included now, they would raise the proportion by
something between 3 and 3·3 per cent, thus bringing
the post-war average, prior to the Midland Bank's
change of ratio, up to about 15 per cent, or nearly
the same as the pre-war figure. Such excess as
remains in favour of the pre-war figure may be due
to the fact that the figures now represent averages for
a single day in each week (different for different
banks), whilst the pre-war figures, being only for a
single day in each month (different for different banks),
may have been raised by " window-dressing " even
higher above the true average figure than they are
now.

As to the division of the banks' reserves between

---

[1] The deposits of these banks were then £122,000,000, which was about
30 per cent of the aggregate deposits of the country.

cash and Bank of England deposits, it is possible to make an estimate. One bank (The Union of London and Smith's) was accustomed in pre-war days to state separately its cash in hand and its cash at the Bank of England, showing about half its reserves in each form. At the present time (1928) it would seem that fully two-thirds of the aggregate reserves of the Banks must be held in Notes and not more than a third as cash at the Bank of England. For the total deposits at the Bank of England, first published in November 1928,[1] on the occasion of the amalgamation of the Bank and Currency Note Issues, of all British Banks doing mainly domestic business (which include several institutions besides the ten Clearing Banks), stood (Nov. 1928) at no more than £62,500,000 ; whereas the total published reserves of the ten Banks range from £190,000,000 to £200,000,000. If we assume that the published figures are increased by (say) £22,500,000 as a result of window-dressing, we have left a figure of (say) £172,500,000, of which perhaps as much as £115,000,000 is held in the form of Notes and £57,500,000 at the Bank of England. There is no reason why we should not know precisely, but—like so much else in banking statistics—the figures are kept a secret.

The proportion of the published reserves of the nine Clearing Banks to the total Note Issue (Treasury Notes and Bank Notes combined) *plus* the total private deposits at the Bank of England is shown below (p. 61).

The figures in the last column, giving the proportion of State Money and Central Bank Money held in reserve by the nine Clearing Banks to the total of such money, show, recently, a steady and fairly substantial increase. Since "window-dressing" has probably been on the decline these figures may understate the increase

---

[1] That is to say, since 1877. From the passing of the Bank Act in 1844 to 1877 the London bankers' balances were shown as a separate item.

MONTHLY AVERAGES

	Private Deposits at B. of E. (1)	Bank and Currency Notes. (2)	Total of columns 1 and 2. (3)	Index of this. (1923 = 100.) (4)	Deposits of 9 Clearing Banks. (1923 = 100.) (5)	Reserves of 9 Clearing Banks. (1923 = 100.) (6)	Proportion of col. 6 to col. 4. (1923 = 100.) (7)
	£ Mn.	£ Mn.	£ Mn.				
1921	124	435	559	113	108	107	95
1922	118	399	517	104	106	105	101
1923	110	386	496	100	100	100	100
1924	110	389	499	101	100	99	98
1925	111	383	494	100	99	99	99
1926	105	374	479	97	100	100	103
1927	101*	373	474	96	103	101	105
1928	102	372	474	96	106	99	103
1929	99	361	460	93	108	99	106

* This figure is believed to have been vitiated in the spring of 1927 for purposes of comparison, to the extent of at least £5,000,000, by the disappearance of some item arising out of the loan from the Bank of England to the Bank of France which was then paid off.

rather than otherwise. The absolute amount of the published reserves of the nine Clearing Banks was the same in 1929 as in 1924, whereas the total of column (3) had fallen by 8 per cent. This suggests that the notes in the hands of the public must have fallen appreciably, whilst cash deposits—as we have seen (p. 40)—were practically unchanged. Thus the indications are that the use of Notes is still sensibly declining relatively to the use of cheques. The table also brings out in a striking manner the effect of the Midland Bank's change in its reserve ratio; for, although the Bank of England kept the aggregate of State and Central Bank Money in 1929 4 per cent below that of 1926, of which 1 per cent was reflected in a reduction of the reserves of the Clearing Banks, the Member Bank Money increased by 8 per cent.

2. *The United States.*—The United States mainly differs from Great Britain in that the reserve propor-

tions are a matter of law and not merely of custom. The actual reserves maintained are, as we shall see, much the same in practice.

The Member Banks[1] of the Federal Reserve System are required to hold reserves in the form of deposit accounts with their Reserve Bank in the following percentages : [2]

	Demand Deposits (payable on 29 days' notice or less).	Time Deposits* (payable on 30 days' notice or more).
Central Reserve Cities (New York and Chicago) .	13 per cent	3 per cent
63 Reserve Cities . . .	10 ,,	3 ,,
Country Towns . . .	7 ,,	3 ,,

* Before 1914 there was no distinction in the reserve requirements against Demand and Time Deposits respectively. At the inception of the Federal Reserve System the reserve against the latter was fixed at 5 per cent, and was reduced to 3 per cent by an amendment to the Act in 1917.

In practice (for reasons into which I need not enter) it is even more complicated than the above table would suggest to compute the amount of the legal reserve from the published figures of the Demand and Time Deposits. The amounts of the legal reserves, as compared with the actual reserves, are, however, compiled at irregular intervals by the Comptroller of the Currency, in order that he may satisfy himself that the banks are duly complying with the requirements of the law. The legal proportion averaged over

[1] At the end of 1926 the Member Banks numbered 9260. There were also no less than 17,824 non-member banks. But the assets of the Member Banks represented about 60 per cent of the total.

[2] Cash in hand does not reckon towards the required proportion. Consequently its amount has been worked down to the minimum needed as till-money. The actual percentage of demand deposits so held on Dec. 31, 1928, was less than 2 per cent for Member Banks in reserve and central reserve cities and 5 per cent for country banks, so that the difference in the legal proportions between reserve cities and country towns was offset by the larger amount of cash held in the latter.

the net demand deposits generally works out at between 10 and 11 per cent. Since the proportion against Time Deposits is only 3 per cent, the legal proportion against the total deposits falls when there is a relative increase of the Time Deposits, which cause has reduced it from about 9 per cent in 1918 to 8 per cent in 1922, and 7·2 per cent in 1927. As, however, till-money does not reckon in the United States towards the legal reserve, we have to make an addition to the above of about 2 per cent, to render the figures comparable with those given for England. If an allowance be made for the English practice of window-dressing, it would seem, therefore, that the cash and Central Bank deposits, which law or custom requires the Member Banks to hold in proportion to their own total deposits, are now very nearly the same in the two countries, at (say) 9 to 9·5 per cent.

Furthermore, the percentage of reserves actually held in the United States does not normally differ to any material extent from the legal minima. In the unsettled conditions of the war period the actual reserves were occasionally in excess of the minima by as much as 1 per cent of the deposits; but since the war they have seldom exceeded the minima (except on Dec. 31) by more than ·5 per cent of the deposits and are often only ·1 or ·2 per cent above the minima. For example, in the middle of 1926 the reserves actually held by the National Banks (which represent more than 80 per cent of the member banks) were 7·5 per cent, whilst the prescribed legal minimum was 7·4 per cent. This means that the member banks are using their reserve-bank deposits practically up to the hilt.

These results are confirmed by the express statement of the Federal Reserve Board in their Annual Report for 1924 as follows (p. 9) :

" While the proportion of the amount of reserve bank credit outstanding to loans and investments of member banks is only a fraction of what it was in 1920, the ratio between reserve balances maintained by member banks at the reserve banks to member bank deposit liabilities has remained practically constant at about 10 per cent,[1] which represents on the average the minimum required by law."

That the member banks should wish to work as close as possible to their legal minima is explained by the natural incentive to keep down the assets not earning interest. That they should be able to do so is explained by the existence of certain special facilities. In the first place the law allows the banks' reserves to fall below the prescribed figure on a particular day provided the weekly average is sufficient. Any deficiency in reserve can be quickly made good by discounting at the Federal Reserve Bank. Any excess can be immediately loaned in the Call Market, and used in due course to let bills run off. Thus it is not surprising that it should be the practice of nearly all banks (especially in New York, where the Call Market is near at hand) to shave their reserve close to the legal minimum.[2]

Thus the facts show that, in the banking conditions which now exist in England and the United States, the aggregate of bank-deposits (represented by M in our monetary equation) is a multiple, as nearly as possible constant, of the " reserves " of the member banks.[3]

3. *Elsewhere.*—Dr. Burgess (*op. cit.* p. 36) has quoted figures which indicate that the percentage of reserves (including cash) to deposits in several other countries

[1] This must mean, I think, reserves held against net *demand* deposits.

[2] As regards current practice in the United States in the above respects I have to thank Prof. B. H. Beckhart for useful information. Some interesting figures to the same effect as the above are also given by Dr. Burgess (*The Reserve Banks and the Money Market*, pp. 152-155).

[3] Subject, of course, to the appropriate arithmetical modification when different reserve-ratios are maintained against time-deposits and demand-deposits respectively and the proportion in which the total deposits are divided between the two is changing.

is not very different from what it is in England and
the United States.   His estimates, based on the years
1925 and 1926, are as follows :

	Typical Reserve.
United States Member Banks . . .	9·5
Ten London Clearing Banks . . .	11·5
Four French Credit Companies . . .	11·5
Swiss private banks	8·0
Chartered banks of Canada . . .	11·0

In Germany, however, the position is protected
neither by law nor by convention.   In the case of
the principal Berlin banks the percentage of their
deposits covered by cash and balances with banks
of issue has been as follows :

End 1900 . . .	12·5 per cent
,, 1913 . . .	7·4 ,,
,, 1924 . . .	6·1 ,,
,, 1925 . . .	5·0 ,,
,, 1926 . . .	4·4 ,,

At other periods of the year the position is still
worse. For example, on March 31, 1928, the six principal Berlin banks held in cash, foreign currency,
coupons and balances with banks of issue and clearing
banks no more than $2\frac{1}{2}$ per cent of their total deposits,
which was also the percentage held by the 83 leading
credit banks of the country (including the six Berlin
banks) against deposits aggregating £528,000,000.   It
is true that a smaller percentage of the deposits is
repayable at call than in Great Britain (see p. 19
above) ; but the main explanation of this low percentage seems to be the facility with which cash can be
obtained, when it is required, by re-discounting bills at
the nearest branch of the Reichsbank, so that a German
bank's portfolio of bills eligible for re-discount constitutes its real reserve and the proportion of this portfolio to its liabilities the effective check on expansion.
This means, however, that when trade is reviving
and the supply of eligible bills consequently expanding,

it may be unduly easy under the German system to force the Reichsbank into a corresponding creation of additional credit. In other words, the German banking system is somewhat unprotected, compared with other countries, against the development of conditions of profit inflation contrary to the wishes of the Central Bank. The authorities of the Reichsbank are aware of the danger and have occasionally put some pressure in recent times on the Berlin banks to reform their ways.[1] As a last resort in times of emergency, the Reichsbank resorts to the rationing of credit, *i.e.* it sets an arbitrary limit to the amount of eligible bills which it will discount for a given institution. German banking law appears to an outsider to be in urgent need of amendment in the direction of requiring minimum reserves (preferably in the shape of deposits with the Reichsbank) from the member banks.

(ii.) The Interchangeability of Non-Reserve Bank Assets

People often speak as if the aggregate of investments, discounts and advances, etc., held by the Member Banks was, within fairly wide limits, decided by them by an act of intelligent judgment. In arriving at this decision, the banks are supposed to pay attention to the demands of trade, to the soundness of underlying business conditions, to the general condition of their customers' accounts, to the prevalence of speculation, and so forth.

The statistics given above demonstrate, however, that this is a " vulgar error ". Apart from the rare occasions of a deliberate change in the conventional ratio, such as that made by the Midland Bank in

---

[1] Cf. *Report of the Commissioner of the Reichsbank*, Dec. 1927, p. 37 : " The Reichsbank objects to this development (*i.e.* the dwindling percentage of reserves) and has thought it advisable to urge the banks to maintain a sufficient reserve ".

1927, and from the possibility of the Member Banks
being in a position to influence the amount of their
own reserves (a discussion which we are postponing to
Book VII.), what bankers are ordinarily deciding is,
not *how much* they will lend in the aggregate—this is
mainly settled for them by the state of their reserves
—but in *what forms* they will lend—in what proportions they will divide their resources between the
different kinds of investment which are open to them.
Broadly there are three categories to choose from—
(i.) Bills of Exchange and Call Loans to the Money
Market, (ii.) Investments, (iii.) Advances to Customers. As a rule, advances to customers are more
profitable than investments, and investments are
more profitable than bills and call loans ; but this
order is not invariable. On the other hand, bills
and call loans are more " liquid " than investments,
i.e. more certainly realisable at short notice without
loss, and investments are more " liquid " than advances. Accordingly bankers are faced with a never-
ceasing problem of weighing one thing against
another ; the proportions in which their resources are
divided between these three categories suffer wide
fluctuations ; and in deciding upon their course they
are influenced by the various considerations mentioned above. When, for example, they feel that a
speculative movement or a trade boom may be reach-
ing a dangerous phase, they scrutinise more critically
the security behind their less liquid assets and try to
move, so far as they can, into a more liquid position.
When, on the other hand, demands increase for advances from their trade customers of a kind which
the banks deem to be legitimate and desirable, they do
their best to meet these demands by reducing their
investments and, perhaps, their bills ; whilst, if the
demand for advances is falling off, they employ the
resources thus released by again increasing their
investments.

It will be sufficient, in illustration of this, to give the figures for the proportion of the "advances" of the leading English banks, *i.e.* of their loans to their customers, to their deposits.

It is evident that the proportion of the banks' deposits employed in advances to their customers is capable of wide fluctuations in conformity with the demands of trade ; but it does not follow that the banks lend more or lend less *in the aggregate*.

PERCENTAGE OF THE AMOUNT OF THEIR ADVANCES TO THE AMOUNT OF THE DEPOSITS HELD BY THE NINE ENGLISH CLEARING BANKS [1]

	1921.	1922.	1923.	1924.	1925.	1926.	1927.	1928.	1929.
Jan.	46·7	41·2	42·9	45·5	49·5	52·4	53·0	52·8	52·9
Feb.	48·1	41·5	44·8	47·2	50·0	53·8	54·6	54·1	54·5
Mar.	50·3	42·7	46·5	49·0	52·4	55·2	55·8	55·6	56·4
April	49·8	42·9	46·3	49·0	52·8	55·0	55·6	55·3	56·6
May	48·6	42·2	46·2	48·7	53·1	55·2	55·3	55·5	56·4
June	46·0	41·2	46·0	47·9	52·4	53·6	54·3	53·7	55·3
July	45·5	41·7	45·6	48·2	52·1	53·1	54·6	53·3	55·4
Aug.	45·3	42·3	46·1	49·0	52·1	53·4	55·0	53·8	55·7
Sept.	44·4	42·8	46·2	49·3	51·7	54·1	55·2	52·7	55·4
Oct.	43·7	42·9	45·8	49·4	51·5	53·7	53·7	53·6	55·0
Nov.	43·2	43·9	46·0	49·8	51·7	53·8	54·0	53·8	55·4
Dec.	41·9	43·5	45·2	49·0	51·4	52·7	52·9	52·4	54·9
Aver.	46·1	42·4	45·6	48·5	51·7	53·8	54·5	53·9	55·3

(iii.) HOW OUGHT THE RESERVE-RATIO TO BE FIXED ?

In Great Britain the reserve-ratio to be maintained by the banks has never been fixed by law. During the earlier period of English Joint-Stock Banking it was left to the banks themselves to keep

[1] Namely, the Bank of Liverpool, Barclay's, Coutts', Glyn Mills, Lloyds, Midland, National Provincial, Westminster and Williams'. The National Bank, which now publishes monthly figures, is excluded from all the tables in this chapter, since figures for it are not available throughout the period.

such amount as was dictated to them by considerations of prudence and of convenience ; and since the amount so kept was never published except in half-yearly balance-sheets which bore little relation to the normal position, there was no motive for them to keep more. In February 1891, however, Mr. Goschen, the Chancellor of the Exchequer (as he then was), made his celebrated speech at Leeds, in which he took advantage of the uneasiness ensuing on the Baring crisis of the previous year and its attendant circumstances, to argue that the amount of reserves which the banks were in the habit of keeping was insufficient for the safety of the system. The impression produced on public opinion was so great that the banks felt that they must do something. Moreover, Mr. Goschen intimated that he had a scheme of currency reform ready which he proposed to introduce into Parliament. " Owing ", as the *Economist* put it at the time, " to the antagonism of the bankers and the obstructive attitude of the Gladstonian party ", nothing came of the scheme, but the banks somewhat strengthened their reserves and began the publication of monthly statements. Since these monthly statements were primarily for public consumption, and since there were no legal requirements to satisfy, the practice of " window-dressing " them, which has continued to this day, was unfortunately adopted. As time went on, the diminished use of cash for daily business, and the progress of amalgamation of the banks amongst themselves [1] (which may be said to have begun on an intensive scale with the formation of Barclay's Bank in 1896), served to reduce the amount of reserves which the banks really required to meet contingencies, whilst the conventional figure

---

[1] In 1891 there were only four Joint-Stock Banks with deposits exceeding £10,000,000—namely, the London and County with £37,000,000, the London and Western with £27,000,000, the Union with £16,000,000, and the London Joint-Stock with £13,000,000.

increased slightly on account of the banks, for reasons of advertisement and prestige, tending to aim at the ratio which was maintained at first only by the stronger amongst them. By 1926 the position was such that Dr. Leaf, writing as Chairman of the Westminster Bank, described the ratio as " purely arbitrary ".[1]

In the United States the position is, as we have seen, rather different. The ratio, varying somewhat for differing types of banks, is laid down by law. Moreover the ratio is much lower for time-deposits than for demand-deposits. Further, till-money does not reckon at all as part of the lawful reserves, so that in the United States any pretension of the amount of the reserves being governed by the actual requirements of the banks to meet sudden contingencies has been given up.

Why, then, we must ask, should law or custom impose on the banks the maintenance of greater reserves than they really require ? In part, no doubt —like so much else in our currency and credit arrangements—this practice is a mere survival of a past state of affairs, and a result of our purporting to conduct a representative money system as though it were a kind of commodity money system. But there is also a sound practical reason lying behind it. The custom of requiring banks to hold larger reserves than they strictly require for till-money and for clearing purposes is a means of making them contribute to the expenses which the Central Bank incurs for the maintenance of the currency.

Under conceivable monetary systems this might not be necessary. But where there is an international standard to maintain, the Central Bank must keep a certain amount of idle resources, not earning interest or not earning adequate interest, in the form of metallic or other reserves. If, by virtue of the

---

[1] *Banking*, p. 130.

practice adopted by the Central Bank of recognising
certain bills or certain types of security as " eligible ",
there exist perfectly liquid interest-bearing investments, the member banks would be able, in theory,
to cut their reserves very fine—limiting them, indeed,
to their requirements for till-money and the day's
clearing.   It is reasonable, therefore, in such circumstances that the member banks should be compelled to share part of the expense of maintaining
the ultimate reserves of the system as a whole—
without the existence of which the convenient practice of " eligible " bills and " eligible " collateral
might sometimes break down ; and this is effected
by their being compelled to maintain a certain proportion of non-interest-bearing deposits at the Central
Bank or of non-interest-bearing notes.

The greater part of the central metallic reserves of
the modern banking system is still generally provided,
it is true, by the active note-issue in the hands of the
public ; but the silent trend of evolution is, I think,
in the direction of the Government regarding the
note-issue as a legitimate source of revenue [1] and of the
member banks being required to provide their quotas
towards the maintenance of the central reserves.

So long as the proportion of cash reserves which the
member banks are expected to maintain is determined
solely by what they need for their own safety and convenience, there is much to be said for the traditional
British practice of leaving it to the banks to decide for themselves what the appropriate figure is—
especially when a stage has been reached, as is now

---

[1] Since the above was written, the new Bank Note Act (1928) in Great
Britain has assigned the whole of the profits of the fiduciary issue to the
Treasury and the whole of the profits of the non-interest-bearing deposits
of the member banks to the Bank of England. Since the fiduciary issue is
not equal to the active circulation in the hands of the public, whilst the
member banks' deposits at the Bank of England are not the whole of their
conventional reserves, this arrangement is not as logical as it looks. Nevertheless the figures work out in practice not very far from the arrangement
suggested above.

the case in Great Britain, when mushroom banking is extinct.   But as soon as further considerations
are considered relevant—considerations, such as the
above, affecting the safety and efficiency of the banking system as a whole rather than the interests of
individual banks—it is by no means so clear that this
is the best plan.   Post-war developments in the
technique of Central Bank management—developments both inevitable and desirable which we shall
explain more fully in Book VII. below—have brought
us to a transitional stage between the two criteria
of reserve proportions.   Modern methods of Central
Bank control, particularly the use of " open-market
operations ", necessitate that the Central Bank
should be in a position to dispose of resources of a
certain size in relation to the scale of the banking
system as a whole ; and it is right and reasonable
that the member banks should contribute, in the
shape of non-interest-bearing deposits held by them
with the Central Bank, the bulk of the resources
which are required for the safety of the highly
economical and efficient system the existence of which
enables the member banks to be so comfortable and
profitable.   Now it is probable that the normal level
of bankers' deposits, required to make the Bank of
England strong beyond a doubt and able in all circumstances to impose its will on the market without
straining its own earning capacity unduly, is greater
than the member banks strictly require for the safe
and convenient transaction of their own business.
If this is true, then both what one observes and what
one would expect concur in raising a doubt whether
it is desirable to go on leaving the matter entirely to
the discretion of the member banks.

If we were to go back fifty years, we should
probably find that the reserves of the member banks
were at that time no higher than were required by
their own safety and convenience—except, perhaps,

on balance-sheet dates.　Between balance-sheet dates
there was indeed no sufficient motive for locking up
resources unnecessarily.　The growth of amalgama-
tions, the diminished use of cash by the public, and
the general progress of the speed and efficiency of
banking machinery generally during the intervening
period, have tended to diminish the proportion of
reserves which is strictly necessary.　Our banks, however, owing to their conservatism, and owing to the
unwillingness of any one of them to appear to be the
first to lower its reserve ratio below those of its
neighbours, have not taken full advantage of this,
with the result that we have arrived at the existing
rather artificial position in which the banks voluntarily
maintain, for reasons which are probably not very
clear to their own minds, somewhat larger reserves
than they really require.　Nevertheless the natural
desire to make as much profit as is compatible with
safety and with appearances has caused them to
employ such a very undesirable ruse as the " window-
dressing " operations described above, whereby their
real proportions are appreciably lower than their
apparent proportions.　Nor is there, in fact, any
substantial obstacle to their nibbling at their conventional ratios as the result of concerted or sympathetic action continued by slow degrees over a
period.

　　The possibilities of the situation may be illustrated
by an interesting episode which occurred in 1927–29.
The Midland Bank had, as pointed out above, maintained for some years past a reserve proportion a good
deal higher than those of its competitors.　It is not
obvious that this had really been worth while from
its own point of view.　Accordingly, beginning in the
latter part of 1926, a gradual downward movement
became apparent in the Midland Bank's proportion
from about 14·5 per cent in 1926 to about 11·5 per
cent in 1929.　Since the Midland Bank's deposits

amounted during this period to at least £370,000,000, this was equivalent to a release of more than £11,000,000 in cash, and in fact enabled the banks as a whole to increase their deposits (and their advances) by about £100,000,000 without any increase in their aggregate reserves. Thus the result of the total operation is either an acquiescence on the part of the Bank of England in a substantial increase in the volume of bank-money without any increase in the volume of reserves, or a depletion of the Bank of England's resources by £11,000,000—the Midland Bank gaining and the Bank of England losing the interest on this sum.

Now, as it happened, this relaxation of credit was in the particular circumstances greatly in the public interest. For an increase in the total of member bank deposits was needed to balance an increase in their fixed deposits—an increase which the Bank of England, if left to itself, might not have allowed in a sufficient degree. Thus the Midland Bank was, in fact, not only acting in its own interest along lines which no one could criticise (for its ratio of reserve was still higher than the average of the other banks), but was also materially aiding the general situation. Nevertheless such an expansion of the resources of the member banks should not, in any sound modern system, depend on the action of an individual member bank, even though it remains within the power of the Central Bank to counteract its effect by appropriate measures. For we ought to be able to assume that the Central Bank will be at least as intelligent as a Member Bank and more to be relied on to act in the general interest.

I conclude, therefore, that the American system of regulating by law the amount of the Member Bank Reserves is preferable to the English system of depending on an ill-defined and somewhat precarious convention.

Moreover, the possibility of all or some of the " Big

Five " nibbling at their proportions is not the only
reason for regularising the present system so as to
render the control of the Bank of England unchallengeable. At present the reserves of the member banks
consist, as pointed out above, not only of their
deposits at the Bank of England but also of what
they call their " cash ", and it is open to them to
vary freely the proportions in which their total
reserves are divided between the two categories.
Normally the " cash " consists of Bank (or, formerly,
Treasury) Notes, but it might also consist of gold or,
conceivably though never yet in practice so far as I
am aware in the case of English banks, in deposits in
a Central Bank abroad. Now each of these options
contains a possibility of surprise and inconvenience
for the Bank of England, as follows :

(1) So long as the Bank of England calculates its
reserve " proportion " by its present formula, the
position can be artificially influenced within wide
limits if the member banks turn their " cash " into
deposits at the Bank of England or *vice versa*. Indeed
the adequacy or inadequacy of the existing fiduciary
issue in its effect on the Bank's free reserves largely
depends on the policy of the member banks in the
above respect.

(2) If the member banks were to hold a part of
their reserves in actual gold, the effect might be to
diminish either the profits or the free gold of the
Bank of England below the point of safety. A
clause was, indeed, wisely inserted in the Bank Note
Act of 1928 to provide against this contingency, by
which the Bank of England is given the power of
compulsory purchase of any gold so held within
this country. This clause does not, however, prevent
a member bank from reckoning as part of its reserves
gold held abroad or in transit ; and cases are believed
to have occurred recently in which a bank has taken
advantage of this liberty.

(3) There is nothing to prevent an English member bank from holding a part of its reserves " earmarked " with the Federal Reserve Bank of New York. From the point of view of safety, and even of convenience, such deposits would be practically " as good as gold ". But it is obvious that this practice would greatly diminish the Bank of England's power of controlling the volume of Bank-money in England by depriving it of the necessary volume of resources and profits. I am not aware that this option has ever yet been exercised. But the risk is quite a real one. For in the case of Continental member banks the practice of holding some part of their reserves at foreign centres is very common. And sometimes—for example, in Switzerland, as I am informed—the practice is carried so far as to impair very greatly the authority of the Central Bank. In Germany at the present time the large proportion of their liquid resources which the leading member banks hold in foreign centres is capable of interfering seriously with the hegemony of the Reichsbank.

Furthermore, there are a great many banks, including London branches of overseas banks, other than the ten Clearing Banks, publishing no monthly or average figures, which take advantage of the facilities of the London Money Market without necessarily contributing proportionately to the resources of the Bank of England.

Finally, there are certain important technical advantages which are impracticable without a legal reserve proportion, the full significance of which will appear in subsequent pages, namely a differentiation between the reserves required against Demand and Time Deposits respectively, and the power to the Bank of England to *vary* the legal proportions from time to time within prescribed limits.

The question of the principle of establishing legal reserve proportions for all banks is distinct from the question as to what these regulations should be. I suggest, however, something on the lines following :

(i.) The prescribed proportions to cover all bank [1] deposits payable in sterling in Great Britain.

(ii.) Deposits payable on thirty (or, perhaps, fourteen) days' notice or more to reckon as Time Deposits.

(iii.) The prescribed proportions to relate to daily averages over monthly periods.

(iv.) The cash reserves to consist either of Bank of England Notes or of deposit balances at the Bank of England, but not less than 40 per cent of the total to be held in the latter form.

(v.) The normal prescribed proportions of cash reserves to deposits to be as follows :

Demand Deposits	. .	15 per cent
Time Deposits .	. .	3 ,,

(vi.) The Bank of England to have the power on thirty days' notice to vary the prescribed proportions to a figure between 10 and 20 per cent in the case of Demand Deposits and to a figure between 0 and 6 per cent in the case of Time Deposits.

These regulations would greatly strengthen the power of control in the hands of the Bank of England —placing, indeed, in its hands an almost complete control over the total volume of Bank-money—without in any way hampering the legitimate operations of the Joint-Stock Banks. The importance for this purpose of (vi.) will transpire more fully in Chapter 32 (vi.).

Thus in countries where the percentage of reserves to deposits is by law or custom somewhat rigid, we are thrown back for the final determination of M, the Volume of Bank-money, on the factors which determine the amount of these reserves. How far

---

[1] The legal definition of a " Bank " presents some—not insuperable— difficulties which are legal, rather than economic, in character.

are they determined by the Central Bank, with the behaviour of the Member Banks necessarily following in a more or less passive way ? And how far, if at all, is the amount of the reserves influenced by the Member Banks themselves acting on their own initiative ? Only in so far as the latter is true need we modify the statement that the Member Banks do no more than determine in what form they will lend, and not how much they will lend altogether.

The answers to these questions we must postpone to Book VII.

CHAPTER 26

THE ACTIVITY OF BUSINESS

(i.) The Influence of Business Activity on the Velocity of the Business-deposits

It has long been held that, when business is brisk, cash is turned over quicker. Indeed the velocity may increase in such circumstances *more* than in proportion to the transactions ; so that an increase of transactions, instead of being associated with a falling price-level as it would be if " other things remained equal ", is in fact regularly associated in the minds of business men with a rising price-level. We have seen in Chapter 24 that there are obvious reasons why this conclusion should be plausible. When business is brisk the whole process of exchange is accelerated, and this acceleration diminishes the average amount of time for which it is necessary or convenient to retain cash between transactions : receipts and disbursements follow hotter on one another's heels. Moreover, when markets are good, satisfactory sales can be foreseen with greater confidence, so that, at least in the belief of the business world, there is less need for provision against the contingencies of frozen stocks or debts which cannot be collected. There is also the further reason that when business is brisk there may be more strain on the resources of traders for the provision of working capital, so that they economise their holdings of cash to the utmost possible extent. The argument may nevertheless rely too much on the mere fact that in actual experience brisker business is generally accompanied by a rising, not by a falling, price-level. For this fact may be better explained by over-investment causing the second term of the Fundamental Equation to increase, than by influences which directly affect true velocities.

The conclusion, that an expansion in the real volume of transactions tends to be accompanied by an increase in velocity *more* than in proportion, is a view often held. But there is a class of writers who maintain that the variations in the two factors tend to be *equal*—*i.e.* that there is an almost strict proportionality in their movements. Professor Angell has quoted Wieser as an early adherent of this doctrine, and Baron Charles Mourne as a recent advocate of it in France.[1] The exposition on these lines most familiar to contemporary students[2] is, however, that of Mr. Carl Snyder of the New York Federal Reserve Bank.[3]

Mr. Snyder's conclusions are empirical and are based on a computation of the variability of the ratio of American Bank Debits (*i.e.* Bank Clearings) to Demand Deposits in past years, or, in my terminology, of the velocity of the Cash-deposits. He compares this not with the volume of " transactions " but with that of " trade ". Since Mr. Snyder's tables represent the fullest investigation yet made of the

---

[1] *The Theory of International Prices*, p. 327 and p. 279. This volume is a most valuable source for the history of monetary doctrines.

[2] Professor Angell (*op. cit.* p. 180) quotes Professor Worthing (" Prices and the Quantity of Circulating Medium," *Quarterly Journal of Economics*, 1923) as the first recent American writer on these lines.

[3] See his articles " New Measures in the Equation of Exchange " (*American Economic Review*, 1924), " A New Index of Business Activity " (*Journal of the American Statistical Association*, 1924), and " A New Index of the General Price Level from 1875 " (*Journal of the American Statistical Association*, 1924) ; and his book *Business Cycles and Business Measurements*, of which chapter vii. summarises these articles. Mr. Snyder seems to claim somewhat less validity for his generalisations in his book than in the articles which preceded it.

variability of the velocity of the Cash-deposits, it will be useful to reproduce them, whether or not we accept the generalisation which he bases on them.

The following table shows the average annual percentage variability from the normal velocity (defined as the ratio of Clearings (or Debits) to Demand Deposits) for 141 cities, including New York City, as compared with the volume of " trade " :

Annual Average.	Velocity of Circulation. (100 = 1919–1925 average.)	Volume of U.S. Trade.
1919	102	104
1920	102	101
1921	94	92
1922	98	102
1923	99	108
1924	99	105
1925	105	111

Even if we take this table at its face value, there does not seem to be very much in the alleged correlation, except as regards the drop in both of them in the slump of 1921. If, however, we take the velocity of the Cash-deposits for the whole country, instead of 141 cities, the alleged correlation becomes even less impressive, as is shown in the table below, no correlation whatever having been apparent since 1922. If, on the other hand, we take the figures for New York City, also shown below, there is a fair degree of correspondence as regards the *direction* of the movements :

[TABLE

(100 = 1919–1925 average)

	Velocity of Cash-deposits.		Volume of Trade, U.S.
	For Whole Country.	For New York City.	
1919	110	98	104
1920	106	96	101
1921	94	89	92
1922	99	98	102
1923	98	103	108
1924	97	103	105
1925	96	114	111

Thus it might be that if Mr. Snyder had alleged a correspondence between the velocity of the Business-deposits, instead of the velocity of the Cash-deposits, and the volume of Trade, he would have been nearer the truth. On the other hand, this statement also might be too loose ; for, as we have seen, the Business-deposits are employed not only for the handling of " trade " but also for financial and Stock Exchange transactions, the real volume of which may sometimes move with that of trade, but may often not.[1] Thus the statistical foundation of the theory is scarcely sufficient to support it.

(ii.) THE RELATION BETWEEN THE BANK CLEARINGS AND THE VOLUME OF TRADE

Can we obtain out of the Bank Clearings a satisfactory index to the volume of trade or output ? It

---

[1] Mr. Snyder points out that the influence of Stock Exchange transactions on the Clearings is not, even in New York, so great as might have been supposed, since 80 per cent or more of the transactions on the New York Stock Exchange is cleared by the Stock Exchange's own clearing corporation (*Review of Economic Statistics*, Feb. 1928, p. 41). Nevertheless, allowing for cheques between brokers and their clients, the influence must be very considerable.

depends on whether we can isolate transactions relating to the Industrial Circulation from those relating to the Financial Circulation, or at least obtain an approximate index of changes in the former.

Let us write

B (the volume of Bank Clearings) $= Q_1 R_1 + Q_2 R_2$

where R_1 = volume of Wages and current production of goods (finished and unfinished) traded,

R_2 = volume of Bonds, Shares, Real Estate, and other financial obligations changing hands,

each weighted in proportion to its cash-using importance ; and Q_1 and Q_2, the price-levels of each of these, weighted on the same system.

It is then seen that B is only a reliable index to $Q_1 R_1$ in so far as $Q_2 R_2$ is small compared with $Q_1 R_1$, or in so far as it varies in the same way. For the bank clearings of the country as a whole there is no justification for regarding $Q_2 R_2$ as small. But it is sometimes possible to isolate a particular section of the bank clearings for which this assumption is more nearly justified. For example, it used to be a common practice to exclude the London Stock Exchange clearing days from the total clearings in order to obtain a figure which might be a useful indication of the state of British trade ; but since there are now no special settling days in the London gilt-edged market, this correction is no longer sufficient. The most serviceable means of partially isolating $Q_1 R_1$ in England at the present time is to take the Country Clearings and the Provincial Clearings (namely, the inter-Bank Clearings in the chief provincial towns), since by this means the bulk of the purely financial transactions are probably excluded, inasmuch as they pass through London.

Nor does $Q_1 R_1$ vary in the same way as $Q_2 R_2$. The price-index of shares, may, it is true, tend to move in the long run with Q_1, the price-index of wages and commodities, and an exceptional activity of the share market will often accompany an exceptional activity of trade. But at times of a rapidly changing price-level the index of gilt-edged securities will tend to move, not in the same, but in the *opposite* direction from Q_1. This can be illustrated from the post-war price and banking statistics of England. In the following table A is the price of fixed-interest securities and B is the price of industrial Ordinary Shares, as calculated by the London and Cambridge Economic Service; C is the Consumption Index Number for Great Britain (see Vol. i. p. 62); and D is the Board of Trade Index Number of wholesale prices:

(1913 = 100)

	A.	B.	C.	D.
1919	73	168	215	258
1920	64	169	257	308
1921	66	116	223	198
1922	79	132	181	159
1923	82	162	170	159
1924	81	158	172	165
1925	80	180	172	159
1926	79	187	169	148
1927	79	201	166	141
1928	81	237	164	139

Since, moreover, the activity of financial transactions is far more variable than that of industrial transactions, it seems clear that the *total* volume of bankers' clearings will be almost worthless as an index to the volume of trade transactions arising out of current production and consumption, unless we exclude Stock Exchange transactions. This conclusion is confirmed by the figures of the total clearings. The

total bank clearings (B), corrected for price by the
Board of Trade Index-Number of wholesale prices
(D), give the following result :

Year.	B.	D.	B/D.
1913	45	63	71
1920	110	194	57
1921	96	125	77
1922	101	100	101
1923	100	100	100
1924	108	104	104
1925	110	100	110
1926	109	93	117
1927	113	89	127
1928	120	88	136

Now if we were to argue from the Fisher
equation $MV = PT$ that, since $B = MV$, B/D is
an index to the volume of trade, we should arrive
at absurd results. For we should find that the
so-called "volume of trade" was 50 to 100 per
cent greater during the slump of 1921–22 than it
had been during the boom of 1919–20 ; that it was
nearly 50 per cent greater in 1925–26 than before
the war ; that it was 7 per cent greater in the great
strike year, 1926, than in 1925 ; and that it is nearly
double to-day what it was before the war. This is a
reductio ad absurdum of calculations on these lines.
Clearly the inclusion of all kinds of financial transactions and the correction of the price-level by reference
to the Wholesale Standard have made enough difference to vitiate the results completely.

Let us, however, consider whether, if we confine
our calculations to the Country and Provincial Clearings in which Stock Exchange transactions do not
play an important part, the result of correcting their
money volume by an appropriate index-number of
prices will conform with what we know from other
sources about the fluctuations in the volume of trade.

What is the most appropriate index-number for this purpose ? I believe that an index made up mainly of wholesale prices for a period three months earlier and of wages for the current period would be serviceable, though something much better could be contrived by the Board of Trade with the whole apparatus of Government statistics behind it. For present purposes, however, we may take the Consumption Index, the method of compilation of which has been explained above (p. 61), and then obtain a " Clearings Index " of the Volume of Production by dividing the Country and Provincial Clearings (compiled as on p. 40 above) by this Consumption Index.

If now we compare the annual average of the Clearings Index, thus arrived at, with Mr. Rowe's Index of Production, compiled for the London and Cambridge Economic Service, which is mainly based on the consumption of raw materials, and with Mr. Rokeling's [1] Index of the Volume of Employment, the result is as shown in the table opposite.

Generally speaking, the agreement between the fluctuations of these entirely independent calculations —they have not a single direct constituent the same —is remarkable. I believe that the most comprehensive Index of Production for Great Britain might be obtained by taking an average of these three indexes, as shown in the last column opposite. For the somewhat slower rate of recent growth in the Clearings Index compared with the other two, more purely industrial, indexes may be a necessary corrective where we are dealing with the economic activities of the country as a whole ; whilst the recent tendency of the Raw Material Index to outstrip the Employment Index may reflect an increase of efficiency.

[1] This index is part of an Index of Production for Great Britain compiled by Mr. Rokeling (*Economist*, Oct. 6, 1928) as follows :

1920 .	.	. 101	1923 .	.	. 93	1926 .	. . 90
1921 .	.	. 75	1924 .	.	. 100	1927 .	. . 105
1922 .	.	. 88	1925 .	.	. 99		

(1924 = 100)

	Clearings Index (Keynes).	Employment Index * (Rokeling).	Raw Material Index (Rowe).	Composite Production Index (average of the three).
1920	101·5	103	104·5	103
1921	78	89·5	75·5	81
1922	91·5	93·5	89·5	91·5
1923	97	97	91	95
1924	100	100	100	100
1925	101	101	101	101
1926	95	95·5	90	93·5
1927	101·5	104·5	110	105
1928	102·5	104·5	108·5	105
1929	104	106	116·2	108·7

* These figures have been kindly supplied to me by Mr. Rokeling, and are slightly revised from those published by him in the *Economist*. They represent A + B – C – D – E, where A = number of agricultural labourers, B = number of insured workers aged 16-64, C = number of insured workers unemployed, D = number of insured workers absent from sickness, accident, etc., E = number of persons directly involved in trade disputes. They make no allowance for increased efficiency on the one hand, or for short time on the other.

An Index of the Volume of Trade based on the Country and Provincial Clearings corrected for price may indeed be superior in some respects to indexes based on statistics of production and output ; since, as Mr. Snyder has pointed out in dealing with similar statistics for the United States,[1] most indexes of production are overweighted with the basic commodities, whereas the volume of cheque transactions offers a more comprehensive picture embracing all those numerous miscellaneous activities which, whilst they are too small individually to be caught in the mesh of the statistician's net, are nevertheless very important in the aggregate. It is a further advantge of such an index that the figures are available

[1] *Business Cycles and Measurements*, p. 79.

promptly without the necessity for any special calculation.

Mr. Snyder's calculations for the United States confirm the value of the Bank Clearings, outside the chief financial centre, corrected for price (meaning, however, by "price"—as in my own calculations above—not the Wholesale Index but the Consumption Index) as an index of the Volume of Trade. The following table is based on a three months' moving average of the Bank Debits for 140 cities outside New York City[1] corrected for price by Mr. Snyder's "General Price-Level", and on his independently compiled index of the Total Volume of Trade.

	Bank Debits outside N.Y.C. corrected for price.	Volume of Trade.
1919 .	105	104
1920 .	102	101
1921 .	92	92
1922 .	101	102
1923 .	105	108
1924 .	102	105
1925 .	110	111

(iii.) Statistical Summary

The estimates of the preceding chapters are summed up in the following table. Although the reader must not overlook the large element of guesswork, approximation and probable error which this table involves in the present deplorable state of our banking and other statistics, it has, I think, some value

[1] The Harvard Economic Service now exclude, in addition to New York City, the Debits of seven other important cities which are more or less financial, as well as business, centres, for the purposes of their B curve, which is intended to reflect business conditions.

as a general indicator of the variability of the different factors involved.

I have no doubt that in a few years' time such guesses will appear hopelessly amateurish and inaccurate, and will be replaced by scientific estimates. But by indicating what figures it would be interesting to know and by making doubtful attempts at their value, I may stimulate others, who are in a position to get better *data*, to correct me. The compilation of official figures has generally been preceded in England by the rash and imperfect efforts of individuals.

(1924 = 100)

	Total Deposits,* M.	Proportion of Cash-deposits to Total Deposits,† w.	Cash-deposits, Mw.	Velocity, V.‡	Industrial Cash Turnover, MVw.§	Volume of Production, O. (Rowe and Rokeling.)[1]
1920	100	111	111	137	152	104
1921	108	100	108	93	101	82
1922	106	100	106	91	96	91·5
1923	100	102	102	94	96	94
1924	100	100	100	100	100	100
1925	99	98	97	104	101	101
1926	100	96	96	97	93	93
1927	103	96	99	99	98	107
1928	106	94·5	100	98	98	106·5
1929	108	93	100	98	98	111

* As computed on p. 10.   † As computed on p. 10.
‡ As computed on p. 40.
§ This has brought us back again to the index of the Country and Provincial Bank Clearings as computed on p. 40, since we arrived at V by dividing this by Mw.

If we assume that the variations in the amount and in the velocity of the cash-deposits applicable to in-

[1] I have taken the mean of the indexes of Rowe and Rokeling given on p. 87, since to introduce the Clearings Index in this context would be begging the question—though in fact it would not make much difference to the result.

come transactions and current business, apart from
financial transactions, are approximately measured by
Mw and V respectively, *i.e.* that the turnover of the
Industrial Circulation is measured by the Country
and Provincial clearings, then, if there is no Profit
Inflation or Deflation, MVw should furnish us with
an index to the aggregate cost of current output,
and MVw/O should give us an index of the price-
level of current output. If, therefore, our statistics
could be relied on, the divergence between MVw/O
and the actual price-level of output would be a partial
indication of the divergence between cost and value,
i.e., of the degree of Profit Inflation or Deflation. For
with Profit Inflation (or Deflation) present we should
expect the actual price-level to be higher (or lower)
than the price-level indicated by MVw/O. As a first
approximation, therefore, for deducing the degree of
Profit Inflation (or Deflation) let us set side by side
the theoretical price-level given by MVw/O, the Consumption Price-Index (Vol. i., p. 61) and the Wholesale Price-Index (Board of Trade Index) :

	MVw/O.	Consumption Price Index.	Wholesale Price Index.	Profit Inflation or Deflation.*
1920	146	150	186	127
1921	123	132	120	98
1922	105	106	96	91
1923	102	99	96	94
1924	100	100	100	100
1925	100	101	96	96
1926	100	98	89	89
1927	91	96	86	94·5
1928	92	95	85	94·5
1929	88	94	82	93

* Given by dividing the Wholesale Index by MVw/O.

Unfortunately the Consumption Index is not
appropriate for the present purpose, because our Index

of Output excludes services,[1] whereas we have expressly weighted the Consumption Price Index so as to include them. On the other hand, the Wholesale Price Index is too much concerned with imported raw materials and too little with finished goods. If, however, failing anything better, we take the latter as our index of the price-level of output exclusive of services, the degree of Profit Inflation (or Deflation) will be very roughly indicated by dividing this index by MVw/O, as in the table above. By taking 1924 as our base year, we have, it must be noticed, tacitly assumed that this was a year of equilibrium in which neither Profit Inflation nor Profit Deflation was present in any sensible degree.

The possible sources of error have piled up by now to such an extent that I am scarcely entitled to attach any serious value to the final column of the above table. But at least it does not contradict the conclusions of the fundamental argument of Book III. For the degree of Profit Inflation or Deflation, as here shown, is quite in accordance with our reasonable expectations. The boom of 1920, persisting into the first half of 1921 but balanced by the slump of the latter half of that year, the continuing slump of 1922–23, the acute distresses of 1926, and the long drawn out profit deflation of 1927–29 display themselves appropriately.

[1] This also vitiates MVw/O for the above purpose to some extent; but not too much, since the amount of monetary turnover corresponding to the remuneration of services is relatively small.

BOOK VI

THE RATE OF INVESTMENT AND ITS FLUCTUATIONS

CHAPTER 27

FLUCTUATIONS IN THE RATE OF INVESTMENT—
I. FIXED CAPITAL

WHEN there is a disequilibrium between savings and investment, this is much more often due to fluctuations in the rate of investment than to sudden changes in the rate of savings, which is, in normal circumstances, of a fairly steady character. To understand, therefore, the genesis and the severity of the disequilibria which we have analysed in Volume i., it is chiefly necessary to consider what causes the rate of investment to fluctuate and to estimate the order of magnitude of such fluctuations. In this chapter and the two following, we shall treat in turn the causes and the degree of fluctuations of investment in Fixed Capital, Working Capital and Liquid Capital. These chapters are in the nature of a digression, which is doubtfully in place in a Treatise on Money but has to be included because the fluctuations in the rate of investment have not been treated, sufficiently for my purpose, elsewhere.

In the case of Fixed Capital it is easy to understand why fluctuations should occur in the rate of investment. Entrepreneurs are induced to embark on the production of Fixed Capital or deterred from doing so by their expectations of the profit to be made. Apart from the many minor reasons why these should fluctuate in a changing world, Professor Schumpeter's explanation of the major movements may be unreservedly

accepted.   He points to " the innovations made from
time to time by the relatively small number of exceptionally energetic business men—their practical
applications of scientific discoveries and mechanical
inventions, their development of new forms of industrial and commercial organisation, their introduction of unfamiliar products, their conquests of new
markets, exploitation of new resources, shifting of
trade routes, and the like.   Changes of this sort, when
made on a large scale, alter the data on which the
mass of routine business men have based their plans.
But when a few highly-endowed individuals have
achieved success, their example makes the way easier
for a crowd of imitators.   So, once started, a wave of
innovation gains momentum." [1]

It is only necessary to add to this that the pace,
at which the innovating entrepreneurs will be able to
carry their projects into execution at a cost in interest
which is not deterrent to them, will depend on the
degree of complaisance of those responsible for the
banking system.   Thus whilst the stimulus to a Credit
Inflation comes from outside the Banking System, it
remains a monetary phenomenon in the sense that
it only occurs if the monetary machine is allowed to
respond to the stimulus.

Fluctuations such as those just considered are due
to a change in the readiness to invest at a given rate of
interest.   Besides these we also have fluctuations in
the rate of investment due to a change on the side of
the rate of interest.   In a manner which we have
already examined in Chapter 13, a change in the rate
of interest will affect the advantages of owning a
particular piece of Fixed Capital so long as the income
derived from it remains unchanged.   But there will
be no reason for this income to be changed until the
supply of Fixed Capital has been changed relatively

[1] This convenient summary of Professor Schumpeter's views is taken
from Wesley Mitchell, *Business Cycles*, p. 21.

to the demand for it. The process of changing the
supply of Fixed Capital, until the income derived from
it is again in equilibrium with the rate of interest,
amounts, however, to the same thing as a change in
the rate of investment.

Thus, whenever the rate of interest changes for
reasons other than a change in the demand-schedule
for the use or enjoyment of Fixed Capital, it is reasonable to expect a change in the rate of investment.

It is worth while to note in passing that the transition, except when the change required is small, is
likely to be easier in respect of an increase than of a
decrease in the supply of Fixed Capital. For the rate
of obsolescence of existing Fixed Capital sets a limit
to the rate at which the total supply of it can be
decreased ; and since different kinds of Fixed Capital
will be affected unequally (for there is not the same
elasticity of demand for all of them), the actual maximum rate of decrease will be determined within still
narrower limits.

(i.) The Statistical Indications

When we turn, however, to the relevant statistics
to find some exact measure of the degree of these
fluctuations, we find that they are few and unsatisfactory. There is no single set of figures which
measures accurately what should be capable of quite
precise measurement—namely, the rate at which the
community is adding to its investment in Fixed
Capital. The best we can do, therefore, is to take a
number of partial indicators and to judge as well as
we can from their combined results.

It might have been supposed that the volume of
new issues on the investment market would provide a
reasonably accurate index. But this total does not
adequately represent the rate of investment in houses,
which are largely financed in other ways than through

the new issue market ; yet house-building is probably
larger than any other one kind of investment. On the
other hand, many so-called new issues merely represent
the transfer of existing assets from one party to another ; whilst in the case of holding, finance and investment companies there may be a large element
of duplication. Moreover, even in the case of those
classes of investment which are mainly financed by
bond issues, there is a lack of synchronisation between
the date at which the bonds come on to the market
and the date at which the corresponding investment
takes place. Thus bond issues are not a good index
of the *short-period* fluctuations in the types of investment which they finance. The fluctuations in the
rate of investment may, therefore, be either greater
or less than those in the rate of issue. Nevertheless,
fluctuations in the volume of new issues is one of the
partial indicators of which we must take account.

Much the greater part—probably not less than
three-quarters—of the Fixed Capital of the modern
world consists of Land, Buildings, Roads and Railways. Thus—turning from the financial side to the
physical side—any statistics directly bearing on the
activity of productive effort in these directions will
be of some assistance. For the United States there
is a set of statistics of this character which is very
significant for our purpose—namely, the monthly
values of Building Permits. Since the term " Building " includes in this connection Construction and
Contracting Works generally (including, I think, roads,
sewers and the like), these figures go a long way
towards giving us what we want. In Great Britain
we have no comparable figures ; but the volume of
employment in the Building and Contracting industries, and the incomplete quarterly returns of
building published in the *Labour Gazette*, give some
indication of the volume of investment in these
directions.

Since there are to-day comparatively few kinds of investment in Fixed Capital which do not employ a certain amount of iron and steel, some writers [1] have argued that the consumption of these materials—for which fairly accurate figures are available over a long term of years—affords a reliable barometer of the rate of fixed investment. Since, however, technical methods change and different types of investment, even where they consume iron and steel, consume them in widely varying proportions (compare, for example, house-building with ship-building), it is better not to exaggerate the value of this indicator by itself, but to be content with including it as one amongst several.

The result of statistical inquiries along these various lines (*vide* Wesley Mitchell's *Business Cycles, passim,* for a summary of the results) cannot, unfortunately, be reduced to tabular form, so as to allow us to make any satisfactory numerical estimate of the order of magnitude of the fluctuations in the rate of investment in fixed capital between one year and another. They are sufficiently definite, however, to make it clear that the fluctuations are substantial and that they are correlated with the phases of the Credit Cycle in quite as high a degree as our theory would lead us to expect.

(ii.) THEORIES OF THE CREDIT CYCLE BASED ON FLUCTUATIONS IN FIXED CAPITAL INVESTMENT

Indeed the fact of fluctuations in the volume of fixed investment and their correlation with the Credit Cycle has long been familiar, and has been made by numerous writers the basis of a solution of the Credit Cycle problem. Whilst—if my theory is right—these solutions have been incomplete, particularly through their neglect of fluctuations in working capital, most of them, even when they have appeared to reach opposite results, seem to me to have had hold of some

[1] Especially Hull and Spiethoff.

part of the truth. Some of them have attributed the Cycle to under-saving and some have attributed it to over-investment. Take, for example, the following contrast made by Professor Wesley Mitchell (*op. cit.* p. 151) : " Professor Tugan-Baranovski contends that crises come because people do not save enough money to meet the huge capital requirements of prosperity. Professor Spiethoff holds that crises come because people put their savings into too much industrial equipment and not enough consumption goods." If we interpret the first of these statements to mean that Saving falls short of Investment and the second to mean that Investment runs ahead of Saving, we see that the two authorities mean essentially the same thing—and also the same thing that I mean.

Accordingly I find myself in strong sympathy with the school of writers [1]—Tugan-Baranovski, Hull, Spiethoff and Schumpeter—of which Tugan-Baranovski was the first [2] and the most original, and especially with the form which the theory takes in the works of Tugan-Baranovski himself, and of two American amateur-economists (cranks, some might say), Rorty [3] and Johannsen.[4] The fault of Tugan-Baranovski lay

---

[1] For a most excellent short summary of the views of this school see Wesley Mitchell, *Business Cycles*, pp. 20-31.

[2] His theory was originally published in Russian in 1894.

[3] Colonel Rorty's theory of " over-commitments " is more directly applicable to cycles due to the growth of Working Capital at a rate in excess of Savings. But it has the merit of recognising that it is of the essence of the problem in these cases that the purchasing power is created as soon as expansion begins, whereas the goods come along at a later date governed by the duration of the productive process.

[4] Mr. N. Johannsen originally published his theory in *A Neglected Point in Connection with Crises*, 1908, and followed it up with pamphlets in 1925, 1926 and 1928. His doctrine of " Impair Savings ", *i.e.* of savings withheld from consumption expenditure but not embodied in capital expenditure and so causing entrepreneurs who have produced goods for consumption to sell them at a loss, seems to me to come very near to the truth. But Mr. Johannsen regarded the failure of current savings to be embodied in capital expenditure as a more or less permanent condition in the modern world due to a saturation of the Capital Market, instead of as a result of a temporary but recurrent failure of the banking system to pass on the full amount of the savings to entrepreneurs, and overlooks the fact that a fall in the rate of interest would be the cure for the malady if it were what he diagnoses it to be.

in his holding, or at any rate implying, that savings can in some way accumulate during depressions in an uninvested form and that this accumulated fund is then gradually used up during booms, and also in his suggesting that this failure of savings to become materialised in investments at a steady rate is due to the unequal distribution of wealth instead of to Schumpeter's "innovations" in conjunction with a failure of the banking system to respond in such a way as to preserve the desirable degree of stability. But none of these writers clearly apprehend the direct effect on prices of disequilibria between savings and investment and the part played by the Banking System. The pioneer work at this point is due to Mr. D. H. Robertson (*Banking Policy and the Price Level*). Moreover, lacking a version of the Quantity Theory of Money applicable to the problem of Credit Cycles, they have not got to the root of the matter or perceived that Cycles due to a growth of Working Capital are at least as "characteristic" as those primarily due to a growth of Fixed Capital.

CHAPTER 28

FLUCTUATIONS IN THE RATE OF INVESTMENT—
II. WORKING CAPITAL

SUBJECT to the necessary conditions (which will be elucidated in the later sections of this chapter) an increase in the volume of employment will usually require a more or less proportionate increase in the volume of working capital. Thus fluctuations of investment in working capital will be closely correlated with fluctuations in the volume of employment. An increased volume of employment may result either from abnormal activity due, for example, to an investment boom, or to a recovery from a preceding slump. In any case a Credit Cycle will, as we have seen, tend to be associated with an increased investment in working capital—if not in its primary phase, then in its secondary phase. Furthermore, it is generally impossible to increase the volume of employment (even when it is at a level far below the optimum) unless it is practicable to increase *pari passu* the volume of investment in working capital.

Now the practical importance of the fluctuations in the amount of the revolving fund of working capital, which result from these conditions, depends on their order of magnitude. If these fluctuations are substantial relatively to the time-rate at which new investment can be made available to replenish working capital either from new savings or by diminishing the volume of investment in liquid capital, then the ques-

tion before us is of great practical significance ; and
our analysis may furnish us with an important clue
to the explanation of the time-element in booms and
depressions. The phenomena of the boom may represent a struggle, concealed under the veil of the credit
system, to replenish working capital faster than would
be feasible under a régime of stable prices.

If, on the other hand, the possible variations in the
demand for working capital are quite small compared
with the other elements, so that any deficiency can be
rapidly made good out of stocks of liquid capital [1] and
out of current savings, then the practical bearing of
the above analysis is not important.

Let us proceed, therefore, to an attempt to estimate
the various factors *quantitatively*. How much working capital, for example, is required to run the industrial system of Great Britain at full steam ? How
much does it fluctuate between good times and bad ?
What relations does this fluctuation bear to stocks of
liquid goods, to the flow of current savings and of
total investment, and to the variability of investment
in fixed capital ?

(i.) THE STATISTICAL INDICATIONS

In order to reach an approximation to the order
of magnitude of the working capital of Great Britain
(*i.e.* the value of goods in process) under normal
conditions, we have to consider mainly the value of
the output and the average length of time occupied by
the productive process. For example, if the productive process lasts six months on the average, and if the
product grows in value at a steady rate so that its
average value during the six months is half its final
value; then it follows that the working capital required
is equal to three months' output.

It is evident that the amount of working capital

[1] As Mr. Hawtrey maintains; vide *Trade and Credit*, pp. 126 and 156.

required per unit value of output varies enormously between different products, corresponding to variations in the length of process—from next-to-nothing in the case of personal services up to the equivalent of a year's output or more in certain cases.

When we are calculating the working capital required by an individual country, we have also to consider at what stage of the trading and manufacturing process that country has to pay for its imports and at what stage it gets paid for its exports ; for the former is the date at which, for that country, the demand for working capital begins where imports are concerned, and the latter is the date at which the demand comes to an end where exports are concerned. For Great Britain the date of commencement is generally prior to the date of actual import, and the date of termination is generally after the date of export. The " process " of a Chinaman's shirt begins with the preparation of the cotton fields for sowing and ends when the Chinaman goes shopping. The working capital for the first stage is furnished by America ; from the time when the raw cotton is bought, or soon after, it is furnished by Lancashire ; when the auction has been held at Shanghai, or at some near date to that, it is furnished by China. The complete process may average from a year and a half to two years, out of which Lancashire may be responsible for six to nine months, whilst the product will already have acquired a considerable value before Lancashire takes it over. But the distribution between the three parties of the burden of finding the working capital may vary greatly, according as the China merchant pays promptly or slowly, and according to the length of time, mainly governed by the relative rates of interest, during which the cotton-bill is carried in the money-market of New York or in that of London. This example illustrates the difficulty of an exact computation in the case of a trading country. The

case of agricultural produce grown at home, and consumed at home at an even rate through the year,
offers, on the other hand, a simpler example ; it has
been calculated that the working capital required is
equal to about a year's output in the case of a mixed
farm growing cereals, and half a year's output in the
case of a grass and dairy farm.[1]

Another example for which fairly definite figures
can be given is that of copper, statistics being available of the amounts on hand at five successive stages
of its trip towards consumers—the total of blister at
smelteries, blister in transit, blister at refineries, metal
in process of being refined, and refined copper on hand
at refineries being one-third to one-half of the annual
output of virgin copper. This refers only to the metal-
lurgical system. Including copper in transit, in use
by manufacturers and in scrap, Dr. W. R. Ingalls,
director of the American Bureau of Metal Statistics,
believes that " the normal stock of copper in the U.S.
is equivalent to something between 6 months and
12 months' production, and more nearly the latter
than the former ".[2]

It would be an interesting and useful task to make
an accurate statistical estimate of working capital in
each main industry. I am not in a position to do this.
But it will be enough for the present argument if we
can reach a rough approximation to its order of
magnitude.

---

[1] These figures are based on calculations made by Mr. W. C. D. Whetham
and published by him in the *Economic Journal*, December 1925. In the
case of a mixed farm his figures in months are :

For the Mixed Farm.			*For the Dairy Farm.*		
Cereals .	.	13·6 to 14·5	Milk .	.	7·65
Cattle .	.	17·7	Fat pigs .	.	3·9
Milk .	.	8·3	Poultry and eggs	.	3·0
Sheep and wool	.	15·0	Weighted average	.	7·01
Pigs .	.	8·6			
Weighted average	.	13·77			

[2] W. R. Ingalls, *Wealth and Income of the American People*, 1923, p. 150,
quoted by Wesley Mitchell, *Business Cycles*, p. 96.

I propose to set out from the statistics for Great Britain at the level of productive activity and of prices and wages existing in 1924. We must chiefly depend on the figures of foreign trade, the aggregate wages bill, and the results of the Census of Production.

Consider the following statistics for Great Britain, stated in round numbers, relating to the price level and the trade activity of 1924 : [1]

	£ Million
Census of Production 1924—	
Net Output of all Industries covered by Census . . .	1719
Including	
Mining	236
Metal and Machine Trades	380
Textile, Leather and Clothing Trades . . .	305
Gross Output of Building and Contracting . . .	189
Net Output of Agriculture	300
Personal Services and use of Consumption Capital (Houses) .	650
Costs of Transport and Distribution	1000
Imports	1280
Exports	795
Wages Bill . . . . (say)	2000
Bank Advances and Discounts (9 banks)	1030
National Income	4000

These figures suggest, I think, that the working capital of Great Britain in 1924 was probably between £1,500,000,000 and £2,000,000,000. The net output of industry and agriculture *plus* imports came to £3,300,000,000. To finance this for six months would take £1,650,000,000, without allowing for costs of transport and distribution. The above limits are also in reasonable conformity with the other indications quoted above. In particular, they are in the neighbourhood of 40–50 per cent of a year's income. Provisionally, and pending a better estimate, I propose to adopt them as giving the order of magnitude of Great Britain's Working Capital.

Corresponding calculations for the United States suggest that this is not likely to be an over-estimate.

[1] Cf. Flux, " The National Income ", *Stat. Journ.*, 1929, Parts I. and II.

Both in the Census estimate and in the Federal Trade Commission estimate of the wealth of the United States in 1922 the value of goods in process and moving to consumption was estimated at 36 thousand million dollars, which was equal to about half the national income in the year in question. The Standard Statistics Service of New York has compiled some interesting figures as the amount of the "inventories"—which closely correspond to Working Capital as defined above—of industrial corporations in the United States. The inventories of more than 500 of the largest concerns, representing about a third of the industrial capital of the country, were found to amount to about 17 per cent of the total capital of these concerns and about 125 per cent of a year's net income. On this basis the total industrial working capital of the United States in 1927 would be about 9 thousand million dollars. Agricultural working capital and the greater part of trading and retailing working capital (some trading and retailing companies are included in the Standard Statistics list) would have to be added to this. Nevertheless, the Standard Statistics figures suggest to my mind that in 1927 total Working Capital was probably somewhat less than half the national income, whatever it may have been in 1922.

Owing to the greater relative importance of mining and agriculture as compared with manufacture in the United States than in Great Britain, both of which are long-process industries, one might expect working capital to be a somewhat larger proportion of a year's income there than here. On the other hand, the fact that Great Britain buys from and sells to distant markets on a relatively large scale cuts the other way.

We are left, therefore, with the conclusion that the value of working capital probably amounts to between 40 and 50 per cent of a country's annual income.

We must consider, next, the amount by which working capital is impaired at the bottom of a slump as compared with what it is at the top of a boom. Mr. Rowe's [1] index-numbers for the volume of production in Great Britain and Mr. Snyder's [2] for the volume of production in the United States are as follows :

	Great Britain (Rowe). 1907–1913 = 100.	U.S.A. (Snyder). 1910–1914 = 100.
1907	100·1	91·48
1908	93·2	81·75
1909	96·8	90·94
1910	97·1	96·28
1911	101·4	94·66
1912	103·5	101·93
1913	107·5	105·28
1914	..	102·20
1915	..	109·84
1916	..	124·53
1917	..	131·39
1918	..	125·49
1919	..	121·67
1920	97·2	128·97
1921	73·7	110·91
1922	88·7	128·66
1923	92·3	144·10
1924	97·5	141·22
1925	96·4	149·69
1926	79·8	..
1927	99·9	..

Another index of the physical volume of production for the United States is that brought up to date by Mr. Floyd Maxwell and sponsored by the Harvard

[1] Published by the London and Cambridge Economic Service. To preserve the continuity of record I have given Mr. Rowe's figures as originally published. He has since revised materially the figures for the later years. This index has not been corrected for secular trend.

[2] Snyder, *Business Cycles and Measurements,* p. 239. This index is based on 87 items and is uncorrected for trend.

Economic Service (*Review of Economic Statistics*, July 1927, p. 142):

	Agriculture.		Mining.		Manufacture.	
	Adjusted for trend.	Unadjusted. 1899 = 100.	Adjusted for trend.	Unadjusted. 1899 = 100.	Adjusted for trend.	Unadjusted. 1899 = 100.
1899	102	100	101	100	98	100
1900	100	101	97	106	93	101
1901	88	89	97	115	99	112
1902	108	114	98	123	105	122
1903	98	105	100	135	101	124
1904	106	116	94	136	95	122
1905	105	118	105	162	106	143
1906	109	125	105	170	110	152
1907	96	112	109	186	106	151
1908	100	119	87	154	87	126
1909	98	118	101	189	103	155
1910	100	122	102	208	101	159
1911	94	115	95	207	93	153
1912	108	137	102	221	102	177
1913	94	121	102	237	102	184
1914	106	137	95	225	91	169
1915	110	144	99	239	98	189
1916	96	126	108	269	112	225
1917	101	134	112	288	109	227
1918	100	135	110	289	104	223
1919	101	137	95	257	98	218
1920	110	150	105	293	101	231
1921	90	124	82	233	76	179
1922	99	138	87	254	97	237
1923	98	138	116	349	112	281
1924	96	136	106	324	101	259
1925	97	140	106	333	110	290
1926	99	144	113	361	111	301

Indexes of the physical volume of production are still in their infancy, and a high degree of accuracy cannot be claimed for any of the above. They are probably good enough, however, for our present purpose—especially as they show a fair measure of agreement. They suggest that the fluctuation between a boom year and the succeeding slump year has been, in severe cases, between 15 and 25 per cent.

Since these figures are averaged over a year, the variation between the top of the boom and the bottom of the slump is appreciably greater. In *Business Cycles* (pp. 343-354) Prof. Wesley Mitchell has discussed somewhat fully the amplitude of Business Cycles from 1878 to 1923, including thirteen major movements. The general effect of five different indexes of business activity is to indicate, with some considerable show of consistency, that on the average business is about 13 per cent below normal at the trough of a depression and about 13 per cent above normal at the peak of a boom ; the maximum figures in each case being about 25 per cent below and above respectively.

The figures for the fluctuation of employment in Great Britain, based on the Trade Union percentages (1921 and 1922 are 13½ per cent below 1920), are considerably less than the above—as one would expect, because these percentages do not adequately reflect partial employment and reduced intensity of employment. In the United States the decline in the volume of employment from the peak in 1920 to the trough of the depression in 1921–22 was about 30 per cent in Factories, Railways and Mines, and 16½ per cent for employments as a whole—agriculture, retail trade, and domestic and personal service, with a drop of 3 to 4 per cent, bringing down the average.

The fluctuations in business activity do not measure, of course, the fluctuation in the national income, but much exceed it. For the national income also includes personal services and the use of fixed consumption capital, both of which are much steadier than the above, and—in the case of Great Britain—income from foreign investments. Even less does it measure the fluctuation of national consumption ; for in good times investment is increased and in bad times it

is diminished.[1]   For example, Mr. King's figures for
the physical volume of Retail Trade in the United
States do not show a difference of more than 7 per
cent between boom and slump.   This is in accordance
with other indications.   We should not estimate the
order of magnitude of the variation of consumption
between boom and slump at above 10 per cent.

Assuming, then, that the peak of " business
activity " is 25 per cent above normal in the most
severe cases and 13 per cent above in a credit cycle
of average severity, with the trough correspondingly
below, the amplitude of the fluctuation in the demand
for working capital will be by no means so wide, since
it is governed by the average rate of employment of
the factors of production over a period equal to the
length of process and also covers the financing of
normal and seasonal stocks which do not fall away
so severely as employment.   On a balance of considerations we may perhaps assume, at least for
purposes of illustration, that the amplitude of the
fluctuation in the demand for working capital will be
about a third that of the fluctuation in " business
activity ", that is to say, 15 per cent from peak to
trough in severe cases and 10 per cent in the more
usual type of case.   It should be noted, in passing,
that the dates of maximum and minimum demands
for working capital will not coincide with the dates
of maximum and minimum " business activity ", but
will, generally speaking, be subsequent.

If these rough indications can be accepted, the impairment in the fund of Great Britain's working capital
between boom and slump in 1920–22 was of the order
of £250,000,000, measured in the prices of 1924,
namely, 15 per cent of £1,650,000,000, with a figure of
(say) £1,750,000,000 for the boom and £1,500,000,000

[1] Dr. Ingalls (quoted by Wesley Mitchell, *op. cit.* p. 154) thinks that in
1920–22 savings (probably meaning what I call investment) in the United
States shrank to about half their normal figure—say from 14 to 15 per cent
of the national income to a figure of 7 to 8 per cent.

for the slump. As before, I do not claim statistical
accuracy for these figures. But they will serve to
illustrate my argument, as indications of the order
of quantity which we are dealing with in extreme
cases.

What is the relation between £250,000,000 and a
year's normal savings at the same date ? The most
reliable estimates of the present level of savings in
Great Britain put them at about £500,000,000 per
annum. The figure in 1922–23 was probably somewhat lower—say £400,000,000 to £450,000,000. Thus
the depletion of working capital between boom and
slump may on this occasion have represented fully
half of a year's savings.

Generally speaking, the normal percentage of the
national income saved is put at 12 to 15 per cent. If,
therefore, Working Capital is normally 40 to 50 per
cent of the national income and fluctuates 10 to 15
per cent, the fluctuations in Working Capital are from
a third to a half of a year's savings.

We must not suppose, however, that the whole or
even the greater part of current savings is available
for the replenishment of working capital. For in
equilibrium the whole of current savings, apart from
the normal growth of working capital, is available
for additions to fixed capital, and the investment
market is mainly organised with this situation in view.
Moreover, some additional foreign investment is going
on all the time ; new building never stops ; and in
these and other ways a substantial part of new savings
is being drawn away at all times into fixed capital.
Moreover, some of the goods already in process will
be destined to emerge in the shape of fixed capital.

When, therefore, the time comes for the replenishment of working capital, it may be *impossible* to effect
this rapidly without rupturing the equilibrium of prices
and incomes. Even if appropriate steps are taken in
good time, two years or more may elapse before work-

ing capital can be restored ; and if such steps are not taken, a longer interval will be required.[1]

It may be equally impossible when employment is diminishing to compensate the impairment of working capital by increased investment in other directions. Thus the mere fact of a falling rate of employment will almost necessarily diminish the rate of investment ; although the full extent by which net investment falls off at such a time may be concealed from us by our being so accustomed to measure investment mainly by reference to the volume of new capital issues and the addition to the stock of fixed capital in the shape of houses and the like, which do not fall off so markedly. For example, the *Economist's* total of new issues on the London Market (excluding British Government issues which were for the purpose of funding short-dated debt) were as follows :

	Nominal Total.	Price Level.*	Total corrected for Price Level.
1919	£211,000,000	162	£130,000,000
1920	330,000,000	194	170,000,000
1921	186,000,000	125	149,000,000
1922	204,000,000	100	204,000,000
1923	194,000,000	100	194,000,000

* Wholesale Index.

Thus if new issues were an accurate indication of the rate of investment, the latter would have been actually greater in the slump year 1921 than in 1919. But when we remember that the fund of working capital was being rapidly built up after the war, during 1919 and part of 1920, and was being not less rapidly depleted in 1921, the figures bear a different complexion. The following calculation is not based on statistical data, but is a not unplausible guess as

---

[1] Professor Wesley Mitchell's tabulations (*Business Cycles*, p. 338) indicate that the mean duration of a period of advance is just under two years and the maximum duration about three years.

to what may have happened—intended to illustrate my argument rather than to state an historical fact :

(Price Level of 1923)

	Net Addition to Fixed Capital, including Foreign Investment.	Working Capital.	Total Net Investment.
	£	£	£
1919	280,000,000	+ 120,000,000	400,000,000
1920	370,000,000	+ 120,000,000	490,000,000
1921	275,000,000	− 250,000,000	25,000,000
1922	330,000,000	+ 75,000,000	405,000,000
1923	370,000,000	+ 50,000,000	420,000,000
1924	390,000,000	+ 100,000,000	490,000,000

Since the top of the boom came in the middle of 1920 and the bottom of the slump in the middle of 1921, our net investment during the first half of 1921 may well have been negligible. At the end of 1924 an additional working capital of at least £50,000,000 may still have been required to permit full employment of the factors of production available at that date. The replenishment of the stock of working capital in the United States after 1921 was for various reasons much faster.

Let us check this against the *Economist's* rough estimate of the net National Income (Oct. 4, 1924)— again only for purposes of illustration :

(£1,000,000's—prices of 1923)

	Economist Net Income.	Net Investment (as above).	Consumption.
1920	3,480	490	2,990
1921	2,816	25	2,791
1922	3,140	405	2,735
1923	3,470	420	3,050

These figures are open to many criticisms—I believe

all the *Economist's* figures to be too low absolutely but the figure of income in 1921 to be relatively too high—but for showing the possible order of magnitude of the fluctuations between one year and another they have their value.

Now the point of these illustrative figures is as follows. It was impossible for the volume of production and employment early in 1922 to recover to the level of the spring of 1920, unless the revolving fund of working capital could be restored *pari passu*, or unless there was a very substantial fall in real wages.[1] But once this fund had become impaired by the events of 1920–21, a very rapid restoration of working capital could not occur except by a great increase of total investment or by a substantial reduction in the proportion of income emerging in a fixed form. Now the first was not practicable without severe inflation, except over a period of time. Nor, for several reasons, was the second—for example, it was not practicable to abandon new building ; moreover, the usual proportion of goods in process at the time would be already destined to emerge in fixed form, and time —probably the best part of a year—would be required to modify this ; and finally, a certain proportion of the Factors of Production being specialised for the production of fixed capital, an attempt at curtailing fixed investment too drastically would do as much harm to the volume of employment in one direction as it did good in another. Furthermore, owing to the world-wide character of the slump, it was not easy to attract fresh working capital from abroad in the shape of raw materials and half-finished goods, as Germany did in 1925. Thus a monetary policy designed to facilitate a rapid increase in the rate of production and employment would have involved, almost certainly, an excess of investment over saving.

[1] In Great Britain the greater part of the fall in real wages was in fact postponed until the middle of 1922.

It is evident, therefore, that fluctuations in the amount of Working Capital are so large that they can, on occasion, be an *important* factor in bringing about a disequilibrium between the rates of Saving and of Investment.

The above discussion deals mainly with the statistical and quantitative side of Working Capital. The Theory of Working Capital has, however, suffered much neglect in its general aspects. In working out the argument of this Treatise, I found that I had to give considerable thought to this subject, if only to clear up my own mind. In the subsequent sections of this chapter I have ventured to introduce a summary of the results.

(ii.) The Theory of Working Capital

The definition of " Working Capital " given in Chapter 9 (Vol. i.) needs to be expanded. I define Working Capital as being the aggregate of goods (and the *cost* of Working Capital as the *cost* of the aggregate of goods) in course of production, manufacture, transport and retailing, including such minimum stocks, whether of raw materials or of finished products, as are required to avoid risks of interruption of process or to tide over seasonal irregularities (*e.g.* intervals between harvests or fluctuations of individual harvests about the mean). It does *not* include surplus stocks, which constitute liquid capital. But it includes without distinction goods in process, such as food and textiles, which will emerge as liquid income, the consumption of which will be spread over a short time, and goods in process, such as houses and railways, which will emerge as fixed capital, the consumption of which must be spread over a period, and are not immediately available.

The amount of Working Capital, thus defined, depends upon :

(1) The rate of in-put (*i.e.* the rate at which the product has been started into the machine of process) over a period of past time equal in length to the duration of the process.

(2) The intensity with which the Factors of Production are being and have been employed on a unit of the product at each stage of the process.

(3) The duration of the process upon which the Factors of Production are employed.

(4) The rate per unit of time of the cost of production, *i.e.* the rate of earnings of the Factors of Production per unit of efficient work applied to the product; which we may call, for short, the rate of wages.[1]

(5) The value of the stocks which must be carried to tide over the irregularities of the Seasons.

It is not difficult to reach from this a formula for the total volume of Working Capital,[2] in the most general case. If we define the " rate of employment " at any time as the sum of the number of units of product at each stage of process each multiplied by the intensity of employment at that stage,[3] then it is obtained by integrating (in respect of time) the rate of employment multiplied by the rate of wages, back to the beginning of all the processes not yet finished. It may, however, be more illuminating to use for illustration the simplest case—namely, where the rate of in-put of the product and the rate of the intensity of employment of the Factors of Production have both been constant. In this case the volume of working capital required is equal to the rate of employment multiplied by *half* the duration of process multiplied by the rate of the cost of production (working capital = employment × ½ length of process × rate of wages). Thus, since the wages bill per unit of time is equal to the volume of employment

---

[1] " Wages " here includes the remuneration of *all* the Factors of Production.

[2] I am neglecting, in the next few paragraphs, the working capital required to carry seasonal stocks.

[3] " Employment " here means the employment of *all* the Factors of Production.

at that time multiplied by the rate of wages, we may also express this by saying that the volume of working capital is the wages bill at any time multiplied by half the duration of process (working capital = wages bill × ½ length of process). Further, in the simplest case, where the rate of in-put and the intensity of employment at each stage of process are both steady, it follows, since the wages bill is equal to the rate of in-put, multiplied by the rate of wages, multiplied by the length of process, that working capital = rate of in-put × rate of wages × *half the square* of the length of process. The factor *one-half* comes into the above expressions, because, if the rate of process is constant at all stages of the process, the aggregate of product in process at any time is on the average *half*-finished. But this particular figure is for purposes of illustration only. If employment is applied more intensively at some stages of the process than at others (which is likely to be the case), or if the rate of in-put has been unsteady, some other figure would be appropriate.

Let us take these factors in turn.

(1) When products have been started into process at a steady rate, and there has been no change in the intensity of employment or in the duration of process, so that the rates of in-put and out-put are both steady, it follows that the rate of employment corresponds to the rate of out-put, and the amount of employment multiplied by the rate of wages is equal to the cost of production of current out-put, so that earnings are equal to cost of out-put. If, however, the rate of in-put is not steady and employment fluctuates, the position is not so simple, and the expression "volume of production" becomes ambiguous. It is sometimes not clear whether we mean by it the volume of employment or the volume of out-put. In the "long-run" the average volume of out-put must obviously be governed by the average volume of employment. But during fluctuations they will temporarily separate.

For during a slump the volume of employment will fall off much faster and sooner than the volume of out-put; and during a boom it will recover much quicker. Similarly, the aggregate demand for working capital will fall off during a slump, and will recover during a boom, more rapidly than out-put but less rapidly than employment. Statistics of out-put indicate what employment *has been*; statistics of employment indicate what out-put *will be*; whilst the demand for working capital depends upon those past figures of employment which are not yet so distant as to have been reflected in out-put. It will be best, therefore, to use " volume of production " to mean, not the current volume of out-put, but the volume of employment of the Factors of Production. Thus— taking the duration of process, for purposes of illustration, at six months—the level of employment at the *beginning* of a period of six months could be deduced from the statistics of average daily out-put during the six months; whilst to obtain the volume of working capital at the beginning of the six months we must take the daily average out-put during the six months, each daily item being *weighted* according to the length of time between that day and the end of the six months.[1]

Mistakes are often made, both by those who seek to explain past events and by those who seek to forecast future ones, through their paying insufficient attention to the time-lag between the three manifestations— out-put, demand for working capital, and employment. The following is an example. The imports of raw material into Great Britain may be regarded as a rough indication of the rate of in-put, and manufactured exports as a rough indication of the rate of out-put. Thus in the early stages of the slump when in-put is

---

[1] Although I am no longer assuming in this example that the rate of in-put is steady, I am still making the simplifying assumption that the intensity of employment is steady at each stage of the process.

falling, but out-put has not yet fallen, we should expect exports to gain on imports. In the early stages of the boom, on the other hand, when in-put is rising, but out-put has not yet risen, we should expect imports to gain on exports.

(2) When trade is brisk, particularly when it first begins to recover after a slack period, it may be possible to increase the intensity of employment, *i.e.* the amount of the factors of production applied per unit of time to a unit of product in process, with the result of accelerating the rate of process and shortening the duration of process. If the reviving demand is for " early delivery", so that a premium can be obtained for extra speed, the business world has, indeed, a strong inducement to accelerate the rate of process by increasing the intensity of employment. It follows that an extra demand for working capital corresponding to an increased volume of employment may be partly offset by a faster rate of process. If the duration of process is halved by doubling the intensity of employment, the demand for working capital is (eventually), other things being equal, halved.

On the other hand, when the volume of goods in process is approaching the maximum of which the available instruments of process are capable, there is apt to be a retardation of rate, owing to the fact that, the relative supply of the different instruments of process being not perfectly balanced, the rate is limited by the capacity of that one of which the supply is least adequate. In other words, "congestion" takes place at some stage of the process.

(3) The average duration of process may increase as a result, either of diminished intensity of employment (which we have just dealt with), or of a change in technical processes (which is likely to take place slowly rather than suddenly), or of an increase in the scale of production of goods having, for technical reasons, a long duration of process, relatively to the production of goods

having a short duration of process. This last may sometimes, but not always, be important over short periods. A boom in textiles requires more working capital per unit of value of ultimate product than a boom in steel rails. A boom in China tea requires more working capital than a boom in local blackberries.

(4) The effect on the cost of working capital, measured in money, of an increased rate of wages of the Factors of Production, may be of great importance. If, for instance, as the demand for labour increases, wages rise, then each unit of production will require, for its wages bill, more expenditure than before.

A relative rise of wages in certain industries may have effects on the cost of working capital of considerable importance, if it takes place in industries which require much working capital relatively to those which require less. Probably the greater part of the normal demand for working capital comes from building, from textiles in process, and from that part of the produce of the earth which is subject to seasonal harvests but is consumed at a steady rate through the year—much out of proportion to the importance given to these in many index numbers of wholesale prices. A slump in textiles and a relatively low price for farm products (unless due to abundant harvests), such as was experienced in 1921–23, which meant low wages to the Factors of Production, taken as a whole, in these industries, must have greatly diminished the demand for working capital. The revival of wheat prices (and of cereals generally) in 1924 must have greatly increased it.

Changes in the relative wages of the Factors of Production in different industries and changes in the volume of production are probably the two preponderant causes, as a rule, in bringing about sharp fluctuations in the money-cost for working capital. But there

are also the fluctuations arising out of changes in the
amount of seasonal stocks to be carried, which we
must now consider.

(5) According to the definitions of this chapter,
Working Capital has to provide for carrying seasonal
stocks between harvests (for such carrying is a
form of " process ") and also for fluctuations in the
" carry-over " from one harvest to another, in so
far as such carry-over is required by the unavoid-
able variations of individual harvests round the mean
harvest. On the other hand, a net prospective surplus,
taking one season with another, due to a mistake
involving a relative over-production, belongs to liquid
capital.

Since, however, a good harvest tends to diminish,
and a bad harvest to increase, the relative price of the
crop affected, the aggregate value of the working
capital required to carry the crop may or may not
move in the same direction as the size of the crop.
To illustrate this, let us suppose that a normal wheat
harvest is 100 and a normal carry-over 20, that the
amount of wheat consumed has to be carried for six
months on the average and that the carry-over has
to be carried for twelve months. With a normal
carry-over and a normal harvest of 100 let the price
be p, with a 110 harvest p_1 and with a 90 harvest p_2.
Let us assume that consumption is constant at 100
in all these cases. Then the amount of £-months
working capital required is :

Normal harvest . . $6 \times 100 \times p + 12 \times 20 \times p = 840\,p$
Good harvest following
  normal position . . $6 \times 100 \times p_1 + 12 \times 30 \times p_1 = 960\,p_1$
Bad harvest following
  normal position . . $6 \times 100 \times p_2 + 12 \times 10 \times p_2 = 720\,p_2$

Suppose $p_1 = \frac{7}{8}p$ and $p_2 = \frac{7}{6}p$: in that event the
demand for working capital is the same in each case.
If the variability of price, in relation to supply, is less,

then the good harvest takes most capital (whether working or liquid) ; if the variability of price is greater, then the bad harvest takes most capital. For simplicity of illustration it is here assumed that the prices p, p_1 and p_2 rule throughout the season. Prior to harvest, however, the cost of production, which may not vary much between the three cases, will in fact govern the cost of working capital, and the prices assumed will primarily affect the value of working capital required between harvest and consumption. Further, the fluctuations in the value of working capital required may be partly supplied out of the corresponding windfall profits or losses accruing to farmers.

Some interesting statistics for wheat in the United States, which have a bearing on the above, have been compiled by the Food Research Institute of Stanford, California (*Wheat Studies*, Feb. 1928, " Disposition of American Wheat since 1896, with special reference to changes in year-end stocks "). Over a period of thirty years the Institute finds that in the thirteen large crop years, with an average excess of 80 million bushels, 38 million went into increased exports, 4 million into increased consumption, and 38 million into increased stocks ; whilst in the seventeen small crop years, with an average deficiency of 63 million bushels, 30 million came from decreased exports, 4 million from decreased consumption,[1] and 29 million from decreased stocks. Since the average crop during this period was 777 million bushels and the average end-year stock 166 million, the average large crop was 113 per cent, the average small crop 92 per cent, and the average end-year stock 21 per cent of the average crop. The maximum end-year stock over the thirty years, apart from the abnormalities of the war years, was 25 per

---

[1] Incidentally this shows a *very* inelastic demand on the part of con-sumers, maximum consumption being only one per cent above minimum consumption in spite of wide fluctuations of price.

cent and the minimum was 8 per cent of an average crop.[1]

(iii.) PRODUCTIVE AND UNPRODUCTIVE CONSUMPTION

The substitution of the production of fixed capital for the production of consumption goods necessitates investment ; and the previous decisions, which have resulted in this increase of fixed capital, since they have caused more income to emerge from the process of production in a non-available form and less in an available form than would otherwise have been the case, require a reduction in the level of current consumption below what it need have been otherwise.

An increase in working capital resulting from an increased volume of production and employment (and not from a lengthening of the productive process) also necessitates investment ; but in this case investment does not require any reduction in the level of consumption below what it would have been if the increase in production had not taken place.

That is to say, an increase in working capital due to increased employment does not involve an equal abstention from, or a reduction of, current consumption by the community as a whole, as does an increase in fixed capital, but mainly a redistribution of consumption from the rest of the community to the

---

[1] Those who pay attention to the correlations between harvests and credit cycles may be interested in the following. Taking July stocks of wheat of less than 100 million bushels as abnormally small, and of more than 150 million as abnormally large, the July's of minimum stocks are 1898, 1905, 1908 and 1909, and the July's of maximum stocks are 1896, 1899, 1900, 1907 and 1923 (leaving out the war years). All of the former dates are on the upward phase of a credit cycle, and all of the latter, except 1899, are on a downward phase. The result is paradoxical, and I do not know what conclusion, if any, to draw from it. It might be found, however, that, as a result of the disproportionate influence of a large crop on prices owing to the necessity of bringing exports down to a price attractive to the world market, the purchasing power of the agricultural community is markedly superior in small stock years.

newly employed. Investment, which requires a re-distribution of current consumption but no reduction in its aggregate, may be said to substitute productive consumption for unproductive consumption.

Thus we may define " unproductive consumption " as consumption which could be forgone by the consumer without reacting on the amount of his productive effort, and " productive consumption " as consumption which could not be forgone without such a reaction. Further, it may be possible to redistribute consumption in a way which increases production, whenever the unfavourable reaction on the producer whose consumption is reduced is less than the favourable reaction on the producer whose consumption is increased.

Thus whenever available income is transferred from an individual *qua* unproductive or relatively unproductive consumer to an individual *qua* productive or relatively productive consumer, it follows that the amount of production is increased, and *vice versa*. When, therefore, such a transference is effected, there is, in spite of there being no decreased consumption of available income, an increment to the wealth of the community in the shape of an increment of non-available income which serves to increase the volume of net investment—this increment being brought about by increased production and not by diminished consumption.

Nevertheless, this too requires diminished consumption *on the part of particular individuals*, namely, those who would otherwise have consumed what is actually being consumed by the newly employed factors of production. This reduction of unproductive consumption and substitution of productive consumption instead may be brought about, as we have seen, either by individuals voluntarily saving a part of their money-incomes or by a reduction in the purchasing power of these money-incomes as the result of a rise in prices which transfers some part of their real-incomes into the control of individuals who will direct it towards productive consumption.

At any time, therefore, a community has two sets of decisions to make—the one as to what proportion of future income shall be available for consumption and what proportion shall consist of fixed capital, the other as to what proportion of present income shall be consumed productively and what proportion shall be consumed unproductively. The first set of decisions is that which is ordinarily in mind when we think of saving and of investment. But it is on the second set that employment and unemployment depend. Full employment of the factors of production requires a redistribution, not a reduction, of the aggregate of consumption. It would seem obvious that circumstances can conceivably exist in which—failing any other method of redistributing consumption—it would be better to redistribute it by a Profit Inflation (an Income Inflation, be it noticed, is quite useless for this purpose, unless it is used for the purpose of granting a direct dole to a particular industry or locality to enable a wage to be paid to productive labour greater than the marginal value of its product) than to allow Unemployment to continue ; in which, that is to say, the evil of not creating wealth would be greater than the evil that the wealth, when created, should not accrue to those who have made the sacrifice, namely, to the consumers whose consumption has been curtailed by the higher prices consequent on the Profit Inflation.

Additions to fixed capital, to liquid capital and to working capital are, all of them, only possible as the result of allowing an interval of time to elapse for the community as a whole between the date of the disutility of doing work and the date of the actual enjoyment of income. But the form of investment which results from additional employment of the factors of production without immediate additional consumption for the community as a whole does not, nevertheless, consist in the community's abstaining from the consumption of available income, but in their allowing it to be consumed by persons who are engaged in a productive process which will not yield its income in return until after the lapse of a certain length of time.

So long as unemployment and unproductive consumption are allowed to exist side by side, present total net income and future available income are less than they might be ; and nothing is required to mend the situation except a method of transferring consumption from one set of individuals to another.

(iv.) THE TRUE WAGES FUND

In a static equilibrium of production there is no need for any net addition to working capital. For working capital is a revolving fund, the maintenance of which requires no new saving or investment, when once it has been established at the requisite level. Even when a steady addition is needed to working capital year by year, to provide for increased population or for a longer technique of production, such gradual additions are not likely to absorb a large proportion of current savings.[1]   Nor in a state of perfectly balanced equilibrium between production and consumption is there a need for any liquid capital.   Thus it is natural to measure new investment mainly by reference to the net additions to fixed capital.

Counsel has been darkened in this matter by a famous confusion of the Classical Economists and by the failure of their successors, who detected the confusion, to perceive the truth which lay, nevertheless, at the centre of the confusion.   The Classical Economists

---

[1] If working capital is increasing at 3 per cent per annum, this is probably not more than 10 per cent of the annual savings.   *Vide* p. 112 above.

emphasised the distinction between fixed capital and what they called " circulating capital ".[1] But they did not clearly distinguish my third category of capital, namely, " goods in process " or working capital, which is not identical with their " circulating capital ". They appreciated the necessity of a fund to support labour during the period of production; but they overlooked the *continuous* character of production and out-put, and confused the working capital, which is provided by *continuously* feeding the flow of available income back into the machine of process, with the liquid capital or goods in stock at the *commencement* of any period of process. They did not clearly perceive that the capital to keep labour in employment is found, not in the stocks of goods *already* available, nor by abstention from the consumption of available income, but by decisions which have the effect (*a*) of determining what proportions of the goods emerging from the machine of process are in fixed and in liquid form respectively, and (*b*) of applying the flow of available income in one way instead of in another, namely, by supporting productive consumers instead of unproductive consumers.

According to their doctrine of the " Wages Fund ", as it is generally called,[2] it was impossible to set labour to work upon the handling of " goods in process ", or rather to pay wages to labour for such work, in excess of the " circulating capital " or fund of ready goods which had been previously saved and was, therefore, available to support labour during the interval of time which must elapse before the goods in process could emerge in the form of income, ready for use.[3]

---

[1] For the precise meanings which Adam Smith, Ricardo, and J. S. Mill severally attached to this term, see Marshall's *Principles of Economics*, p. 75.

[2] For a critical account of the history of this doctrine see Marshall's *Principles of Economics*, Appendix J.

[3] This doctrine, besides the mistake of confusing " working capital " with " liquid stocks ", also involved a secondary error, in that it confused the fund available for supporting and rewarding *all* the factors of production

Mill's statement, that wages mainly depend on the proportion between "the number of the labouring class who work for hire" and "the aggregate of what may be called the Wages Fund which consists of that part of circulating capital which is expended in the direct hire of labour", was incorrect, mainly because, in Marshall's words,[1] " it suggested a correlation between the *stock* of capital and the *flow* of wages, instead of the true correlation between the *flow* of the products of labour aided by capital and the flow of wages ". But it has proved injurious to clearness of thought to demolish this doctrine without putting anything into its place.

For if "circulating capital" is identified not merely with liquid capital or "goods in stock", but with liquid stocks *plus* the flow of *available* income accruing during the period of process, then the Doctrine of the Wages Fund embodies an important truth, without which the nature of the productive process through time and its relation to capital and to saving cannot be understood. It is the flow of income, available for consumption by the factors of production, which constitutes the true *Wages Fund*; and it is the distribution of this Fund between relatively productive and relatively unproductive consumption which determines the volume of employment and of output.

---

with the fund available for the payment of wages in particular—overlooking the fact that, even though the Fund remained constant, its proportionate division between the several factors of production could, nevertheless, be varied. Indeed it was criticism of this mistake, rather than of its more fundamental error, which finally led J. S. Mill to abandon the Wages Fund.

[1] *Principles of Economics*, p. 545.

CHAPTER 29

FLUCTUATIONS IN THE RATE OF INVESTMENT —
III. LIQUID CAPITAL

IF the impairment of working capital during the slump were balanced by a corresponding accretion of suitable kinds of liquid capital, then the replenishment of working capital during the boom could be effected by drawing on the high stocks of liquid capital. Business would never lack the *means* of working at full steam, and the problem of recovery would merely be one of furnishing business with the *motive* to work at full steam. But inquiry in this case will be found to lead us to the opposite conclusion to that which we have reached in the case of working capital. Instead of the fluctuations in the amount of Liquid Capital being larger than one might expect, we shall find that they are small and that there are cogent reasons why we cannot expect much assistance from this source to balance fluctuations of investment in Fixed Capital.

The question of the actual order of magnitude of fluctuations in the stocks of liquid goods is of considerable importance, because it is not obvious *à priori* that these may not furnish a balancing factor capable of looking after short-period increases and decreases in the rate of investment in fixed and working capital without any change being required in the rate of total investment. Indeed, Mr. Hawtrey's theory of the Credit Cycle is largely based on this supposition. A short criticism of this point of view may be a useful

130

introduction to an appreciation of the significance of this chapter.

(i.) MR. HAWTREY'S THEORY OF LIQUID STOCKS

Mr. Hawtrey has gone a good deal farther than I have been prepared to go in arguing that the Credit Cycle is " a purely monetary phenomenon ". When he writes, " *All* causes of fluctuations in productive activity are conditioned by the monetary factor. Only those can bear fruit for which the monetary climate for the time being is favourable," [1] I agree with him. But he does not sufficiently distinguish, I think, between the financial incentive as determined by the monetary factor, and the material means as determined by the supply of real income available for productive consumption. At times he seems to overlook the latter altogether and to write as if the output of available income was simultaneous with the work done, so that no working capital is necessary at all —*e.g.* : " If all producers were under-employed, all would be willing to accept additional orders without asking higher prices. The additional money put into circulation would be applied to buying the additional goods produced, and there would be no reason for a general increase of prices at any stage between producer and consumer." [2]

But when his attention is called to the difficulty, he replies that an appropriate monetary policy is capable, generally speaking, of extracting the required real resources out of the stocks of liquid capital. He argues that dealers in commodities who are holding part of their stock-in-trade with borrowed money are very sensitive to changes in bank-rate and are easily induced to reduce their stocks by a higher bank-rate and to increase them by a lower rate : " The amount of a dealer's stock-in-trade is elastic and variable. He is very ready to hold either more or less, according to

---

[1] *Trade and Credit*, p. 169.   [2] *Op. cit.* p. 74.

the state of markets and of credit.   Let markets be favourable, and he will seek to hold more ; let credit become dearer, and he will seek to hold less." [1]   These stocks supply the material for a revival of trade : " Increased working capital, in the form of goods in course of production, is provided at that stage not by a ' windfall ' conferred on producers through a rise in prices, but by supplies of money, which enable consumers to draw on the finished products in stock. This is not at anyone's expense, so long as the stocks are adequate to bear the strain without a rise in price. Goods previously idle pass into consumption, and are replaced for the time being as an item of working capital by goods in course of manufacture." [2]   Mr. Hawtrey adds, however, subsequently : " It should be mentioned that the fluctuations in stocks do not *necessarily* always correspond with the alternations of activity and depression.   Traders are *willing* to hold larger stocks at a time of activity than at a time of restricted production, and when either condition has persisted for some time, they tend to adjust their stocks by making their selling prices in the one case above and in the other below replacement value." [3]

Now it is not obvious on the face of it that the course of events might not be as Mr. Hawtrey supposes, fluctuations in Working Capital being balanced by opposite fluctuations in Liquid Capital.   If, however, we look into the matter more deeply, we shall find that there are good reasons, both of fact and of theory, for the contrary opinion.   There are three reasons, of which the last is the most fundamental in the sense of being the most inevitable, tending to show that— though in the early stages of the slump there may be some fairly substantial accretions to hoards of liquid capital—before the slump has touched bottom the

---

[1] Vide *Trade and Credit*, p. 126 ; cf. also *Trade and Credit*, p. 10, and *Currency and Credit*, pp. 24-26.

[2] *Trade and Credit*, p. 156.   [3] *Op. cit.* p. 160.

decrease in working capital far outstrips any increase in liquid capital, with the result that the liquid stocks existing at the bottom of the slump only suffice to provide for the very earliest stages of the recovery.

(ii.) THE OBSTACLES TO AN ACCUMULATION OF LIQUID CAPITAL

1. The first argument follows from the fact that during the slump production falls off much more sharply than consumption—that is to say, the slump does not merely result in less production and correspondingly less consumption, but also in the substitution of unproductive consumption in place of productive consumption. Especially is this the case if unemployment relief is maintained at a high level. The facts do not suggest that this excess-consumption is fully balanced by a diminished investment in fixed capital. If these observations are correct, it follows that the impairment of working capital must exceed any accretion of liquid capital.

2. The second argument is the result of direct investigations into the volume of stocks of commodities at different dates. At one time I thought it possible that some part of the clue to the Credit Cycle might be found in a close study of the fluctuations of the stocks of liquid goods. It is not a matter about which the available statistics are very satisfactory. But the study of what material could be found indicated that the true surplus stocks of liquid capital, which are at any time existing, are too small to have any decisive influence on the replenishment of working capital. As regards the stocks of staple raw materials I refer the reader to my memoranda on " Stocks of Staple Commodities " [1] and to the material collected by the United States Department of Commerce and published in

---

[1] *Special Memoranda of the London and Cambridge Economic Service* on " Stocks of Staple Commodities ", published in April 1923, June 1924, July 1925, Feb. 1926, March and Sept. 1927 and August 1929.

their monthly *Survey of Current Business*. In looking at these figures the reader must remember that not the entirety of the stocks of raw materials in existence at any time fall within my definition of liquid capital. A considerable proportion is a part of working capital. For those stocks, which are in course of transport or are being carried between the seasons, or are required to average out the fluctuations of harvests or are a necessary safeguard against interruptions to the continuity of production, must be regarded as a part of working capital, and not of liquid capital. The truly redundant surplus of liquid goods, not required for any of these purposes, seldom reaches, even in the case of an individual commodity, the equivalent of more than a very few months' consumption at the most ; and for the average of commodities the maximum is, of course, much smaller.[1]

Furthermore the figures corroborate the expectation that (in the case of a slump which has been brought about by other causes than an excessive investment in fixed capital) stocks tend to attain their maximum in an early phase of the slump and are at a low point when the improvement of trade is definitely beginning. For example, both the English and the American figures indicate that stocks of staple commodities were at their highest point in 1921 and fell steadily during 1922 and 1923 towards an inconveniently low figure. Thus the revival of 1924 and 1925 could not accelerate its progress by drawing from surplus stocks of liquid capital. This confirms expectation because, when the slump begins, the falling off of production does not show itself immediately at the finishing end of the machine of process,

---

[1] It has been calculated (*Rubber Quarterly*, Nov. 1928) that world stocks of American cotton, taken over the year, average about two months' supply, or two and a half months' including mill stocks ; sugar stocks, a month and a half's supply ; tea stocks, three and a half months' ; tin, less than two months' ; copper, three months'. It is only the excess over some such normal stocks as these which represents the truly redundant surplus.

whilst it does show itself immediately in the amount which is being fed back into the mouth of the machine : so liquid stocks increase. Later on, however, the diminished production results in diminished available output, whilst current consumption does not fall off so much as does production—with the result that there can be no increase of liquid stocks, but rather the contrary. It is precisely this shortage both of available output and of liquid capital which may retard the process of recovery, even after the influences which originally caused the slump have long ceased to operate. The extent to which we live on our fat during the slump and the impairment of our stock, both of liquid and of working capital during the slump's progress, are obscured from sight by the common practice of measuring *net* investment mainly by reference to the growth of fixed capital.

3. The third ground—which we develop below— for believing that stocks of liquid goods at the end of a slump are not sufficient to provide material aid towards recovery follows from the heavy cost of carrying them—of which fluctuations in the interest charges, to which Mr. Hawtrey attaches so much weight, are perhaps the least important.

(iii.) The " Carrying " Costs

The costs of carrying redundant stocks through time are made up of :

(1) Allowance for deterioration in quality or in suitability (through the unpredictability of the precise specifications which will be required when demand recovers) ;

(2) Warehouse and Insurance charges ;

(3) Interest charges ;

(4) Remuneration against the risk of changes in the money-value of the commodity during the time through which it has to be carried by means of borrowed money.

(1) The first of these gravely interferes with stocking many classes of commodities at all. Perishable commodities, articles of fashion, which include a great proportion of articles of clothing, even many semi-finished products of the iron and steel and engineering industries, cannot be carried in stock except at the risk of such heavy loss that it is better, where possible, to suspend further production altogether until the stocks have been absorbed. Nevertheless there are certain staple raw materials where this factor is not important.

(2) The second factor always costs something, and is occasionally important as in the case of oil and coal. The lack of storage facilities may often operate as a limiting factor in the carrying of oil pending the revival of demand; whilst with coal this difficulty is even more important, further work at the pits soon becoming impossible if accumulations of stock are not carried away.

(3) The third factor requires no special elucidation.

These three factors are those of which account is ordinarily taken. In the case of commodities which are suitable for storage, they seldom cost altogether less than 6 per cent per annum, and 10 per cent per annum may be regarded as a normal figure.

Now if we assume that through a miscalculation of supply and demand redundant stocks have accumulated equal to six months' consumption, the price must fall sufficiently far below the anticipated normal price to provide the carrying charges through the period which is expected to elapse before the redundant stocks are completely absorbed. For example, if a reduction of price of 17 per cent below the anticipated normal curtails new production sufficiently to absorb the stocks in two years, that is to say by 25 per cent over the average of the two years,[1] the costs so far

---

[1] Since the price will gradually rise and since new production will, therefore, gradually recover correspondingly during the two years, the initial curtailment of new production will have to be greater than 25 per cent.

considered, assuming them to be at the rate of 10 per cent per annum, will be just covered.

(4) But we have not yet considered the fourth factor. The anticipated normal price, and also the length of time which will elapse before the stocks are absorbed, are matters, not of certainty, but of conjecture. Hence there is a risk which someone must bear. Thus, in the above example, the price will have to fall *more* than 17 per cent below the anticipated normal price, in order to provide an inducement to a speculator to run the risk that the carrying-period may be longer and the eventual price lower than is now expected.

It is difficult to measure the rate of the anticipated profit which is necessary to encourage the speculative holding of stocks of commodities on a large scale for a considerable period. But I am sure that it is very high. Six months' stocks of an important commodity represent an enormous sum of money ; the amount of capital available for speculative operations of this kind is limited ; when stocks have accumulated through a miscalculation of supply and demand, and a slump is in progress, outside speculators are discouraged and timorous, whilst professional dealers in the commodity are impoverished. Moreover, brokerages and other expenses of dealing are considerable. I do not think, therefore, that even in the broadest and steadiest markets the services of the speculative holder can be obtained on a large scale in bad times for an expectation of less than 10 per cent per annum, and in the case of some commodities a much higher rate of remuneration is necessary.[1] If we add this 10 per cent (as a minimum) to our previous 10 per cent to cover other costs, the existence of surplus stocks which will

---

[1] The evidence collected by F. C. Mills in *The Behavior of Prices* (*passim*) as to the violence of the fluctuations which normally affect the prices of many individual commodities, shows what a great risk the short-period speculator in commodities runs, for which he requires to be remunerated on a corresponding scale.

not be absorbed for two years may be expected to
force the price 30 per cent below the anticipated
normal.[1]

Let me give two numerical examples :

(1) In 1920–21 the surplus stocks of American
cotton amounted to some 7,000,000 bales—about
seven months' supply. Taking 24 cents per lb. as an
estimate, at that time, of the normal price, the value of
the surplus stocks at this price would be $840,000,000,
in addition to the normal stocks which had to be
carried during the current year.[2] In fact the price
fell to about 16 cents and three years elapsed before
the surplus was absorbed, at the end of which time the
price rose to about 28 cents. Thus this enormous
fluctuation of prices in a fundamental commodity
represented no more than 20 per cent per annum to
meet all the costs, including risk, of carrying surplus
stocks for three years. In view of the difficulty of
predicting with any confidence in the autumn of 1920
the normal money price of producing an adequate
supply of cotton three years later, the magnitude of
the fluctuation can be explained on reasonable grounds.
Looking at the facts from another angle, the crops
during the three years averaged about 20 per cent
below normal requirements. If the price had never
fallen below 20 cents the crops would probably have
been larger, so that four years might have elapsed
before the surplus was absorbed ; in which case the
difference between 20 cents and 24 cents would barely
have paid the interest. Thus the price must fall far
enough to curtail production sufficiently to allow the
surplus to be absorbed within a period not so long as
to eat up, by the costly passage of mere time, too much
of the speculative holder's anticipated gross profit.

---

[1] $(1 + \cdot 4) \times (1 - \cdot 3) = 1$ (approx.).

[2] The *total* stocks of cotton, when the crop of 1920 had just been harvested,
amounted to about 17,000,000 bales, which at 24 cents would have been
worth $2,000,000,000—an enormous sum on which to find persons willing
to run the risk of price changes.

For seven months' redundant stocks to force the price to two-thirds and the output to four-fifths of the normal is not immoderate and is well within the present rules of the game.   It will be observed that the more inelastic the conditions of supply, and the larger the proportion of the production which is yielding a substantial rent, the greater must be the fall in price which redundant stocks will cause.

(2) At the end of 1920 the redundant stocks of copper amounted to about 700,000 tons, or more than eight months' consumption.[1] The estimate of the normal price, at that time, was about 14·5 cents per lb., and in 1921 the actual price fell to 11·7 cents per lb. It would, however, have fallen to a lower level if no concerted action had been taken.   Copper is produced under conditions of very variable return.   A fall in the average price to 12 cents would probably, at that time, have reduced output about 25 per cent, and a fall to 10 cents by a further 25 per cent.   It follows from these hypotheses (I need not trouble the reader with the arithmetical details) that the price would have had to fall in 1921 to at least 10 cents to produce an equilibrium position, having regard to the output at various price-levels, if it had been unrestricted, and the consequent length of time which the absorption of the stocks would have taken.   In fact the American producers took concerted action, and in April 1921 the bulk of the mines of the United States closed down and were only gradually restarted in the course of 1922. World production was thus reduced to less than 50 per cent of the normal, the bulk of the stocks was absorbed in 1921 and 1922, and by the end of 1922 the price had risen to a normal figure.[2]   The course of prices, from a minimum of 11·7 cents early in 1921 to

---

[1] A year earlier the stocks had been even greater ; but since Government War Stocks had not yet been released, the weight of the stocks was not known or effective in the market.

[2] I am ignoring the subsequent price rise above the normal in the spring of 1923 and the moderate over-production which again resulted.

a maximum of 14·7 cents late in 1922, did not represent any unusual net profit to the speculative holder, considering the risks he had been running in those disturbed times.

(iv.) THE EQUATION RELATING PRICE FLUCTUATIONS TO " CARRYING " COSTS

In fact, the mechanism of short-period organisation, as it exists at present, leads necessarily to the result that redundant stocks exercise a disproportionate effect on prices and therefore on new production : such stocks exercise a tremendous pressure on the market to get themselves absorbed as soon as possible. If x is the total cost per annum of carrying stocks measured as a proportion of the normal price ; y is the proportion of the redundant stocks to a year's consumption ; p the proportionate fall of prices below the normal at its maximum ; and q the proportionate fall of new production below the normal (*i.e.* below the figure at which production and consumption are assumed to be balanced with a normal price) at its maximum, *i.e.* due to a proportionate fall p in prices ; then p, the initial price fall, is given, subject to certain simplifying assumptions, by the equation

$$pq = xy.$$

It is easily seen that the assumptions required for the validity of this equation in its simplest form (which is complicated, but not altered in essence, by more generalised assumptions) are, first, that the price should rise steadily from its initial minimum back to the normal, and, secondly, that the increase of consumption due to a given fall of price below the normal is equal to the decrease of production due to the same cause (from which it conveniently follows that the *maximum* fall in the rate of production below normal is equal to the *average* rate of absorption of stocks).[1] The theory of short-period prices has been so much neglected that this simple equation, which helps to explain the violence of the fluctuation of the *relative* prices of staple commodities, is, so far as I know, unfamiliar.[2]

This equation also shows why in certain cases valorisation schemes to provide by concerted action for the carrying of stocks are inevitable and defensible, as well as protecting from loss the group which organises them. Where production is inelastic, or where a particular product is so large a proportion of the national business that alternative occupations cannot be found, a miscalculation leading to heavy redundant stocks may prove ruinous, if matters are allowed to take their course on principles of *laissez-faire*. The B.A.W.R.A. organisation for carrying the stocks of Australian and South African wool after the war was of inestimable benefit to the producers, and indeed to the world at large, by preventing a debacle in the industry which would have caused a famine in wool later on. The Coffee Valorisation of the Brazilian Government and the Tin Valorisation of the Government of the Federated Malay States, brought into existence by the post-war troubles and the slump of 1920–21, were fully justified on the same grounds. Similarly, though on different lines, the Copper Restriction in the United States, and the Rubber Restriction in the Straits Settlements and Ceylon, were called into existence to meet the same problem in a different way (*i.e.* these aimed at bringing about a restriction of output drastic

---

[1] For if a measures the time taken to absorb the redundant stocks and to restore the price to normal, there must be sufficient profit to a speculator, who buys at the beginning of this period of time and sells at the end of it, to pay for his carrying charges, *i.e.* $a \cdot x = p$. Furthermore, since at the outset stocks are being reduced at the rate $2q$ (q by reason of curtailment of output and q by reason of increase of consumption) and the price rises steadily, the *average* rate of reduction of stocks is q, *i.e.* $a \cdot q = y$, whence the above result.

[2] Mr. F. C. Mills's book *The Behavior of Prices* contains a splendid collection of data for a study on the side of facts of the phenomena which have been dealt with above on the theoretical side.

enough to effect the absorption of stocks within a reasonable period). Where there are large stocks, a restriction of new production *must* be brought about somehow—either by so great a fall of price as to compel restriction, or by an organised voluntary restriction which will bring about the same result with a less fall of price. There can be no doubt, in such cases, of the advantage to producers of a policy of organised restriction. Such a policy only becomes dangerous if the price level aimed at is too high in relation to normal production costs, or if the producers, who join the scheme of restriction, do not account for a sufficient proportion of the total capacity for production (as actually happened in the case of the Rubber Restriction).[1]

(v.) THE THEORY OF THE "FORWARD MARKET"

Let me restate the argument in terms of the "forward market". In the case of organised markets for staple raw materials there exist at any time two price-quotations—the one for immediate delivery, the other for delivery at some future date, say six months hence.[2] Now if the period of production is of the order of six months, the latter price is the one which matters to a producer considering whether he shall extend or curtail the scope of his operations ; for this is the price at which he can at once sell his goods forward for delivery on the date when they will be ready. If this price shows a profit on his costs of production, then he can go full steam ahead, selling his product forward and running no risk. If, on the other hand, this price does not cover his costs (even after allowing for what he loses by temporarily laying

---

[1] On the other hand, rubber presented a strong *prima facie* case for restriction, because, once the trees are planted and in bearing, the commodity is produced under conditions of highly inelastic supply.

[2] The " forward " price is for delivery *and payment* at the future date, not for immediate cash.

up his plant), then it cannot pay him to produce at all.

If there are no redundant liquid stocks, the spot price may exceed the forward price (*i.e.* in the language of the market there is a " backwardation "). If there is a shortage of supply capable of being remedied in six months but not at once, then the spot price can rise above the forward price to an extent which is only limited by the unwillingness of the buyer to pay the higher spot price rather than postpone the date of his purchase. When the buyer has himself entered into forward contracts as a result of having previously miscalculated the state of supply, he may be compelled to pay a very substantial premium. It would be easy to quote cases where the backwardation for periods of three months has risen to the equivalent of 30 per cent per annum.

But it is not necessary that there should be an abnormal shortage of supply in order that a backwardation should be established. If supply and demand are balanced, the spot price must exceed the forward price by the amount which the producer is ready to sacrifice in order to " hedge " himself, *i.e.* to avoid the risk of price fluctuations during his production period. Thus in normal conditions the spot price exceeds the forward price, *i.e.* there is a backwardation. In other words, the normal supply price on the spot includes remuneration for the risk of price fluctuations during the period of production, whilst the forward price excludes this. The statistics of organised markets show that 10 per cent per annum is a modest estimate of the amount of this backwardation in the case of seasonal crops which have a production period approaching a year in length and are exposed to all the chances of the weather. In less organised markets the cost is much higher—so high indeed as to be prohibitive to most producers, who prefer to run the price risk themselves rather than pay it. It will be seen that, under the present régime of very widely fluctuating prices for individual commodities, the cost of insurance against price changes—which is additional to any charges for interest or warehousing—is very high.

What is the position in the case important to the argument of this chapter, namely where there exist redundant liquid stocks ? In this case there cannot exist a backwardation ; for if there was one, it would always pay to sell the stocks spot and buy them back forward rather than incur the warehousing and interest charges for carrying them during the intervening period. Indeed the existence of surplus stocks must cause the forward price to rise *above* the spot price, *i.e.* to establish, in the language of the market, a " contango " ; and this contango must be equal to the cost of the warehouse, depreciation and interest charges of carrying the stocks. But the existence of a contango does not mean that a producer can hedge himself without paying the usual insurance against price changes. On the contrary, the additional element of uncertainty introduced by the existence of stocks and the additional supply of risk-bearing which they require mean that he must pay more than usual. In other words, the quoted forward price, though above the present spot price, must fall below the anticipated future spot price by at least the amount of the normal backwardation ; and the present spot price, since it is lower than the quoted forward price, must be much lower than the anticipated future spot price. If the stocks are expected to be absorbed within a year, the present spot price must fall (say) 20 per cent below the anticipated future spot price ; but if the stocks look like lasting for two years, then the present spot price must fall (say) 40 per cent.

(vi.) CONCLUSION

This has brought us back to our former argument. Owing to the existence of high carrying charges of one kind or another, our present economic arrangements make no normal provision for looking after surplus liquid capital. If, as the result of a previous mis-calculation, such stocks come into existence, the price of the goods continues to fall until either consumption increases or production falls off sufficiently to absorb them. In no case can surplus stocks exist alongside of normal production. Recovery—broadly speaking—cannot begin until stocks have been absorbed, with the result that the process of recovery cannot be much facilitated by the existence of stocks.

The conclusion of this section may be summarised by saying that our present economic system abhors a stock of liquid goods. If such a stock comes into existence, strong forces are immediately brought into play to dissipate it. The efforts to get rid of surplus stocks aggravate the slump, and the success of these efforts retards the recovery.

Incidentally it is evident that a fluctuation of 1 or 2 per cent in bank-rate will represent so small a part of the total carrying charges that it is not reason-able to assign to the *expense* of high bank-rate a pre-ponderating influence on the minds of dealers in stocks. In so far as low and high bank-rate are regarded by dealers as *symptoms* of impending rising or falling prices, it is another matter. But this influence will often tend to operate just the wrong way—inducing them to increase stocks when trade is reviving and to reduce them when it is falling away.

Thus the theory of Liquid Capital gives us, in relation to the swift downward movement of the slump, the counterpart of what the theory of Working Capital gave us, in relation to the slow upward movement of the boom. Just as the improvement in the volume of production can only take place gradually, owing to the time which it takes to build up Working Capital again ; so must the falling off in the volume of production take place suddenly, when there is surplus Liquid Capital, owing to the short time within which Liquid Capital must be absorbed.

An important factor of instability is thus introduced into our economic life. Industry is extraordinarily sensitive to any excess or deficiency, even a slight one, in the flow of available output ready to be fed back into the productive process. If there is a deficiency, full employment is impossible at the existing level of real wages ; if there is an excess, equally, though for quite a different reason, full employment is impossible at the existing level of real wages. In the event of a deficiency the means for full employment is lacking ; in the event of an excess the incentive is lacking.

The bearing of the above on our theory of the Credit Cycle is evident. When the rate of Saving is exceeding the rate of Investment, goods are coming forward at a faster rate than that at which they can be purchased at prices corresponding to their costs of production. Now it might be that a very moderate fall in prices would restore equilibrium in such cases by inducing increased investment in Liquid Capital— which would take the redundant goods off the market and at the same time bring Saving and Investment back into step. But the foregoing argument proves that the fall of prices must be substantial and must proceed until it is accompanied by a fall of production. Owing, however, to the length of the period of production, the falling off in the rate of in-put will begin by aggravating matters. For it will cause the rates of employment and of earnings to fall off *before* the rate of output declines. Thus the stock of Working Capital will fall away and the disparity between

Saving and Investment will be still further aggravated —unless the effect of the slump is to cause Saving to decline faster than earnings, an alleviation which is not to be relied on.   We have, therefore, an adequate theoretical explanation of the violence and rapidity of the slump once it has begun.

CHAPTER 30

It will better illustrate the ideas of this Treatise if, instead of applying them to hypothetical cases, we consider, very briefly, in their light, certain well-known episodes in the history of prices.

It has been usual to think of the accumulated wealth of the world as having been painfully built up out of that voluntary abstinence of individuals from the immediate enjoyment of consumption which we call Thrift. But it should be obvious that mere abstinence is not enough by itself to build cities or drain fens. The abstinence of individuals need not increase accumulated wealth;—it may serve instead to increase the current consumption of other individuals. Thus the thrift of a man may lead either to an increase of capital-wealth or to consumers getting better value for their money. There is no telling which, until we have examined another economic factor.

Namely, Enterprise. It is enterprise which builds and improves the world's possessions. Now, just as the fruits of thrift may go to provide either capital accumulation or an enhanced value of money-income for the consumer, so the outgoings of enterprise may be found either out of thrift or at the expense of the consumption of the average consumer. Worse still;—not only may thrift exist without enterprise, but as soon as thrift gets ahead of enterprise, it positively discourages the recovery of enterprise and sets up a vicious circle by its adverse effect on profits. If Enterprise is afoot, wealth accumulates whatever may be happening to Thrift; and if Enterprise is asleep, wealth decays whatever Thrift may be doing.

Thus, Thrift may be the handmaid and nurse of Enterprise. But equally she may not. And, perhaps, even usually she is not. For enterprise is connected with thrift not directly but at one remove; and the link which should join them is frequently missing. For the engine which drives Enterprise is not Thrift, but Profit.

Now, for enterprise to be active, two conditions must be fulfilled. There must be an expectation of profit; and it must be possible for enterprisers to obtain command of sufficient resources to put their projects into execution. Their expectations partly depend on non-monetary influences—on peace and war, inventions, laws, race, education, population and so forth. But the argument of our first volume has gone to show that their power to put their projects into execution on terms which they deem attractive, almost entirely depends on the behaviour of the banking and monetary system.

Thus the rate at which the world's wealth has accumulated has been far more variable than habits of thrift have been. Indeed, it is not certain that the average individual has been of a much more saving disposition during the sixteenth and seventeenth centuries, when the foundations of the modern world were being laid, than in the Middle Ages, or during the railway booms of the nineteenth century, when its material superstructure was being raised, than in the dead period of the eighteen-nineties.

It is, I think, a fair generalisation to say that a community is "saving" a high proportion of its current income if the proportion of saving to income is as high as 15 per cent, and that 5 per cent, on the other hand, is a low proportion. Now, if we take 10 per cent as an average figure for a modern community's savings, the current increment of capital wealth is three times greater if commodity inflation is taking 5 per cent from the real value of current incomes, than if commodity deflation is adding 5 per cent to their value. Moreover, if employment is 10 per cent greater under the spur of profit than under the drag of losses, the aggregate of incomes is as great in the former case as in the latter— the increment of wealth coming wholly out of increased activity and not out of diminished consumption ; not to mention the augmentation of real income, due to this increment of capital, in succeeding years. Were the Seven Wonders of the World built by Thrift ? I deem it doubtful.

It would be a fascinating task to re-write Economic History, in the light of these ideas, from its remote beginnings;—to conjecture whether the civilisations of Sumeria and Egypt drew their stimulus from the gold of Arabia and the copper of Africa,[1] which, being monetary metals, left a trail of profit behind them in the course of their distribution through the lands between the Mediterranean and the Persian Gulf, and, probably, farther afield ; in what degree the greatness of Athens depended on the silver mines of Laurium —not because the monetary metals are more truly wealth than other things, but because by their effect on prices they supply the spur of profit ; how far the dispersal by Alexander of the bank reserves of Persia, which represented the accumulated withdrawals into the treasure of successive empires during many preceding centuries, was responsible for the outburst of economic progress in the Mediterranean basin, of

---

[1] Copper was astonishingly cheap and abundant in the ancient world; so much so that it must, in view of the costs and difficulties of smelting, have been obtained in an ore of very high purity. Perhaps Egypt had command of an outcrop of one of the extraordinarily rich seams which are now being discovered in the Congo and Northern Rhodesia, and built on this the greatness of Thebes.

which Carthage attempted and Rome ultimately succeeded to reap the fruits ; [1] whether it was a coincidence that the decline and fall of Rome was contemporaneous with the most prolonged and drastic deflation yet recorded ; [2] if the long stagnation of the Middle Ages may not have been more surely and inevitably caused by Europe's meagre supply of the monetary metals than by monasticism or Gothic frenzy ; [3] and how much the Glorious Revolution owed to Mr. Phipps.[4]

I have not the knowledge or the time to lead the

[1] The large supplies of bullion from the possession of the Spanish mines were also, of course, a vital element in the Roman economic system, after the Sierra Morena had been taken from Hannibal. Polybius reports that in his day 40,000 miners were employed.

[2] The supply of the precious metals in the ancient European world reached its maximum in the time of Augustus. It has been estimated (by Jacob, *Production and Consumption of the Precious Metals*)—with what reliability I do not know—that by A.D. 800 the stock had fallen to one-eleventh of what it had been. I am informed that the best accredited modern historians—*e.g.* Rostovtzeff, *Social and Economic History of the Roman Empire*; Tenney Frank, *An Economic History of Rome* (2nd ed., p. 504); Dopsch, *Naturalwirtschaft und Geldwirtschaft* (p. 88)—are not prepared to admit that lack of the precious metals played any material part in the fall of Rome. But the subject may deserve re-examination.

[3] The Moors reopened the Spanish mines and founded on this basis their famous civilisation. From then on the *status quo* could be about maintained with the aid of the mines of Saxony, the Harz and Austria.

[4] The expedition of Mr. Phipps (afterwards Sir W. Phipps) to recover a Spanish treasure ship which was believed to have sunk some fifty years before off the coast of Hispaniola, is one of the most extraordinary records of improbable success. He returned to London in 1688, having fished up out of the sea a sum estimated at between £250,000 and £300,000 and paid a dividend to his shareholders of 10,000 per cent (even Drake had only distributed a dividend of 4700 per cent). The excitement and stimulus occasioned by this event was the proximate cause of the remarkable Stock Exchange boom which reached its climax in 1692–95 and ended with the foundation of the Bank of England, a Stock Exchange list (with 137 securities quoted) on modern lines, and the reform of the currency by Locke and Newton. The stimulus which this gave to home investment offset the loss of foreign trade due to William's French war, and created an atmosphere of optimism and prosperity which must have been invaluable for the stability of the new régime. This investment boom is of particular historical interest in that it was the first of the public utility booms so typical of later periods (*e.g.* the railway booms of the nineteenth century), being characterised by a number of water-works flotations. (For these particulars, as well as for many others mentioned in this section, *vide* W. R. Scott, *Joint-Stock Companies to 1720, passim.*)

reader through the long histories of the rise and decline of Wealth; nor in most cases has enough statistical material survived to allow my conjectural analysis to be subjected to a searching test. But if we come to the modern age, certain episodes can be selected to illustrate these theories and to test them in some statistical detail.

(i) SPANISH TREASURE

The first episode which I select—the rise of European prices during the sixteenth and seventeenth centuries as a result of the flow of precious metals from America—is one for which I am particularly ill-equipped. But the suggestiveness of what little I know about this period is so great that I cannot refrain from putting it forward for the examination of experts.

According to Professor Earl J. Hamilton,[1] small quantities of gold began to reach Spain from the West Indies in 1503; the first Aztec spoils from Mexico arrived in 1519; and Pizarro's Incan booty from Peru dates from 1534. But these dispersals of old treasure were trifling in amount—far less than the spoils of Alexander nearly two thousand years before —compared with the new output of the mines of Potosi and elsewhere, which came into bearing with the aid of improved methods of extraction between 1545 and 1560. After 1630 the new supplies of gold

[1] I am much indebted in what follows to the preliminary account of his researches into the history of Spanish treasure which Professor Earl J. Hamilton has recently contributed to various learned journals. A summary of them is best found in his article, published in *Economica*, November 1929, "American Treasure and the Rise of Capitalism (1500–1700)". But see also his "American Treasure and Andalusian Prices, 1503–1660", *Journal of Economic and Business History*, Nov. 1928; "Imports of American Gold and Silver into Spain, 1503–1660", *Quarterly Journal of Economics*, May 1929; and "Wages and Subsistence on Spanish Treasure Ships, 1503–1660", *Journal of Political Economy*, Aug. 1929. These investigations are of high historical importance. I shall use his material without special acknowledgment in each instance.

and silver were considerably abated relatively to the demand. Thus the years from (say) 1550 to 1600 were the period of revolutionary price changes, and by 1630 this particular phase of monetary history was at an end.

Now, the pre-Peruvian supplies, whilst insufficient to upset the price-level throughout Europe, were quite enough to start a definite upward movement in the locality where they were first received; and—after a few ups and downs with a mild upward trend in the first two decades of the century—the main movement commenced in Spain as early as 1519. It was in that year that Andalusian prices began the violent progress upward which continued without serious interruption for the next eighty years,[1] culminating just before the century closed (say in 1596) with a price-level five times as high as that which was ruling when the century began.[2] The next seventy years were marked by a series of violent cyclical movements, the price-level returning at the top of the major booms to the fivefold figure of 1596, but never materially exceeding it and averaging well below it.

This was in Spain. In France the movement followed a few years later and culminated at the same date, but at only half the rate, the price-level at the end of the century being two and a half times what it had been at the beginning. In England the progress of events was later still;—the sensational rise of prices did not really begin until after 1550, perhaps

[1] Professor Hamilton's table of the money allowances for rations, calculated at the time by the accountants of the House of Trade at Seville on the basis of actual prices, provides a very satisfactory summary :

1505–25	. 10 to 12	1539–44	. 20 to 25	1565–80	. 26 to 34
1530	. 15	1552–63	. 25 to 30	1581–1623.	. 51
1532–37	. 17				

[2] The very high level to which prices rose in Spain, compared with the rest of Europe, was probably due in part to the strenuous efforts of the government to impede the export of bullion, to the inevitable consequences of which they were doubtless quite blind.

not until 1560,[1] and did not culminate until 1650,
when prices were more than three times what they had
been at the end of the fifteenth century. England,
if the evidence is to be trusted, escaped the serious
depression of prices which afflicted both France and
Spain in the first two decades of the seventeenth
century.[2] We were just in a financial position to
afford Shakespeare at the moment when he presented
himself ! [3]

Such is a rough outline of the course of prices. But
it is the teaching of this Treatise that the wealth of
nations is enriched, not during Income Inflations
but during Profit Inflations—at times, that is to say,
when prices are running away from costs. We must,
therefore, turn to the course of wages (as the only
available indication of the movement of costs), where
our statistical material is inevitably inferior to that
which is available for prices. Professor Earl J. Hamilton's own index for Spanish wages looks to me convincing ; but those which he quotes from Wiebe's
Zur Geschichte der Preisrevolution des xvi. und xvii.

---

[1] Prior to the exploits of Drake and others, referred to below, the new
treasure could only affect English prices by dribbling in *viâ* the Antwerp
money market.

[2] According to W. R. Scott (*op. cit.* vol. i. p. 465), the years 1603 to
1620 were years of good trade, the depression not developing until 1620–21.

[3] Shakespeare, like Newton and Darwin, died rich. In his last years,
according to tradition, " he spent at the rate of a thousand a year "—which
was high living in the early seventeenth century. But whether or not Pope
is right that Shakespeare

> For gain not glory winged his roving flight,
> And grew immortal in his own despite,

his active career chanced to fall at the date of dates, when any level-headed
person in England disposed to make money could hardly help doing so.
1575 to 1620 were the palmy days of profit—one of the greatest " bull "
movements ever known until modern days in the United States (with some
bad years, of course, due to harvests, plague, commercial crises and chances
of war—1587, 1596, 1603)—Shakespeare being eleven years old in 1575 and
dying in 1616. I offer it as a thesis for examination by those who like
rash generalisations, that by far the larger proportion of the world's
greatest writers and artists have flourished in the atmosphere of buoyancy,
exhilaration and the freedom from economic cares felt by the governing
class, which is engendered by profit inflations.

Jahrhunderts, mainly based on Thorold Rogers' figures for England and d'Avenel's figures for France, must surely overstate the case.

In Spain, it would appear, Profit Inflation commenced in 1519, when the Aztec spoils arrived, and terminated as early as 1588, the year of the Armada.[1] During this period of seventy years prices and wages were both rising steeply, but prices were always able to keep comfortably ahead of wages, especially during the first forty years of it. It was from 1520 to 1560 that the conditions were set in Spain for the very rapid accumulation of wealth. But after 1588 there was no money to be made there, except in two or three boom years ; and in the first three decades of the seventeenth century, Spanish wages (according to Professor Hamilton's figures) not only ruled above prices, so that a Profit Deflation was set up, but reached a prodigious level relatively to wages in the rest of Europe. The relation of money-wages in Spain to those in France and England during the generation of Spain's political eclipse, was much the same as the relation to-day between money-wages in England and those in France.[2]

For the course of wages in France and England

---

[1] See Professor Hamilton's chart of prices and wages in Andalusia, published in *Economica*, November 1929, p. 354.

[2] The extreme rise of wages in Spain from 1540 to 1600, quite out of line with what was happening in the rest of Europe, was doubtless much aggravated by the loss of population into the armies and into America (and to a minor extent by reason of the large celibate population and the expulsion of the Moriscos), and by the drift of peasants into the towns to join the body of overseas adventurers or to earn the high wages obtainable for personal services. All this and the consequent difficulty of keeping the land in cultivation have long been the commonplaces of historians. But I am not aware that statistical *data* were available prior to the researches of Professor Hamilton ; and historians, as is their wont, have attributed these things to moral and political causes, such as idleness, superstition and luxury, neglecting, for the most part, monetary influences—just as to-day the troubles of England are attributed to the idleness of the workers, the obscurantism of the trade unions and the inefficiency of the employers, factors which would be worth more as explanations if they could be shown to be peculiar to the present age.

differed widely from what it was in Spain. Evidently in Spain the new purchasing power came straight into the hands of the aristocratic and ruling classes, and was soon used by them to bid up the cost of services —the new American wealth was being fully reflected soon after the middle of the sixteenth century in an enhanced level of wages (*i.e.* in Income Inflation) and not, any more, in capital accumulation (*i.e.* no longer in Profit Inflation). But in the rest of Europe the new purchasing power arrived by different channels, namely, those of private commerce.[1] The merchants of those countries which had been least affected by the new treasure were able to sell at a great profit to those which had been more affected ; and more particularly those countries which had established trading relations with the Levant and with Asia were then able to export the treasure thus received on terms which were quite immensely profitable. During the seventeenth century it was the English and French capitalists, not the Spanish, who were adding enormous increments to their country's wealth.

Indeed, the booty brought back by Drake in the *Golden Hind* may fairly be considered the fountain and origin of British Foreign Investment. Elizabeth

---

[1] Including in this privateering ! For, in the case of England, a large part of the imports of bullion were due to Drake's capture of Spanish treasure ships and many similar exploits by others. These expeditions were financed by syndicates and companies and represented business speculations, the success and fruits of which supplied a stimulus to enterprise of all kinds. The boom-period in England definitely began with the return of Drake's first important expedition (his third voyage) in 1573, and was confirmed by the immense gains of his second expedition which returned home in 1580, whilst his third expedition of 1586 was not entirely negligible. The value of the gold and silver brought back in the *Golden Hind*, which was carefully concealed at the time, has been very variously estimated by historians at anything from £300,000 to £1,500,000. Professor W. R. Scott inclines strongly towards the higher figures and produces evidence to show that it must have exceeded £600,000 at the least. The effect of these great influxes of money in establishing " the eleven years of great prosperity ", from 1575 to 1587, must have been predominant. It is characteristic of our historians that, for example, the *Cambridge Modern History* should make no mention of these economic factors as moulding the Elizabethan Age and making possible its greatness.

paid off out of the proceeds the whole of her foreign debt and invested a part of the balance (about £42,000) in the Levant Company; largely out of the profits of the Levant Company there was formed the East India Company, the profits of which during the seventeenth and eighteenth centuries were the main foundation of England's foreign connections; and so on. In view of this, the following calculation may amuse the curious. At the present time (in round figures) our foreign investments probably yield us about 6½ per cent net after allowing for losses, of which we reinvest abroad about half—say 3¼ per cent. If this is, on the average, a fair sample of what has been going on since 1580, the £42,000 invested by Elizabeth out of Drake's booty in 1580 would have accumulated by 1930 to approximately the actual aggregate of our present foreign investments, namely £4,200,000,000—or, say, 100,000 times greater than the original investment. We can, indeed, check the accuracy of this assumed rate of accumulation about 120 years later. For at the end of the seventeenth century the three great trading companies—the East India Company, the Royal African and the Hudson's Bay—which constituted the bulk of the country's foreign investment, had a capital of about £2,150,000; and if we take £2,500,000 for our aggregate foreign investments at that date, this is of the order of magnitude to which £42,000 would grow at 3¼ per cent in 120 years.[1]

Returning to the last quarter of the sixteenth century in England, the reader must remember that it was not the absolute value of the bullion brought into the country—perhaps not more than £2,000,000 or £3,000,000 from first to last—which mattered, but the *indirect* effect of this on profit and enterprise, the increment of the country's wealth in buildings and

---

[1] None of the above calculations are exact, but are all in orders of magnitude.

improvements being probably several times the above
figures. Nor must we overlook the other side of the
picture, namely the hardship to the agricultural population, which became a serious problem in the later
years of Elizabeth, due to prices outstripping wages ;
for it was out of this reduced standard of life, as well
as out of increased economic activity (tempered by
periodic years of crisis and unemployment), that the
accumulation of capital was partly derived.

For wages in France and England—and this is of
the essence of the story—were not rising comparably
to prices, as they were in Spain. Indeed, if the
statistics quoted by Wiebe are to be taken at their
face value, the violence and duration of the profit
inflations in France and England were so great that
real wages in 1600 were only half what they had been
in 1500. Professor Hamilton accepts these figures,
but they are scarcely credible, if they are intended
to mean that the standard of life of the average
worker had fallen during a century of unexampled
progress to half what it had been a hundred years
before.[1] It is not safe to believe more—and this is
quite sufficient to illustrate our argument—than that
the greater part of the fruits of the economic progress and capital accumulation of the Elizabethan and
Jacobean age accrued to the profiteer rather than to
the wage-earner. Putting it shortly, we may say that
Profit Inflation in Spain lasted from 1520 to 1590, in
England from 1550 to 1650,[2] and in France from 1530
to 1700 (with a serious depression intervening from

---

[1] On the other hand, it is important to remember that real wages were
abnormally high in England at the commencement of the fifteenth century,
much above the subsistence level, so that there was plenty of room for a
fall. Professor Clapham tells me that, merely on the basis of the wheat-
wage ratio, the figures suggest, for what they are worth, that the broad
movements of real wages in England might be represented by the following
proportions : 1340, 1 ; 1450–1510, 2 + ; 1540–70, 2 ; 1570–1600, down
towards 1 ; 1600–50, 1 + ; 1650–1700, 1½.

[2] It will be remembered that Adam Smith in the *Wealth of Nations*
gives 1570 as the date when prices were first affected in England, and 1636
as the date by which the full effect had been produced.

1600 to 1625). In England real wages were rising rapidly from 1680 to 1700, whereas there is no evidence of a similar improvement in France. Never in the annals of the modern world has there existed so prolonged and so rich an opportunity for the business man, the speculator and the profiteer. In these golden years modern capitalism was born. There is also another generalisation which, in passing, we may note—one relating to the *length* of the economists' " short periods ". A " short period ", it would seem, thinks nothing of living longer than a man. A " short period " is quite long enough to include (and, perhaps to contrive) the rise and the fall of the greatness of a nation.[1]

If we take Wiebe's figures for prices and wages in England and France, as adapted by Prof. Hamilton, and re-adapt them to the extent of assuming that so-called money-wages (which probably did not even account for nearly the whole of the actual economic reward of the labourer) represented only half of the costs of production and that the other half moved parallel with prices, we have the following tables for the ratio of prices to costs in England and France.

England.—(Prices and Costs assumed to be in equilibrium on the average of the years 1500–1550.)

Price/Costs Ratio.

Period	Ratio	Group	Span
1500–1550	100		
1550–1560	116		
1560–1570	112		
1570–1580	116	116	1550–1590
1580–1590	120		
1590–1600	137		
1600–1610	139		
1610–1620	135		
1620–1630	141	136·5	1590–1650
1630–1640	134		
1640–1650	133		

---

[1] Adam Smith did not under-estimate the length of short periods. " Ninety years ", he wrote, " is time sufficient to reduce any commodity, of which there is no monopoly, to its natural price."

Price/Costs Ratio.

1650–1660 . . . 122 ⎫		
1660–1670 . . . 125 ⎬ 124	1650–1680	
1670–1680 . . . 124 ⎭		
1680–1690 . . . 115 ⎫ 114·5	1680–1700	
1690–1700 . . . 114 ⎭		

These figures are very rough and doubtless inaccurate in detail. But they may serve to indicate
what were *par excellence* the epochs of the profiteer
and *therefore* (assuming habits of thrift to be constant)
of an abnormal rate of capital-accumulation.

The French statistics tell much the same story, except for the failure of wages to rise even so late as 1700.

France.—(Prices and costs assumed to be in equilibrium on the average of the years 1500–1525.)

Price/Costs Ratio.

1500–1525	100
1525–1550	103
1550–1575	110
1575–1600	139
1600–1625	118
1625–1650	128
1650–1675	123
1675–1700	124

In Spain the degree of Profit Inflation was never
so considerable, and was already evaporating by the
end of the sixteenth century. The following table is
based on Professor Hamilton's chart of prices and
wages in Andalusia without any adjustment.[1]

Spain.—(Prices and costs assumed to be in equilibrium on the average of the years 1500–1520.)

Price/Costs Ratio.

1500–1520	100
1520–1530	111
1530–1540	122
1540–1550	125
1550–1560	126

---

[1] This table is based on Professor Hamilton's *Chart*, published in
Economica, November 1929 (p. 354), and on a *table* of figures which he has
kindly supplied to me.

Price/Costs Ratio.

1560–1570	106
1570–1580	112
1580–1590	115
1590–1600	106
1600–1610	94
1610–1620	84
1620–1630	84

In all of the above three tables attention should be paid to the *changes* from one decade to the next, rather than to the absolute figures.

Now, the broad conclusion to which I would draw the particular attention of historians is the extraordinary correspondence between the periods of Profit Inflation and of Profit Deflation respectively with those of national rise and decline. The greatness of Spain coincides with the Profit Inflation from 1520 to 1600, and her eclipse with the Profit Deflation from 1600 to 1630. The rise of the power of England was delayed by the same interval as the effect of the new supplies of money on her economic system, which was at its maximum from 1585 to 1630. In the year of the Armada, Philip's Profit Inflation was just concluded, Elizabeth's had just begun. And if we compare France with England, the contrast between the financial strength of Louis XIV. and the financial weakness of James II. is seen to be due to the fact that wages in France did not rise relatively to prices in the last two decades of the seventeenth century as they did in England.[1] Indeed, the situation presents a remarkable parallel with the situation to-day, when the financial strength of the French government relatively to that of the British government is mainly due (the only other factor favourable to France being the writing down of the war debts) to the extraordinarily low level at which it has been possible to

[1] In the last decade of the century, the situation of Dutch William was saved by the remarkable investment boom in London, due to various special causes, which we have already mentioned in passing (p. 151 above).

hold money-wages in France since the return in both countries to the gold standard. France has been re-built since the war and her foreign investments greatly augmented, neither by exceptional efficiency nor by exceptional thrift, but by a steep Profit Inflation which has already lasted for a full decade.

Let not the reader suppose that I am including in this survey the whole of economic well-being. A relatively low level of real-wages is necessarily a characteristic of a period of Profit Inflation, because it is partly at the expense of current consumption that the abnormal growth of capital-wealth which accompanies a Profit Inflation is derived. It does not follow, therefore, that a Profit Inflation is to be desired ;—it is a much safer conclusion that a Profit Deflation is to be avoided.

Thus a Profit Inflation is almost certain to bring about a more unequal distribution of wealth—unless its effects are balanced by the direct taxation of the rich of the kind which characterises modern England but no other place or period. The offsets to be considered on the other side are the spirit of buoyancy and enterprise and the good employment which are engendered ; but mainly the rapid growth of capital-wealth and the benefits obtained from this in succeeding years. Before we decide where, for any epoch or country, the balance of advantage lies, we must weigh these advantages against the disadvantages. Now, Mr. F. P. Ramsey showed in his " Mathematical Theory of Saving" (*Economic Journal*, December 1920) that the ideally right rate of accumulation is almost certainly much faster than the 10-15 per cent of the annual income which I have attributed above to the typical modern community. Thus, if we consider a long period of time, the working class may benefit far more in the long run from the forced abstinence which a Profit Inflation imposes on them than they lose in the first instance in the shape of diminished

consumption. Moreover, the amount of the diminution in their current consumption corresponding to a
given increment of capital-wealth is no greater if it
comes about in this way than if it is due to voluntary
saving ;—it is only the distribution of the resulting
wealth which is affected, and, *so long as wealth and its
fruits are not consumed by the nominal owner but are
accumulated*, the evils of an unjust distribution may
not be so great as they appear.

All this applies *a fortiori* to a community very poor
in accumulated wealth, such as Europe at the end of
the fifteenth century. It is unthinkable that the
difference between the amount of wealth in France
and England in 1700 and the amount in 1500 could
ever have been built up by Thrift alone. The intervening Profit Inflation which created the modern
world was surely worth while if we take a long view.
Even to-day a tendency towards a modest Profit
Inflation would accelerate our rate of progress, as compared with the results of a modest Profit Deflation,
towards Mr. Ramsey's theoretical B, which stands for
" Bliss ", so as to make it nearer to what, if we considered our successors, it ought to be.

Nevertheless I am not yet converted, taking everything into account, from a preference for a policy
to-day which, whilst avoiding Deflation at all costs,
aims at the stability of purchasing power as its ideal
objective. Perhaps the ultimate solution lies in the
rate of capital development becoming more largely
an affair of state, determined by collective wisdom
and long views. If the task of accumulation comes
to depend somewhat less on individual caprice, so as
to be no longer at the mercy of calculations partly
based on the expectation of life of the particular
mortal men who are alive to-day, the dilemma between Thrift and Profit as the means of securing the
most desirable rate of growth for the community's
aggregate wealth will cease to present itself.

(ii.) The Depression of the Eighteen-Nineties

We must now take a long leap forward. The relevance of the foregoing theory, as to how investment in excess of savings generates a boom, to the credit cycles associated with the over-rapid investment in railways in the middle nineteenth century is obvious. Passing by both this and the very instructive deflation which followed the wars of Napoleon, let us now pass to the famous and curious depression of the eighteen-nineties.

The course of events in Great Britain between 1890 and 1896 has always seemed to be one which the old-fashioned Quantity Theory of Money was ill calculated to explain. It is, indeed, a matter for some surprise that the events of this period did not cast more doubt, than seems to have been the case, on the adequacy of the monetary theories which were then in vogue, and were, indeed, at that time only disputed by the most discredited of cranks. Instead of this, a somewhat mythical account has been built up of the actual facts of the period.

The story, on which we were brought up, tells how the decline of prices which culminated in 1896 was due to a shortage of gold occasioned by the failure (prior to the development of the South African mines) of new mining to keep up with the demand arising from the adoption of the gold standard by a number of countries. Now for the decade ending about 1886 this explanation is probably accurate. From 1886 to 1890 there was some recovery in the price-level, when a further decline set in which reached its lowest point in 1896. It is the decade from 1886 to 1896 with which I am concerned, and chiefly with the years of declining prices from 1890 to 1896. Between 1890 and 1896 Sauerbeck's Wholesale Index fell about 18 per cent, and the *Economist's* about 14 per cent.

Thus the fall of prices was severe. Yet if we look

into the figures it seems somewhat preposterous to ascribe this decline to a shortage of gold—at least so far as Great Britain was concerned. Between 1890 and 1896 the total stock of gold in the Bank of England was doubled, the Bank's reserves were nearly trebled, and its deposits nearly doubled. For two and a half years (Feb. 1894 to Sept. 1896) the Bank-rate stood unchanged at 2 per cent. Meanwhile the deposits of the Banks other than the Bank of England increased by 20 per cent. In short, the period was marked by an extreme abundance of gold and an extreme ease of credit. At the same time trade was stagnant, employment bad and prices falling.

It is evident, therefore, that there must have been a prodigious decline in prices relatively to money. Relatively to the Wholesale Index (I would use a more appropriate index if I had one) bank balances rose nearly 50 per cent. But there was no evidence of Income Deflation. On the contrary, rates of money wages were moving slightly upwards, and other money-incomes were also on the up-grade, apart from a slight sagging in 1892–93 owing to the very severe unemployment in those years, as is shown by the following table of Dr. Bowley's : [1]

	Index of Rates of Money Wages.	Total of Wages Bill.	Income above Tax Exemption Limit.
		£ million.	£ million.
1889	82	530	640
1890	84	550	640
1891	86	555	635
1892	87	545	625
1893	87	545	630
1894	88	560	645
1895	87	580	660
1896	88	595	680

[1] *Economic Journal*, 1904, p. 459.

It follows, then, from the theory of previous chapters that there must have been a very severe Commodity Deflation during these years. The rate of savings, that is to say, was seriously outrunning the cost of investment. If we look to the *Economist's* tables of new investment,[1] we find striking corroboration of this :

	New Issues.	Exports of Home Produce (% change in each year compared with preceding year).
	£ million.	
1880–1889 (annual average)	102	. .
1889	168	+ 3·71
1890	141	− 0·51
1891	76	− 5·30
1892	59	− 3·43
1893	42	− 2·10
1894	74	+ 3·35
1895	84	+ 8·57
1896	84	. .

From 1888 to 1890 there had been an investment boom, and during those years the new capital issues were abnormally high. But the falling off in new investment from 1891 to 1896 carried the activity far below the normal. The new issues in 1892 and 1893 fell to *half* the annual average for the decade 1880–1889, and the total for 1893 was lower than for any year so far back as the statistics go (*i.e.* to 1870). For the six years 1891 to 1896 new investment per annum *via* the new issue market was 40 per cent less

[1] The figures given in the table are those for actual money-calls in respect of new issues of capital, so that they exclude conversions, capital rearrangements, etc. They include loans issued in England, part of which, and sometimes an important part, was subscribed abroad. I have set, alongside this, the change in the value of our exports of home produce. The purchases of our overseas customers seem to have been quickly influenced in those days by the amounts we were lending them.

than in the six years 1885 to 1890, and 32 per cent less than in the decade 1880–1889.[1] There is no reason to suppose that the falling-off of investment *viâ* the new issue market was compensated by increased investment in other directions. On the contrary, it is estimated that in 1894 the United States repurchased about $60,000,000 of American securities from the London market.

So much for the rate of investment. When we turn to the rate of savings, there is no reason to presume any decline. Dr. Bowley estimates that aggregate money-incomes in 1891–1896 were 15 to 20 per cent higher than in the 'eighties, and the improvement in real incomes was, of course, greater still. If the total national savings in terms of money were about £150,000,000 in 1880, they probably approached £200,000,000 by 1896. Other indications show that the early 'nineties in England was a very thrifty period. In spite of a substantial rise in the value of money, the deposits of the Post Office Savings Banks doubled in terms of money between 1888 and 1897, and the deposits in ordinary Banks increased 30 per cent.[2] Moreover, the Sinking Fund was active in paying off the National Debt.

The reasons for the falling-off in the rate of investment and for the unreadiness of this rate to recover in spite of interest rates so low as to be unparalleled either before or since, were complex and various. But their general character is fairly obvious to anyone who reads the financial history of the period. The investment boom of 1888 to 1890 terminated in the Baring crisis in the latter year. This caused a severe shock to the confidence of investors not only in South

---

[1] The annual averages of new issues were :

1880–1889	.	.	.	£102,000,000
1885–1890	.	.	.	117,000,000
1891–1896	.	.	.	70,000,000

[2] If we could distinguish the savings-deposits from the cash-deposits I should expect to find that the former had doubled.

American securities but also in the stocks of Investment Trusts which had been very active in the previous years, behaving, in effect, as company promoters, and had come, in some cases, seriously to grief.[1] In India and the United States the future of the Currency was in grave doubt—the former until the closing of the Mints in 1893 which was only gradually followed by a renewal of confidence, and the latter until the victory of the " sound " money party in 1896 ; whilst Australia was overwhelmed by her great banking crisis in 1893. Thus foreign investment was brought almost to a standstill, whilst there were no special activities or new inventions [2] to absorb the redundant savings at home.

We may conclude, therefore, with considerable confidence that from 1891 to 1896 the rate of savings in Great Britain was considerably in excess of the rate of investment, and that savings by individuals were abortive to the extent of (say) some £50,000,000 per annum ; that is to say, savings by individuals out of their money-incomes added up to £50,000,000 per annum more than the increment to the national wealth, the factors of production enjoyed the equivalent of this in an increased consumption per unit of output, and producers, for example farmers, were heavy losers as a result of the successive falls in prices, not compensated by a corresponding fall in their production costs. Those factors of production which remained employed, enjoyed higher real earnings than they would have otherwise, but on the other hand an abnormal proportion of them was thrown out of work.

[1] The *Economist* wrote in its " Commercial History " for 1892 : " The disclosures of the methods of trust company finance in especial have done more than anything else to spread and perpetuate a feeling of distrust, and will, it is to be feared, continue to exercise that baneful influence for some time to come. The public, therefore, have refused to be tempted into taking part in new industrial or other undertakings."

[2] It is interesting to recall that the beginning of the recovery in 1896 was associated with the boom in the Cycle Trade.

All this while, the real-deposits entrusted to the banks, probably in the shape of fixed savings-deposits in the main, were increasing faster than money-balances ; and the fall of prices could only have been avoided by a much greater expansion of the volume of bank-money.

I consider, therefore, that the history of this period is a perfect example of a prolonged Commodity Deflation—developing and persisting in spite of a great increase in the total volume of Bank-Money. There has been no other case where one can trace so clearly the effects of a prolonged withdrawal of entrepreneurs from undertaking the production of new fixed capital on a scale commensurate with current savings.

Quantitatively the eventual effect on the price-level seems to have been greater than could reasonably be accounted for by the abortive saving alone. But this was to be expected on account of the cumulative effects and secondary reactions of such a prolonged Deflation, which we have discussed above. Also one would expect the effect on the Wholesale Indexes, which we have quoted on p. 164, to be greater than on the Consumption Index, the movements of which we do not accurately know, since the latter includes many insensitive items which the former excludes. If Great Britain had been a closed system, the excess of saving over investment might have been enough by itself to account for a fall, in the primary phase, of 4 to 5 per cent in the Consumption Index. But in fact the phenomena were international—the same things were also happening elsewhere, with complicated inter-actions both in the primary and in the secondary phases on international wholesale prices. Moreover, in the later stages the drain of gold to London caused by the cessation of foreign investment probably induced an Income Deflation abroad, as well as a Profit Deflation, which operated as a further depressing influence on international prices ; just as at the end of 1929 the

French and American price-levels felt the effect of the
international deflation caused by the drain of gold *into*
those countries earlier in the year.

Could the Bank of England have prevented the
Deflation ?   In the matter of Bank-rate it did what
lay in its power to make credit easy.   It is not obvious
what further action it could have taken in accordance
with the notions of those days, when " open-market "
policy had not been heard of.   As it was, the Bank's
" proportion " rose to 70 per cent both in 1893 and in
1894.   The purchase of securities in those years might
have done something to make the tide turn sooner.
But Consols were already at a high price, and it must
be doubtful whether purchases of Consols by the
Bank of England would have done anything material
to stimulate investment.   It may have been a case
where nothing but strenuous measures on the part of
the Government could have been successful.   Borrowing by the Government and other public bodies to
finance large programmes of work on Public Utilities
and Government guarantees on the lines of the recent
Trade Facilities and Export Credit Acts were probably
the only ways of absorbing current savings and so
averting the heavy unemployment of 1892-95.   But
any such policy was of course utterly incompatible
with the ideas and the orthodoxies of the period.

(iii.) THE WAR BOOM, 1914–18

Not even *prolegomena* to the financial history of the
war have yet been written.   Perhaps this history
never will be written in any adequate way.   For too
many of the essential statistics were suppressed at the
time and are still difficult or impossible to procure ;
and our memories of the magnitudes of figures and
the order of events are growing weak.   But looking
back I am struck by the inadequacy of the theoretical
views which, so far as I remember, we held at the time

as to what was going on, and the crudity of our applications of the Quantity Theory of Money. I do not recall that anyone mentioned clearly and explicitly what now seems to me to have been the essential feature of the situation ; yet it would surely have occurred to us if we had been familiar with the effect on prices when investment outruns savings. I shall not attempt to make a statistical study of this period, but simply to state in broad outline the general character of what was happening.

The war inevitably involved in all countries an immense diversion of resources to forms of production which, since they did not add to the volume of liquid consumption goods purchasable and consumable by income-earners, had just the same effect as an increased investment in fixed capital would have in ordinary times. The investment thus required was —especially after the initial period—on such a scale that it exceeded the maximum possible amount of voluntary saving which one could expect, even allowing for the cessation of most other kinds of investment including the replacement of wastage. Thus forced transferences of purchasing power in some shape or form were a necessary condition of investment in the material of war on the desired scale. The means of effecting this transference with the minimum of social friction and disturbance was the question for solution.

Our premisses are, therefore, that the consumption of the factors of production per unit of output had to be diminished,[1] and that this diminution could not be brought about on a sufficient scale by voluntary savings out of their earnings. It follows that their real-

---

[1] How far the authorities were from realising this at the time is shown by a speech (*vide* Beveridge, *British Food Control*, p. 9) made by the President of the Board of Trade (Mr. Runciman) early in 1915, in which he suggested that the line of escape from rising prices must be found in raising wages, whilst the general opinion at that time was that prices should be kept down but consumption left uncontrolled.

earnings per unit of output had to be diminished. There were three ways of doing this—(i.) to diminish money-wages whilst keeping prices steady, (ii.) to let prices rise more than money-wages so as to reduce real-wages, (iii.) to tax the earnings of the factors of production.

The financial purists recommended the third course, —that is to say, to raise by taxation the whole, or almost the whole, of the excess requirements beyond what could be met by voluntary saving. But I do not think that they appreciated what this would have meant in practice, if it had been unaccompanied by rising prices. The object was to curtail *general* consumption, and it would have been quite insufficient to curtail the excess consumption of the relatively rich, since their consumption, especially in time of war, is not a large enough proportion of total consumption. Thus the taxation would have had to be aimed directly at the relatively poor, since it was above all their consumption, in view of its aggregate magnitude, which had somehow or other to be reduced. It would have meant, that is to say, a tax of (say) 5s. in the £ on all wages, perhaps more. No government engaged in war could be expected to add to its other difficulties the political problems of such a tax.

It was a choice, therefore, between the remaining alternatives—between lowering money-wages or letting prices rise. Now the main initial effect of both these measures would be the same—the resources released would not accrue in the first instance to the Government (except to the extent that it was operating by a mere expansion of the currency), but to the entrepreneurs in the shape of exceptional profits. This would happen just the same in either case, because the margin between the money-proceeds of production and its money-costs would be widened. Thus the entrepreneurs would become, assuming the adoption of either of these alternatives, the collecting agents, so to speak, for the resources abstracted from the earners of incomes. The booty having fallen into the laps of the entrepreneurs, the Government would have the choice of taking it from them by loans or by taxation. Once the booty had been transferred from earners to entrepreneurs, the instrument of taxation, let it be noticed, could be adequate to the case, even though it were to fall mainly on the rich in the forms of income-tax, super-tax and excess-profits tax.

As between a policy of lowering money-wages or one of letting prices rise, it would be natural—and sensible —to prefer the latter. In the first place, a policy of forcing money-wages down would be open to almost as much political and psychological objection as taxing them. Moreover, many forms of earnings, particularly on the part of capital, are protected by contracts which cannot be upset except by repudiation, so that an *all-round* reduction of money-earnings would be difficult or impossible to enforce. But, outweighing political and equitable arguments, there was a further practical reason in favour of rising prices which should weigh heavily with a government at war. At such a time it is necessary to divert productive resources of all kinds from one employment to another on a large scale and as rapidly as possible. It would be next door to impossible to achieve this except by invoking the assistance of the price-mechanism, *i.e.* by placing credit facilities at the disposal of the new employments and allowing them to bid for productive resources against the old employments, thus allowing some measure of Income Inflation. Any government which, in the interests of financial "purism", were to cut itself off from this expedient, would lose the war.[1]

I conclude, therefore, that to allow prices to rise by

---

[1] " Nearly every manifestation of discontent on the part of the munition workers had in the end been met by increases of wages—(' let 'em have it and let's get the stuff ') " (*vide* Winston Churchill, *The Aftermath*, p. 33).

permitting a Profit Inflation is, in time of war, both inevitable and wise. But the object, we must remember, is to let prices rise *more* than earnings ; we desire primarily, that is to say, a Profit Inflation, not an Income Inflation. Some degree of Income Inflation must be allowed, to assist the redistribution of productive resources between different uses, as suggested above. But our main objective, namely, the transference of real income from consumers to the government, is defeated in so far as our Profit Inflation tumbles over into an Income Inflation. The conclusion of this part of our argument is now clear. Our object is that prices should rise more than incomes. Thus we should endeavour to control earnings more strenuously than prices.

Having, therefore, ruled out policies which are, in time of war, either impracticable or unwise, we are left with the real alternative between " vice " and " virtue " in war finance. It is expedient to use entrepreneurs as collecting agents. But let them be agents and not principals. Having adopted for quite good reasons a policy which pours the booty into their laps, let us be sure that they hand it over in the form of taxes, and that they are not enabled to obtain a claim over the future income of the community by being allowed to " lend " to the State what has thus accrued to them. To let prices rise relatively to earnings and then tax entrepreneurs to the utmost is the right procedure for " virtuous " war finance. For high taxation of profits and of incomes above the exemption limit is not a substitute for Profit Inflation but an adjunct of it.

Whilst I am not aware that the theory of the matter was ever expressed quite in this way, this is very nearly the system which the British Treasury had actually evolved by the method of trial-and-error towards the end of the war. They had got as near to the ideally right procedure as could be expected.

They are only to be criticised for not applying the procedure early enough and for not following up their other taxes by a Capital Levy in 1919. Consequently entrepreneurs were still able to establish claims against the future income of the community on a scale which was unjustifiably heavy yet not quite intolerable—with the result that we carry them still. Indeed, instead of abating these claims by a Capital Levy in 1919, we spent the subsequent years up to 1925 in riveting them on our necks still more heavily by raising the value of the currency in terms of which they had been contracted.

The war-finance of other European countries was far less " virtuous " on the above criterion of virtue— not so much because the element of Profit Inflation was far greater, but because the entrepreneurs were enabled to retain (on and in paper) a much greater proportion of their booty. But such is the duplicity of Fate that these " vicious " courses worked out better in the end than British moderation. For the result was to make the burdens so intolerable that they had, by mere force of events, to be entirely or largely obliterated through a depreciation of the currency in which they were contracted. There is nothing worse than a moderate evil ! If wasps and rats were hornets and tigers, we should have exterminated them before now. So with Great Britain's obligations to her *rentiers* arising out of the war.

The war-period was also marked by an excessive preoccupation on the part of " sound " financiers with the aggregate volume of bank-money. We have remarked above how it was universally believed at the time that inflation would be avoided if old ladies, who had had money on fixed deposit with their banks for years, could be induced on patriotic grounds to surrender these to the Treasury in exchange for war loans—for in that way any increase in the total volume of bank-money would be avoided ! As soon as we think in terms of the income-deposits and of the flow of incomes and of consumption-expenditure through these deposits, such crude errors of thought become avoidable. Other patriots tried to think out ways by which the same volume of money turn-over could be conducted by means of a smaller volume of Currency Notes !

(iv.) The Post-war Boom, 1919-20

At the end of the war, the working capital for the normal productive processes of peace-time was depleted throughout the world to a degree which was probably unprecedented. A proportion of the goods in process suddenly became useless for the purposes for which they had been intended, and stocks of consumption goods had fallen everywhere far below their normal level. There was, therefore, a big prospective demand for goods given the purchasing power ; and there was also a big supply of labour from the demobilised armies. If, therefore, this labour was to be employed at the prevailing money-wage with the various war-time restrictions removed, a rise of prices was inevitable. Moreover, there were all kinds of delayed requirements for investment in instrumental goods and other fixed capital such as houses.

Consequently the impulses to investment at a rate in excess of savings were tremendously strong. At the same time the pressure to find employment at a satisfactory rate of money-wages for those who had been previously occupied on war-service or in the manufacture of munitions was, for obvious reasons, hardly less strong. A Profit Inflation was, therefore, inevitable unless war-time restrictions were continued and reinforced, and unless the process of absorption of demobilised men into employment was protracted over a considerable period. In the circumstances of the day it was quite out of the question that the banking authorities should put adequate obstacles in the way of a Profit Inflation. And who will say that, even if this had been practicable, it would have been desirable on the whole ? In the later stages the banking authorities were—in my judgment, writing after the event—highly culpable in allowing the Profit Inflation to develop into so violent an Income Inflation, in not taking steps sooner to check the secondary phase of the cycle, and in continuing the steps which they did take long after they were doing harm.

To one looking back, therefore, it does seem inevitable that the war should not only have been accompanied by one Profit Inflation, but should also have been followed by another. Though complicated in various ways, the boom was in the main due to investment running ahead of saving as a result of the urgent necessity of replenishing working capital at a rapid rate. Though a very strong Income Inflation was stimulated in the secondary phase, the extent of the Profit Inflation and the subsequent Profit Deflation is well indicated by the measure in which prices outran wages from the spring of 1919 to the middle of 1920, and wages out-ran prices after the middle of 1920 to the end of 1921.

Unfortunately the available statistics are not suitable for exhibiting the movement in an accurate manner. In 1919 cost-of-living index-numbers were still affected by price-controls, and there are no true Consumption Index-Numbers in existence which indicate adequately the rise of prices of finished consumption goods in the autumn of 1919 and the spring of 1920. Moreover, the phenomenon was on this occasion pre-eminently world-wide in character, whilst, on account of the very high prices obtainable for finished goods, industrial countries such as Great Britain stood to gain at the expense of the rest of the world, with the result that the increase of prices relatively

to wages was probably less in such countries than in
the world at large. If this is true, British statistics
will under-estimate the degree of Profit Inflation as
applying to the world at large. On a balance of considerations, I think that the movements of the Board
of Trade Wholesale Index-Number relatively to Prof.
Bowley's Index of British Wages, will give us, at the
least, an interesting side-light on the position. These
movements are shown in the following table :

	1. Board of Trade Whole- sale Index.	2. Bowley's Wage Index.	3. Ratio of (1) to (2).	4. Ratio of (1) to (2) corrected for increasing efficiency of Labour.
1919 1st Quarter	249	207	120	120
2nd ,,	242	209	116	116
3rd ,,	255	217	118	118
4th ,,	288	221	130	130
1920 1st ,,	309	231	134	135
2nd ,,	324	250	130	131
3rd ,,	314	267	118	119
4th ,,	284	273	104	106
1921 1st ,,	227	276	82	84
2nd ,,	202	268	75	77
3rd ,,	190	244	78	80
4th ,,	174	228	76	78
1922 1st ,,	162	215	75	78
2nd ,,	160	202	79	82
3rd ,,	157	189	83	86
4th ,,	156	179	87	90
1923 1st ,,	158	177	89	93
2nd ,,	160	174	92	96
3rd ,,	157	174	90	94
4th ,,	161	173	93	97
1924 1st ,,	166	174	95	100
2nd ,,	164	177	93	98
3rd ,,	165	179	92	97
4th ,,	170	179	95	100

Now Bowley's Wage Index is an Index of actual
wages paid, not of efficiency-wages. I suggest that

we might get a rough correction for this by assuming
that in 1919 efficiency was at the same level as before
the war and that it was increasing at the rate of 1
per cent per annum after that date.   On this assumption the Wholesale Index had risen as the result of the
Profit Inflation of the war by 18 per cent (taking the
mean of the first three-quarters of 1919) relatively to
British efficiency-wages.   The Profit Inflation of the
post-war boom had increased this disparity to 33 per
cent by the first half of 1920 [1] (taking the mean of the
first two quarters of 1920).   After the middle of 1920
there set in a Profit Deflation which in a very few
months obliterated the previous Profit Inflation and
then produced a positive Profit Deflation which at
its worst (*i.e.* during 1921 and the first quarter of
1922) was just about as severe as the previous Profit
Inflation had been.   Meanwhile—but not until the
Profit Deflation had been going for about a year—
there set in on top of it (as our previous argument
would lead us to expect, failing special steps to the
contrary) an Income Deflation (*i.e.* from the middle
of 1921 to the end of 1922).   By the middle of 1922
the Income Deflation had come to an end and the
Profit Deflation was gradually reversed, until in 1924
(as shown in column (4) of the table) equilibrium was
restored.[2]   A map of these proceedings is given in
the table on the following page.

I should add that all this—even more than usual—
is subject to correction by more minute investigators
of the facts of the post-war period.   I throw out my
hypothesis as a target for statisticians and historians
more diligent than myself.   But the above is—if it
is a correct picture of what happened—in reasonable
accordance with the order of events as predicted by

---

[1] *I.e.* there was by this date an Income Inflation of about 150 per cent
(on pre-war) and a Profit Inflation of 33 per cent on the top of this.

[2] After which came the return-to-gold deflation described in the next
section of this chapter.

			Income Position.	Profit Position.
1919	1st Quarter			
	2nd	,,		
	3rd	,,		Profit Inflation
	4th	,,	Income Inflation	
1920	1st	,,		
	2nd	,,		
	3rd	,,		Diminishing Profit
	4th	,,		Inflation
				Equilibrium
1921	1st	,,	Stationary	
	2nd	,,		
	3rd	,,		Profit Deflation
	4th	,,		
1922	1st	,,	Income Deflation	
	2nd	,,		
	3rd	,,		
	4th	,,		
1923	1st	,,		Diminishing Profit
	2nd	,,		Deflation
	3rd	,,		
	4th	,,	Stationary	
1924	1st	,,		
	2nd	,,		
	3rd	,,		Equilibrium
	4th	,,		

the theory of previous chapters. The Income and
Profit Inflations of 1919 were, of course, a continua-
tion of the Inflations of the War Period. Apart from
this we see that banking policy operated by initiating
a Profit Inflation or Deflation, as the case might be,
which slopt over into an Income Inflation or Deflation six to nine months later.[1] For the banking
system has but little power to influence the income
situation direct; it can only do so *viâ* the profit
situation.

Looking back, we see that the extreme prolongation
of the slump was due to the Profit Deflation which
occurred in the first half of 1921. This was doubtless

---

[1] This was at a time when wage-rates were fairly mobile. The Profit
Deflation attendant on Great Britain's return to the pre-war gold parity
had failed to produce an Income Deflation five years later.

inspired by the object of cancelling some part of the Income Inflation of the war and post-war periods —as was, indeed, effected from the middle of 1921 to the end of 1922 and again subsequently to 1924. But from the standpoint of national prosperity it was a mistake. We might have avoided most of the troubles of the last ten years—and been, perhaps, just about as rich as the United States—if we had endeavoured to stabilise our monetary position on the basis of the degree of Income Inflation existing at the end of 1920, *i.e.* about 175 per cent up as compared with pre-war. Incidentally this would have left the real burden of the War Debt at less than two-thirds of its present figure. The policy actually adopted increased the severity of the Debt problem by 50 per cent, and gave us a decade of unemployment which may have diminished the production of wealth by more than £1,000,000,000.

(v.) Great Britain's Return to the Gold Standard

In the course of the six months which preceded and the six months which followed Great Britain's Return to the Gold Standard in May 1925, it was necessary to raise the gold-value of sterling by about 10 per cent at a time when gold itself was not depreciating in value.[1] This meant that the flow of money-incomes per unit of output, *i.e.* of rates of earnings generally, had to be diminished by 10 per cent—except in so far as a depreciation in the value of gold itself might come to the assistance of the transition. In other words, there had to be an Income Deflation in the strict sense of the word.

Now for at least fifty years before the war—perhaps for more than a hundred years—we had had

---

[1] In the year ending May 1925 gold, as measured by international indexes, depreciated somewhat—perhaps by as much as 5 per cent ; but in the next two years it recovered the whole of this fall in value.

no experience of a rapid and cold-blooded Income Deflation on anything like this scale ; whilst for several reasons the Deflation of 1921–22 was not a satisfactory precedent. What, on the contrary, we had experienced many times was a Profit Deflation, generally accompanied in some measure by an Income Deflation, following after a boom and representing a return to a previous equilibrium. Whilst it is arguable that there existed at the end of 1924 a slight tendency to a mild Profit Inflation accompanied by a still milder Income Inflation, the Deflation required for the return to gold amounted to far more than the mere counteraction of this tendency. But the authorities at the Treasury and at the Bank of England knew nothing about the difference between an Income Deflation and a Profit Deflation, with the result that they greatly over-estimated the efficacy of their weapons of credit restriction and bank-rate—which had often shown themselves effective against a Profit Inflation—when applied with the object of producing out of the blue a cold-blooded Income Deflation.

By withdrawing credit from entrepreneurs the power of the latter to give employment was curtailed ; by the increased cost of credit, by the fall of wholesale prices, which ensued on the raising of the value of sterling on the foreign exchanges, and by the reduction of purchasing power at home, profits were diminished and the incentive to production became less. Thus, in the first instance, the use by the Bank of England of its traditional weapons brought about a Profit Deflation. Prices duly fell. The Governor of the Bank of England felt himself able to inform the Chancellor of the Exchequer that the task was accomplished.

Yet this was far from the truth. Equilibrium required that the flow of money-incomes and the rate of money-earnings per unit of output should be appropriately reduced. But in the first instance the fall of prices reduced, not costs and rates of earnings, but profits.   The entrepreneur bore the brunt, and the only means by which the Bank of England's policy could restore equilibrium was to make him smart so severely that he would pass on the pressure to the proper quarters.   The entrepreneur, faced with prices falling faster than costs, had three alternatives open to him—to put up with his losses as best he could ; to withdraw from his less profitable activities, thus reducing output and employment; to embark on a struggle with his employees to reduce their money-earnings per unit of output—of which only the last was capable of restoring real equilibrium from the national point of view.   In the long run, however, these alternatives might be compatible, if efficiency could be sufficiently increased, with a maintenance of money-earnings per unit of the factors of production.

The entrepreneur tried all three.   To a surprising extent and for a surprising length of time, he submitted to the first, namely the cutting down, or cutting off, of his profits.   The leading industries—the old textile industries, the heavy industries working coal, iron and steel, the railways and the farmers—just took their losses and went on taking them, not merely for months but for years.   The usual profits of these industries were diminished by tens of millions of pounds.   The joint-stock form of organisation, by which the control has largely passed to salaried persons, probably prolonged the period of inertia longer than if the whole of the losses had fallen on the actual managers.

It follows that the full development of unemployment was also longer postponed than might have been expected.   But the entrepreneur availed himself from the outset of the second expedient as well—the expedient of curtailing his less profitable activities. Five years after the consummation of the return to gold the curtailment of employment was still in operation in an unabated degree.

There remains the third expedient—of reducing the rates of money-earnings per unit of output. It may be that in earlier periods the pressure of sub-normal profits and the unemployment of factors of production may have operated more rapidly than they do now to achieve the objective of an Income Deflation. I believe that the resistances to a severe Income Deflation, which is not merely a reaction from a recent Inflation, have always been very great. But in the modern world of organised Trade Unions and a proletarian electorate they are overwhelmingly strong. The attempt by the entrepreneurs to bring this expedient into operation culminated in the General Strike of 1926. But political and social considerations stood in the way of allowing the advantages won by the defeat of the Strike to be pushed home. Wage-rates in particular industries have fallen heavily, but Dr. Bowley's general index of weekly wage-rates was practically as high in 1930 as in 1924. Thus one could only hope for an increase in efficiency by which lower money-earnings per unit of output might be compatible with unchanged money-earnings per unit of the factors of production. At long last, perhaps, this will be the way of escape.

Meanwhile the loss of national wealth entailed by the attempt to bring about an Income Deflation by means of the weapons appropriate to a Profit Deflation was enormous. If we assume that only half the unemployment was abnormal, the loss of national output may be estimated at more than £100,000,000 per annum—a loss which persisted over several years.

(vi) British Home and Foreign Investment after the Return to Gold

The difficulties just mentioned, in which Great Britain was involved from 1925 onwards, were complicated and aggravated by another factor. Since this well illustrates the argument of Vol. i. Chap. 21, an account of it will be in place here.

We saw in Chapter 21 that in equilibrium the rate of interest is such that the amount of foreign lending at that rate is exactly equal to the amount of the favourable foreign balance, as determined by comparative money-costs of production at home and abroad, and also such that the amount of home investment at that rate is exactly equal to the excess of the country's total savings over the amount of the foreign lending. Now, the return to gold at the pre-war parity had an adverse effect on the foreign balance because it increased the gold-costs of production here relatively to gold-costs elsewhere. But alongside of this there has been another tendency at work, namely an increase in the attractiveness to the investor of foreign investment as compared with home investment ;—which has meant that we have been needing for equilibrium not merely as great a foreign balance as before 1925, but a greater one. Thus two separate forces have been at work pushing the amount of foreign lending L (failing the deterrent effect of an artificial rate of interest in excess of the natural-rate) ahead of the foreign balance B ; for L (if left to itself) has been trying to increase, whilst at the same time B has been diminishing.

If, in such circumstances, it proves impracticable to increase B adequately, then there is no remedy except to reduce L by raising the market-rate of interest above the natural-rate. And it is the inevitable result of this that the amounts of home and of total investment will be forced below the equilibrium level.

Thus there was a double reason for the Profit Deflation and Unemployment which set in. Moreover, this second reason worked in a vicious circle. For the business losses resulting from the Profit Deflation served to increase still further the relative attractiveness of foreign investment, thus making it still more necessary to maintain an artificially high rate of interest and so riveting still more firmly on our necks the Profit Deflation, consequent on the deficiency of total investment relatively to savings, and the Unemployment which Profit Deflation brings.

When once the effort materially to reduce money-wages had been abandoned, there remained four possible ways out of the impasse :

(i.) The first and most attractive method was to increase B, the foreign balance, by decreasing money-costs of production as a result, not of reduced money-wages, but of increased efficiency. This was called " Rationalisation ". Obviously the more " rationalisation " in this sense, the better ;—that goes without saying. But improvements of this kind are a slow business at best ; in order to help foreign trade the increase of efficiency relatively to money-wages must mature *faster* at home than abroad ; foreign tariffs are a severe obstacle ; and in 1930 there was a world-wide cyclical depression as a further handicap.

(ii.) The second method, which was popular for obvious reasons in industrial quarters, was to increase B by diminishing the volume of imports through the agency of tariffs or analogous measures. The application of this remedy in present circumstances would probably not result either in a diminution of our exports to an extent equal to the diminution of imports, or in a diminution of home investment, but in some increase of foreign investment, which increase would be mainly a net gain to the wealth of the community. (This comparison with what would happen in the absence of a tariff is, of course, on the assumption that the remedy of reducing money-wages, fluidity in which is essential to the free-trade position, was not available.)

(iii.) The third method was to increase home investment by what would amount in effect to a subsidy of some kind, so as to bridge the difference between the market-rate of interest, which it was necessary to enforce in order to restrict foreign lending, and the natural-rate of interest at which a profitable outlet could be found at home for the excess of total saving over the amount of foreign investment as determined by B. For it was obviously better that this excess of savings should eventuate in investment of some kind than that it should be wasted in the shape of business losses. But it was difficult for those concerned to appreciate this. For if the market-rate of interest was (say) 5 per cent, it naturally appeared wasteful to spend money on capital developments which would only yield (say) 4 per cent;—as it would have been if it were a question of choice between investing at 5 per cent or investing at 4 per cent, whereas in fact for the community as a whole the real choice was between an increment of capital wealth which would yield 4 per cent and no increment at all. It will be observed that this remedy amounted in effect to establishing by means of a subsidy, or other equivalent arrangement, a differential rate of interest for home investment as compared with foreign investment.

(iv.) The fourth method was to stimulate investment throughout the world, both at home and abroad, by an international cheap money policy. This policy would help our exports, and therefore increase our foreign investment, by raising world-prices or at least by avoiding a further fall ; whilst the fall in the rate of interest would at the same time increase our home investment. Thus in both ways it would bring the aggregate of investment nearer to the volume of savings and thus tend to terminate the era of business losses and unemployment. This method, however, required international co-operation, which was not forthcoming until after the Wall Street slump at the end of 1929. Moreover, no adequate results could be expected until the cheapening of short loans had reacted on the quantity and prices of the long-term lending available, which for various special reasons did not occur quickly. Finally, so far as Great Britain was concerned, it was not prudent to rely on this remedy for doing more than remove the aggravation, which the world-wide cyclical depression of 1930 had brought with it, of more deep-seated troubles.

All these methods had their value, and some of them may have produced useful results by the date when the reader is reading these lines. But however this may be, I feel a further and more permanent preoccupation concerning the economic prospects of Great Britain under a régime of *laissez-faire*.

Great Britain is an old country with a higher standard of working-class life than exists in most other parts of the world. The population will soon cease to grow. Our habits and institutions keep us, in spite of all claims to the contrary, a thrifty people, saving some 10 per cent of our income. In such conditions one would anticipate with confidence that, if Great Britain were a closed system, the natural-rate of interest would fall rapidly. In the rest of the world, however (though the United States may find herself in the same position as Great Britain much sooner than she expects), the fall in the rate of interest is likely to be much slower. Equilibrium under *laissez-faire* will, therefore, require that a large and increasing proportion of our savings must find its outlet in foreign investment. Provided that the income from our previous foreign investments increases faster than our current savings, the position will in time come to look after itself without our having to increase our exports, because on this assumption it will be possible in course of time to " finance " the new investment out of in-creased interest from previous investment. But it looks as if there may be an interim period during which it will be impossible, assuming *laissez-faire* in the distribution of our total savings between home investment and foreign investment, to maintain a position of equilibrium without a fairly large increase in our exports relatively to our imports. The existence, as I write, of an international slump may lead me to exaggerate the difficulty of this. But having regard to the tariff-walls against us, to the gradual disappearance, in a world of mass-production and of the universal adoption of modern techniques, of the special advantages in manufacture which used to be ours, and to the high real-wages (including in this the value of social services) to which our workers are accustomed as compared with our European competitors, one cannot but feel a doubt whether the attainment of equilibrium on the lines of an expanding trade surplus will in fact be practicable.

It may be that the attainment of equilibrium in accordance with our traditional principles would be the best solution,—if we could get it. But if social and political forces stand in the way of our getting it, then it will be better to reach equilibrium by such a device as differential terms for home investment relatively to foreign investment, and even, perhaps, such a falling off from grace as differential terms for home-produced goods relatively to foreign-produced goods, than to suffer indefinitely the business losses and unemployment which disequilibrium means. Of the two types of devices indicated above, I much prefer that of differential rates for home and foreign lending to that of differential prices for home and foreign goods ; for I believe that there is a much greater scope for this device without risking injurious reactions in other directions, and, in some cases indeed, with positive social advantage. But I am coming round to the view that there is also room for applying usefully some method of establishing differential prices for home and foreign goods.

(vii.) THE UNITED STATES, 1925–30

This period is interesting in that it provides (up to the spring of 1928) an example rare in monetary history, namely, one in which high rates of productive activity and of investment were developed without the rate of savings falling behind. By the middle of 1928, however, there is evidence that a Profit Inflation had commenced, culminating in boom conditions by the spring of 1929 and rapidly terminated by a collapse in the autumn of 1929. The following table gives some leading statistics up to the date of the collapse:

Average of Year (1926 = 100).	Reporting Member Banks.			Bureau of Labour Index of Wholesale Prices.	Standard Statistics Index of Industrial Productivity.	Standard Statistics Prices of Common Stocks.
	Loans and Investments.	Demand Deposits.	Time Deposits.			
1926	100	100	100	100	100	100
1927	103·5	102·5	109·5	95	97·5	118
1928	111	104·5	121	98	100·5	150
1929 (Jan.–Sept.)	114	102·5	121·5	97	110	198

Now for two reasons these statistics were peculiarly difficult to interpret. Anyone who looked only at the index of prices would see no reason to suspect any material degree of inflation; whilst anyone who looked only at the total volume of bank-credit and the prices of common stocks would have been convinced of the presence of an inflation actual or impending. For my own part I took the view at the time that there was no inflation in the sense in which I use this term. Looking back in the light of fuller statistical information than was then available, I believe that, whilst there was probably no material inflation up to the end of 1927, a genuine profit inflation developed some time between that date and the summer of 1929.

The index of wholesale prices was misleading, because this index is much influenced by the international price-level and in the rest of the world there was from 1926 onwards a deflation rather than otherwise. The

rise of the American index in 1928 took place against
the tide, since prices were falling slightly in that year
in the outside world. Manufactured articles, moreover, were probably undergoing a decrease in their
cost of production as a result of efficiency increasing
faster than wages, so that even a stable price-level
might have represented some measure of commodity
inflation. At the same time the banking statistics
were misleading owing to the unprecedented requirements of the financial circulation; whereas the demand
deposits were scarcely keeping pace with the value of
output. For conclusive evidence, therefore, it was
necessary to examine the direct evidence as to the rate
of net investment. For this purpose I give below
some indicators of the annual rate of net investment
in (a) fixed capital at home and (b) working capital.
I am neglecting foreign investment because the fluctuations in this were certainly very small compared with
the fluctuations in these two items, and also investment in liquid capital, partly because statistics are
lacking and partly because these fluctuations also are
likely to be relatively small. Moreover, I have made
no adjustment for changes in prices, which were not
great enough, however, over the period covered to
make a vast difference to such a crude calculation as
I am making. I hope that the skilled statisticians of
the United States will prepare a more correct index of
net investment than that which I give below.

The following are the Dodge Corporation statistics
of the value of construction contracts awarded
(1928 = 100):

1919 .	.	. 44	1925 .	.	. 94
1920 .	.	. 47	1926 .	.	. 98
1921 .	.	. 43	1927 .	.	. 96
1922 .	.	. 61	1928 .	.	. 100
1923 .	.	. 67	1929 .	.	. 88
1924 .	.	. 74	1930 [1]	.	. 74

[1] Figures for 37 States for first 8 months of 1930 compared with the
corresponding figures for the first 8 months of 1928.

These statistics, which exclude projects under $5,000, are estimated to cover at least 60 per cent of the total volume of investment in fixed capital represented by public and private building, public utilities and other construction. The relation of the Dodge figures to the best total figures which can be compiled is shown below : [1]

Year.	Dodge Figures.	Estimated Total. Public and Private Construction in U.S.	
	($1,000,000)	($1,000,000)	(1928 = 100)
1923	4,768	6,368	64
1924	5,237	7,305	74
1925	6,623	8,911	90
1926	6,901	9,350	94
1927	6,787	9,542	96
1928	7,065	9,936	100

We have in this prodigious volume of construction from 1925 to 1928 [2] a sufficient explanation, in accordance with the theory of this Treatise, of the immense prosperity of the United States culminating in 1928–29. Nevertheless the high rate of capital construction in 1925–27 does not seem to have led to a notable profit inflation in those years. This must be partly attributable to a high rate of savings compared with previous years. But it was also due, I think, to the smallness of the net increment required for the revolving fund of working capital during those years. Assuming a time-lag of six months in our fixed capital index, we need for comparability over annual periods (July–June) the increment of working capital in the January–June half-year over the working capital in the previous January–June half-year. The Standard

---

[1] Material recently collected in a volume entitled *Planning and Control of Public Works*, compiled by the National Bureau of Economic Research, is very useful for assessing the value of the Dodge statistics. The more complete estimate quoted above is taken from p. 126 of this work.

[2] The above figures probably ante-date the time of actual construction by some six months throughout.

Statistics Index of Industrial Production for the first half of each calendar year is as follows :

1923 . . . 116	1927 . . . 120
1924 . . . 107	1928 . . . 118
1925 . . . 116	1929 . . . 132
1926 . . . 120	1930 . . . 113

Thus the increased requirements of working capital were inconsiderable from 1925 up to the middle of 1928 ; but from the middle of 1928 to the middle of 1929 they were large, whilst from the middle of 1929 to the middle of 1930 the decrement was still larger.

Let us now attempt to make a combined index, though necessarily very crude and rough, of the order of magnitude of the fluctuations in investment in fixed and working capital taken together. Our previous calculations (p. 107) suggest that every point of the above Index of Production may represent about $100,000,000 of working capital ; and as it happens every point of the above Index of Capital Construction also represents about $100,000,000. Let us, therefore, add the increment of the former, which measures the net additional requirements of the year, to the absolute value of the latter (with a lag of six months) :

Year.	Investment in Fixed Capital.	Net Investment in Working Capital.	Aggregate.
1923–24	64	− 9	55
1924–25	74	+ 9	83
1925–26	90	+ 4	94
1926–27	94	. .	94
1927–28	96	− 2	94
1928–29	100	+ 14	114
1929–30	88	− 19	69

This table supplies some evidence, therefore, for the conclusion that, whilst the investment covered by these figures had been extremely stable in the three years 1925–26 to 1927–28, its amount jumped 20 per cent in 1928–29 (in value $2,000,000,000) and receded 45 per cent [1] in 1929–30 (in value $4,500,000,000). The preliminary figures for the first quarter of the year 1930–31 indicate a further fall, the index of fixed investment being about 75, and that of industrial production falling 13 points further to about 100. Thus the boom of 1928–29 and the slump of 1929–30 in the United States correspond respectively to an excess and to a deficiency of investment, and appear, therefore, to conform reasonably well with what the theory of this Treatise would lead us to expect.

Part of the explanation of the maintenance of equilibrium between investment and saving from 1925 to 1928, when the former was on a great scale, whilst the public were commonly reported to be in an extravagant rather than in a saving mood, is to be found in the great expansion of corporate saving, *i.e.* of saving effected by Joint-Stock institutions through their practice of dividing amongst their shareholders an amount far short of their total profits. Both in Great Britain and in the United States it is estimated that about two-fifths of aggregate savings are made in this way. In the case of the United States these internal resources of Joint-Stock Corporations have been accumulating at a time when, owing to changes in methods of doing business, the amount of working capital required has been decreasing rather than increasing, whilst expansion in fixed plant has been proceeding at a moderate rate. Thus industry had large liquid reserves which were available to be placed at the disposal of other developments, *e.g.* building and instalment buying, either direct or through the banking system. There was also another peculiar feature in the situation. One might have

---

[1] This figure may have been partly offset by an increase of investment in liquid capital, *i.e.* increase of stocks.

expected that the very high short-money rates enforced by the Federal Reserve Banks would have
had a more rapid effect in retarding investment and
so bringing the period of business prosperity to an
earlier conclusion.   That this was not so, is to be
ascribed partly to the fact that high short-money rates
reacted less than usual on bond-rate, but largely to the
fact that the very high prices of common shares,
relatively to their dividend yields, offered Joint-Stock
enterprises an exceptionally cheap method of financing
themselves.   Thus, whilst short-money rates were very
high and bond-rates somewhat high, it was cheaper
than at any previous period to finance new investment
by the issue of common stocks.   By the spring of 1929
this was becoming the predominant method of finance.
Thus easy terms were maintained for certain types of
investment, in spite of the appearance of very dear
short-money.

With the Wall Street collapse in the autumn of 1929
one of the greatest " bull " Stock Exchange movements in history came to an end.   But we may remark
that this was preluded by the development of " two
views " on an enormous scale.   Whilst one section were
still keen to buy stocks and carry them on borrowed
money, even at very high rates of interest, another section were " bears " of the position (in the sense in which
I have used this term) and preferred to hold money
rather than stocks.   If we take the volume of Brokers'
Loans on the New York Stock Exchange as the measure
of the " bull-bear " position, *i.e.* of the degree to which
" two views " had developed, we find that at the end
of September 1929, which was the culminating point,
the total of these loans had risen to $8,549,000,000.
Three months later the collapse of stock prices had
brought the " two views " together, at a level of values
where the two parties could agree with one another
more nearly, and the total of the Brokers' Loans fell

to less than half the above, namely $3,990,000,000.[1]
We have not had on any previous occasion so perfect
a statistical test of the way in which, when stock
prices have risen beyond a certain point, the machinery
of the "two views" functions. But the fact that
the technique of the New York market allows an
important proportion of the "bear" position to be
lent directly to the "bulls" without the interposition
of the banking system, together with the low reserve
which the Member Banks are required to hold against
Time Deposits, facilitated immense fluctuations in the
magnitude of this position without the disturbance to
the Industrial Circulation which would result almost
inevitably in such conditions as characterise the British
system. Nevertheless the high market-rate of interest
which, prior to the collapse, the Federal Reserve
System, in their effort to control the enthusiasm of the
speculative crowd, caused to be enforced in the United
States—and, as a result of sympathetic self-protective
action, in the rest of the world—played an essential
part in bringing about the rapid collapse. For this
punitive rate of interest could not be prevented from
having its repercussion on the rate of new investment
both in the United States and throughout the world,
and was bound, therefore, to prelude an era of falling
prices and business losses everywhere.

Thus I attribute the slump of 1930 primarily to the
deterrent effects on investment of the long period of
dear money which preceded the stock-market collapse,
and only secondarily to the collapse itself. But the
collapse having occurred, it greatly aggravated matters,
especially in the United States, by causing a disin-
vestment in working capital. Moreover, it also promoted the development of a profit deflation in two
other ways—both by discouraging investment and by

---

[1] The grand totals of loans on securities both through brokers and
direct from banks were (in $1,000,000) : June 29, 1929, $15,055 ; Oct. 4,
1929, $16,660 ; June 30, 1930, $12,170 (H. V. Roelze, *Review of Economic
Statistics*, Aug. 1930).

encouraging saving. The pessimism and the atmosphere of disappointment which the stock-market collapse engendered reduced enterprise and lowered the natural-rate of interest ; whilst the "psychological" poverty which the collapse of paper values brought with it probably increased saving.

The last point is important, and we may pause upon it for a moment. It may suggest a generalisation of permanent value. A country is no richer when, for purposes of swopping titles to prospective gain between one of its citizens and another, people choose to value the prospects at twenty years' purchase, than when these are valued at ten years' purchase ; but the citizens, beyond question, *feel* richer. Who can doubt that a man is more likely to buy a new motor-car if his investments have doubled in money-value during the past year than if they have been halved ? He feels far less necessity or obligation to save out of his normal income, and his whole standard of expenditure is raised. For their paper profits and their savings out of current income are not kept by most men (as perhaps they should be) in entirely separate compartments of the mind.

In the actual example before us the market value of the securities listed on the New York Stock Exchange rose from $70,000,000,000 in April 1929 to $90,000,000,000 in September 1929, and had fallen back to $64,000,000,000 by December 1929.[1] The public cannot be expected to see their nominal wealth increase by $20,000,000,000 in six months and then lose $26,000,000,000 in three months, and to maintain precisely the same style of life during the second period as during the first. I conclude that they are more likely to " save " (in my sense of word) when they are " losing " than when they are " making " hundreds

---

[1] The number of shares listed was greater in December than in September, and greater in September than in April ; but this does not make a material difference to the argument.

of millions of dollars a week ;—more likely to refrain from new extravagances and to pay off the instalments of their former purchases.

(viii.) The " Gibson Paradox "

For some years past Mr. A. H. Gibson has published a series of articles, mostly in the *Bankers' Magazine*,[1] emphasising the extraordinarily close correlation over a period of more than a hundred years between the rate of interest, as measured by the yield of Consols, and the level of prices, as measured by the Wholesale Index-Number. I have long been interested by Mr. Gibson's figures, and have often endeavoured to determine some theoretical hypothesis which would explain them. For some time my failure made me try to believe that Mr. Gibson's surprising results were to be attributed to nothing more than the well-established and easily-explained tendency of prices and interest to rise together on the upward phase of the credit cycle, and to fall together on the downward phase *plus* a generous allowance of mere coincidence. But it was never easy to sustain this view. For the extraordinary thing is that the " Gibson Paradox "—as we may fairly call it—is one of the most completely established empirical facts within the whole field of quantitative economics, though theoretical economists have mostly ignored it. It is very unlikely indeed that it can be fortuitous, and it ought, therefore, to be susceptible of some explanation of a general character.[2] The analysis of the preceding chapters will furnish us, however, with a hypothetical explanation which is worth mentioning.

---

[1] *Vide*, in particular, *Bankers' Magazine*, Jan. 1923 and Nov. 1926.

[2] Mr. Gibson's own explanation—that " it is obviously due to the fact that the less the cost of living the greater must necessarily be the margin available for investment "—must, I am afraid, be rejected unreservedly. He forgets that money-earnings *plus* profits move to the same extent as prices.

	Wholesale Index-Number.[1]	Wholesale Index-Number with adjusted Base.	Yield of Consols[2] (£3 : 4 : 6 = 100).
1791–94	108	119 ⎱ +10%	121
1795–99	137	151 ⎰	159
1800–04	145	145	147
1805–09	158	158	148
1810–14	144	144	149
1815–19	128	128	133
1820–24	106	117	119
1825–29	101	111	110
1830–34	91	100	109
1835–39	98	108 +10%	102
1840–44	92	101	100
1845–49	85	93	101
1850–54	85	93	96
1855–60	98	98	100
1860–64	101	101	101
1865–69	100	100	102
1870–74	103	103	100
1875–79	91	100 ⎱ +10%	98
1880–84	83	91 ⎰	93
1885–89	70	84	92
1890–94	68	82	88
1895–99	63	76 +20%	82
1900–04	71	85	88
1905–09	75	90	90
1910–14	82	98	101
1915–19	163	130 ⎱ −20%	135 [3]
1920	251	201 ⎰	165
1921	155	155	162
1922	131	131	137
1923	129	129	134
1924	139	139	136
1925	136	136	137
1926	126	139	141
1927	122	134 +10%	141
1928	120	132	138

[1] From 1820 the index-number is that of Sauerbeck continued by the *Statist*, while for 1791–1819 it is that of Jevons × $\frac{8}{7}$, this multiplier representing the ratio between the index-number of Sauerbeck and that of Jevons for 1820–29.

[2] Up to 1839 mean of highest and lowest of each year; since 1840 average of year.

[3] Consols were held at an artificial price during most of 1915.

The facts are given in the table on the previous page.

The first and third columns of this table are the plain facts completely unadjusted. In the second column certain adjustments of the wholesale index-number have been made, as indicated, which have the effect of damping down its more violent movements. It would be outside all probability if in the course of 130 years there were to be no monetary events which would not require a change of base for the index-number to bring out clearly the tendency of the two columns to move broadly together rather than always to move by just the same amount. The surprising thing is how slight these adjustments are, and that we end up just where we began. They consist in long-period shifts of the base 10 or 20 per cent up or down, corresponding in most cases to well-known events in monetary history.

The adjusted column, whilst making matters clearer to the eye, is not, however, at all necessary to establish the correlation. Mr. W. H. Coates,[1] taking the unadjusted figures, has worked out the Pearsonian coefficient of correlation both for the hundred years 1825–1924 and for the modern period 1908–1924 as follows :

Relatives.		Coefficient of Correlation.	Probable Error.
Statist Index 1825–1924	Gross yield of Consols in same year	+ 0·893	0·014
Statist Index 1824–1923	Gross yield of Consols in succeeding year	+ 0·903	0·012
Statist Index 1908–1920	Gross yield of Consols in same year	+ 0·90	0·03
Statist Index 1907–1923	Gross yield of Consols in succeeding year	+ 0·91	0·03

[1] *Colwyn Report on National Debt and Taxation,* Appendix XI. p. 101.

The broad character of the statistics since 1820 can be summarised as follows. Prices and Interest fell together from 1820 to 1850, rose together from 1851 to 1856, fell together in 1857–58, rose together from 1858 to 1864, fell together from 1866 to 1869, fell together from 1873 to 1896, rose together from 1896 to 1900, fell together from 1901 to 1903, rose together from 1905 to 1907, fell together in 1907–8, rose together from 1908 to 1914 and 1914 to 1920, and fell together from 1920 to 1923. And over and above these general trends, a number of the minor oscillations of the two are in the same direction.[1] Moreover, the reality of these apparent associations is fully substantiated by Mr. Coates' evaluation of the correlation coefficients.

Now, as I have indicated above, the most obvious explanation which suggests itself is the well-known fact that when trade is expanding on the upward phase of a credit cycle both wholesale prices and the rate of interest tend to rise. Nevertheless this explanation is inadequate. For the correlation is a long-period, or intermediate, rather than a strictly short-period, phenomenon, and is not less striking if the sharp oscillations of the Wholesale Index associated with credit cycles are smoothed out. Indeed the yield on Consols has not invariably responded to the phases of the credit cycle. Moreover, an article by Mr. E. G. Peake (*Bankers' Magazine*, May 1928, p. 720), which employs different statistics from Mr. Gibson's but strongly corroborates his results, shows that the correlation is higher for the long-term rate of interest than for the short-term. Mr. Peake uses the yield on L. and N.W. Railway Debenture Stock in place of Consols (to avoid the complications due to the conversion of the latter), and he also charts the rate of interest on floating money in London and the rate of

---

[1] The figures for each year separately are given by Mr. Gibson in the *Bankers' Magazine*, January 1923.

discount on three months' bank bills. Whilst the
short-period movements of the latter are in the same
direction as those of the Wholesale Index, he finds
that the correlation on the whole is not so close, as is
shown by the following table :

CORRELATION COEFFICIENTS FOR THE YEARS 1882 TO 1913

	Of the previous Year.	Of the same Year.	Of the next Year.
Statist index-number and the average annual rate of interest on floating money . .	+ ·681	+ ·801	+ ·564
Statist index-number and the discount on three months' bank bills	+ ·630	+ ·724	+ ·512
Statist index-number and the yield on L. and N.W. Debenture Stock	+ ·788	+ ·880	+ ·888

Nor can we regard the facts as an example of
Professor Irving Fisher's well-known theorem as to
the relation between the rate of interest and the
appreciation (or depreciation) in the value of money.
Indeed quite the contrary. For the compensatory
movements which Professor Fisher postulates relate
to the sum of money repayable a year hence against
cash loaned to-day which will cover interest *plus* (or
minus) an allowance for the change in the value of
money during the year. Thus, if real interest is 5 per
cent per annum and the value of money is falling
2 per cent per annum, the lender requires the repay-
ment of 107 in terms of money a year hence in return
for 100 loaned to-day. But the movements to which
Mr. Gibson calls attention, so far from being compensatory, are aggravating in their effect on the
relation between lender and borrower. For he shows

us that, if prices are rising (*e.g.*) 2 per cent per annum, this will usually be associated with a tendency for the capital value of long-dated securities to be *falling* 2 per annum ; so that the purchaser of long-dated securities will possess a year later a sum which is worth 2 per cent less in terms of money which is itself 2 per cent less valuable, so that he is 4 per cent worse off, the two factors of change not balancing, but aggravating, one another—whilst the variations in the rate of interest earned during the year in question are too small to make much difference.

My tentative explanation of the phenomenon is as follows :

(1) I think that the market-rate of interest, as measured by the yield on long-dated securities, is very " sticky " in relation to the natural-rate of interest. (The natural-rate of interest, as defined in Chapter 11 and further explained in Chapter 13, is the rate at which savings and investment are exactly balanced.) That is to say, when the natural-rate of interest is falling (or rising), the banking world does not quickly detect this or respond to it, so that there is a tendency for the market-rate to lag behind and to fall (or rise) less than it should if it is to maintain contact with the natural-rate.   In other words, when savings are abundant or deficient in relation to the demand for them for investment at the pre-existing level of interest, the rate does not adjust itself to the new situation quick enough to maintain equilibrium between savings and investment. The usury laws may have played a part in this in the earlier nineteenth century.   To-day the fact that in London bank-lending is not conducted wholly on the principles of a free market may be relevant. Moreover, where the new savings have to find their main outlet in foreign investment, this failure of sensitiveness of the one to the other will be particu-

larly noticeable for the reasons which have been given in Chapter 21.

(2) Since the annual increment in any year to the aggregate of capital is small relatively to this aggregate, movements in the natural-rate of interest are—subject to interruption by such things as wars—long-period movements extending over decades.

(3) When a long-period movement in the natural-rate of interest is in progress, there is, therefore, a prolonged tendency for investment to fall behind saving when this rate is falling because the market-rate does not fall equally fast, and to run ahead of saving when it is rising because the market-rate does not rise equally fast. Since the market-rate lags behind the natural-rate, less than the right degree of stimulus or deterrence is being applied to the rate of investment.

(4) Granted this, it follows from our Fundamental Equation that when the natural - rate is falling there is a long-period drag on the price-level, and contrariwise. This phenomenon is not on the large scale or of the striking character of a Credit Cycle. It is a slight, long-continued drag in a particular direction. Each dose of Profit Deflation (or Inflation) is gradually translated into a dose of Income Deflation (or Inflation), and is then succeeded by a fresh dose of Profit Deflation (or Inflation) ; for so long as investment lags behind (or runs ahead of) saving by a given amount (it is not necessary that there should be an *increasing* disparity between the two), prices will continue to fall (or rise) without limit (cf. Vol. i. Chapter 13).

(5) It is an obvious objection to this explanation that over longish periods the price-level is governed by the supply of money (as modified, of course, by banking practices, velocities of circulation, etc.), and that this is governed by causes quite independent of the rate of interest. I answer to this objection that

the degree of "management", which has existed during the past hundred years, aimed at adjusting the supply of money to the *status quo*, is commonly under-estimated ; also that there is another "sticky" factor in the Fundamental Equation, namely, the money-rates of efficiency earnings.   In fact, Central Banks have shown themselves much more adaptable to changes in the supply of gold, relatively to the demand for it, than is sometimes supposed.   They are all natural gold-hoarders, and are always keen to increase their stocks of it whenever they find them-selves in a position to do so without inconveniencing the business world ; so that abundant supplies of gold can often be absorbed without producing as much effect on prices as might have been expected.   On the other hand, when gold is in short supply, they are reluctant to put strong pressure on the business world to force down money-rates of earnings.   A small dose of this is so unpleasant that the Central Banks will always seek, if they can, to avoid a larger dose, with the result that they will find some way, *e.g.* by slowly modifying their reserve practices or the use of gold in circulation, of making a smaller quantity of gold " do " as well as a larger quantity would have with their old habits and practices.   Moreover, the rate at which countries not previously on the gold standard have come on to it partially or completely, has not been independent of the degree of abundance of free gold available to meet their needs.   Lastly—especially over long periods—the valuation of gold by the East relatively to silver has always operated as a regulator and as a damper down of extreme movements.

In other words, Central Banks have to a certain extent regulated the degree of their greed for gold by reference to its relative abundance, and have tended to acquiesce in that level of gold-reserves with which they happen to find themselves as a result of the volume of supplies of new gold in conjunction with the influence on the price-level of the forces just described.

(6) I conclude that even the long-period movements of the price-level have been influenced by the *second* term of the Fundamental Equation to a much greater extent than might have been expected. If this is true, the Gibson Paradox is explained. If the market-rate of interest moves in the same direction as the natural-rate of interest but always lags behind it, then the movements of the price-level will tend, even over longish periods, to be in the same direction as the movements of the rate of interest. Referring to the table on p. 199 above, monetary influences, as distinct from the influences of Profit Inflations and Deflations, have been limited to the periodic changes of base, up or down 10 or 20 per cent, which have been roughly indicated in the second column of this table.

In general, I am inclined to attribute the well-known correlation between falling prices and bad trade to the influence of Profit Deflations rather than to strictly monetary influences. I mean that a failure of the market-rate of interest to fall as fast as the natural-rate has been more important than a shortage of gold supplies. Our table shows that during the Napoleonic Wars, during the Boer War and during the great expansion of foreign investment which followed it (1901–1914), and during the Great War, the rate of interest did not rise fast enough to keep savings level with investment. Between 1820 and 1900, on the other hand, the rate of interest did not fall fast enough to keep investment level with savings, except during the great mid-nineteenth-century investment boom, 1855–1875. And the same thing has been true since 1920.

Moreover, the evil is cumulative. For savings in excess of investment are wasted and do not materialise in any *net* increase to the wealth of the world. Thus, Profit Deflation not only holds the market-rate of interest above the natural-rate, but, by retarding the growth of wealth, it holds the natural-rate itself at a higher level than it would stand at otherwise.

These paragraphs invite one more comment on the contemporary situation. I repeat that the greatest evil of the moment and the greatest danger to economic progress in the near future are to be found in the unwillingness of the Central Banks of the world to allow the market-rate of interest to fall fast enough. Ten years have elapsed since the end of the war. Savings have been on an unexampled scale. But a proportion of them has been wasted, spilt on the ground, by the unwillingness of Central Banks to allow the market-rate of interest to fall to a level at which they can be fully absorbed by the requirements of investment. The return to the Gold Standard in Europe has been accompanied by a policy of holding the rate of interest at an artificially high level in order to facilitate deflation. The struggle of 1929 between the Federal Reserve Board and Wall Street was, in part, a misguided effort on the part of the former to prevent the rate of interest from finding its natural level.

In Great Britain especially there has been a school of thought which has believed that the way to bring down the rate of interest in the long run (in the interests of the conversion of the War Debt) is to stimulate saving by a Thrift Campaign whilst simultaneously putting obstacles in the way of investment by an " Economy " Campaign—oblivious of the fact that savings which are not invested are spilt and add nothing to the national wealth. It is *investment*, *i.e.* the increased production of material wealth in the shape of capital-goods, which alone increases national wealth, and can alone in the long run bring down the natural-rate of interest.

Looking further ahead, however, and with an œcumenical reference, the prospect for the next twenty years appears to me to be a strong tendency

for the natural-rate of interest to fall, with a danger
lest this consummation be delayed and much waste
and depression unnecessarily created in the meanwhile by Central Banking Policy preventing the
market-rate of interest from falling as fast as it should.
I return to this question in Chapter 37 (iv.).

BOOK VII

THE MANAGEMENT OF MONEY

P

CHAPTER 31

THE PROBLEM OF THE MANAGEMENT OF MONEY

(i.) The Control of Prices through the Rate of Investment

THE Banking System has no direct control over the prices of individual commodities or over the rates of money-earnings of the factors of production. Nor has it, in reality, any *direct* control over the quantity of money ; for it is characteristic of modern systems that the Central Bank is ready to buy for money at a stipulated rate of discount any quantity of securities of certain approved types.

Thus—in spite of the qualifications which we shall have to introduce later in respect of the so-called " open-market " operations of Central Banks—it is broadly true to say that the governor of the whole system is the rate of discount. For this is the only factor which is directly subject to the will and *fiat* of the central authority, so that it is from this that induced changes in all other factors must flow.

This means, in substance, that the control of prices is exercised in the contemporary world *through the control of the rate of investment*. There is nothing that the central authority can do, whether it operates by means of the bank-rate or by means of open-market dealings, except to influence the rate of investment. But our Fundamental Equation has shown that, if the rate of investment can be influenced at will, then this can be brought in as a balancing factor to effect in any required degree, first of all the price-level of output as a whole, and, finally, as a response to the effect of prices on profits, the rate of money-earnings of the factors of production.

Thus the art of the Management of Money consists partly in devising technical methods by which the central authority can be put in a position to exercise a sensitive control over the rate of investment, which will operate effectively and quickly, and partly in possessing enough knowledge and prognosticating power to enable the technical methods to be applied at the right time and in the right degree to produce the effects on prices and earnings which are desirable in the interests of whatever may be the prescribed ultimate objective of the monetary system which is being managed.

This Book will be mainly concerned with the technical methods of control. There is, first of all, the question of the relation of the Central Bank to its own Member Banks and the means of establishing an unchallengeable centralised control over their aggregate behaviour in encouraging or retarding the current rate of investment—which is the subject of Chapter 32. Then there is the question, which we have rather begged in the earlier parts of this Treatise, whether, granted that the Central Institution has established an effective control over its Member Banks, it does really lie within its power to control the rate of investment as completely as we have been supposing—which is the subject of Chapter 37. Meanwhile we shall have been studying in Chapter 33 the limitations which the law does, or should, place on the discretion of the Central Bank itself; in Chapter 35 we give a short account of the international Gold Standard; and in Chapters 34 and 36 we shall examine the difficulties and perplexities which the Central Bank may experience in its relations with similar institutions abroad.

Finally we shall pass, in Chapter 38, to the possibility of a supernational management for the monetary affairs of the world as a whole and to a few reflections in conclusion.

It will be convenient, however, before we pass on to these matters, to pause for a moment to consider a type of error which is, as it seems to me, characteristic of nearly all the heretic monetary reformers, who perceive truly enough the faults of the present system, but overlook certain fundamental principles when they come to propose their remedy.   This error essentially arises, I shall suggest, out of a failure to appreciate the profound and far-reaching character of the relation of the monetary system to the rate of interest and to the rate of capital investment.

(ii.) The Dual Functions of Bankers

A banker is in possession of resources which he can lend or invest equal to a large proportion (nearly 90 per cent) of the deposits standing to the credit of his depositors. In so far as his deposits are Savings-deposits, he is acting merely as an intermediary for the transfer of loan-capital. In so far as they are Cash-deposits, he is acting both as a provider of money for his depositors, and also as a provider of resources for his borrowing-customers. Thus the modern banker performs two distinct sets of services. He supplies a substitute for State Money by acting as a clearing-house and transferring current payments backwards and forwards between his different customers by means of book-entries on the credit and debit sides. But he is also acting as a middleman in respect of a particular type of lending, receiving deposits from the public which he employs in purchasing securities, or in making loans to industry and trade mainly to meet demands for working capital.

This duality of function is the clue to many difficulties in the modern Theory of Money and Credit and the source of some serious confusions of thought.

So long as Commodity Money was the rule, there was no such intimate connection between the supply of units of money and a particular kind of lending. But as soon as Representative Money took the field, the problem came into existence, whatever attempts might be made to force Representative Money to imitate the behaviour of Commodity Money. For the manufacture of Representative Money uses up no real resources, so that, when the public holds more units of Representative Money, those who issue the Money have a sum of money available to lend out equal in value to the real resources the enjoyment or use of which the public is willing to forgo as the price payable for the convenience of holding a larger quantity of cash.

The next stage arrived when those who issued Representative Money (in the shape of Bank Money) combined with this the function of acting as intermediaries for loan-capital, and, furthermore, pooled the resources obtained in this capacity with those which they obtained as purveyors of Representative Money, and then proceeded to lend out as a single fund the joint proceeds of these two distinct operations.

In former times it may have been easier than it is now to distinguish between savings-deposits and cash-deposits. For at first bank-deposits were predominantly savings-deposits, whilst bank-notes served, for the most part, the present purposes of cash-accounts. In some countries this distinction still has considerable validity. But in Great Britain the Bank Act of 1844 stifled the Bank Note and blurred the distinction between the two things beyond recognition. Finally, by modern times the banks had come to control such large resources and had built up so far-reaching an organisation that they were by far the largest professional lenders on short term. Naturally, therefore, they have come to feel it a duty, not less important than their duty to provide money, to meet the community's fluctuating demands for this particular kind of borrowing.

The dilemma of modern banking is satisfactorily to combine these two functions. As a purveyor of Representative Money, it is the duty of the banking system to preserve the prescribed objective standard of such money. As a purveyor of loans on terms and conditions of a particular type, it is the duty of the system to adjust, to the best of its ability, its supply of this type of lending to the demand for it at the equilibrium rate of interest, *i.e.* at the natural rate. Moreover, the preservation of the objective standard is bound up, as we have seen, in a peculiar way, the precise character of which has generally escaped notice, with the rate at which the banking system in its capacity of lender is facilitating investment in new capital. Since, for this reason, the complete attainment of one of its duties is sometimes incompatible with the complete attainment of the other, those in control of the banking system have to make up their minds which object is to prevail, or, if neither is to prevail, to achieve a just compromise between the two.

Now a partial selection of some amongst these truths and a blind eye to others of them have led to the opposed points of view which are characteristic between them of the vast bulk of non-academic monetary literature. On the one hand, there are the bankers, who at least maintain a certain sanity of demeanour by holding on tight to rough rules-of-thumb which they have learnt from experience. On the other hand, there is the most disinterested body of persons in the world, the Army of Heretics and Cranks, whose numbers and enthusiasm are extraordinary. By writing a *Tract on Monetary Reform* and opposing the Return to Gold, the author of this book has gained amongst them a better name than he deserves for being a sympathetic spirit. From all quarters of the world, and in all languages, scarcely a week passes when he does not receive a book, a pamphlet, an article, a letter, each in the same vein and using substantially the same arguments.[1] It is a problem for any student of Monetary Theory to decide how to treat this flood, how much respect and courtesy to show, how much time to spend on it — especially if he feels that the fierce discontent of these heretics is far preferable to the complacency of the bankers. At any rate, we cannot be right to ignore them altogether. For when, as in this case, the heretics have flourished in undiminished vigour for two hundred years—so long in fact as Representative Money has existed— we may be sure that the orthodox arguments cannot be entirely satisfactory. The heretic is an honest intellectualist, who has the pluck to stick to his conclusions, even when they are surprising, so long as the line of thought by which he reaches them has not been refuted to his own understanding. When, as in this case, his surprising conclusions are also of such a kind that, if they were true, they would resolve many of the economic ills of suffering humanity, a moral enthusiasm exalts and strengthens his obstinacy. He follows, like Socrates, with unbowed head wherever the argument leads him. He deserves respect ; and it must be the duty of anyone who writes on this subject to make the attempt to clear the matter up and to reconcile heretics and bankers in a common understanding. Let us see, therefore, if our analysis enables us to produce an argument which will bring the parties together.

There is a common element in the theories of nearly

---

[1] An account of the leading contemporary crank writers on Money in the German language will be found in Haber, *Untersuchungen über Irrtümer moderner Geldverbesserer* (1926).

all monetary heretics. Their theories of Money and Credit are alike in supposing that in some way the banks can furnish all the real resources which manufacture and trade can reasonably require without real cost to anyone, and, if they qualify their claims, it is according to some criterion as to the purpose to which borrowers apply the resources they borrow.

For they argue thus. Money (meaning loans) is the life-blood of industry. If money (in this sense) is available in sufficient quantity and on easy terms, we shall have no difficulty in employing to the full the entire available supply of the factors of production. For the individual trader or manufacturer " bank credit " means " working capital " ; a loan from his bank furnishes him with the means to pay wages, to buy materials and to carry stocks. If, therefore, sufficient bank credit was freely available, there need never be unemployment. Why then, he asks, if the banks can create credit, should they refuse any reasonable request for it ? And why should they charge a fee for what costs them little or nothing ? Our troubles seem to him to arise because the banks have monopolised this power of creating credit in order to enable them, by artificially restricting its supply, to charge a price for it and thus realise a profit. For why, if they possess this magical power, are they so stingy ? Why should industrialists have less working capital than they desire, or be compelled to pay 5 per cent for it ? There can only be one answer : the bankers, having a monopoly of magic, exercise their powers sparingly in order to raise the price. If bakers were a close corporation who could make bread from stones, it does not follow that they would reduce the price of the loaf to the cost of a quartern of stones. Where magic is at work, the public do not get the full benefit unless it is nationalised. Our heretic admits, indeed, that we must take care to avoid " inflation " ; but that only occurs when credit is created which does not correspond to any productive process. To create credit to meet a genuine demand for working capital can never be inflationary ; for such a credit is " self-liquidating " and is automatically paid off when the process of production is finished. Monetary Reform, he concludes, consists in adjusting the creation of credit so as to meet all genuine demands for working capital. If the creation of credit is strictly confined within these limits, there can never be inflation. Further, there is no reason for making any charge for such credit beyond what is required to meet bad debts and the expense of administration. Not a week, perhaps not a day or an hour, goes by in which some well-wisher of mankind does not suddenly see the light—that here is the key to Utopia.

Now the traditional reply of the bankers to all this is singularly unconvincing. The banker does not indeed deny that in some sense or other he *can* create credit. The only clay which he demands for this act of creation is a suitable proportion of gold (or other form of reserves). When a bank has a balance at the Bank of England in excess of its usual requirements, it can make an additional loan to the trading and manufacturing world, and this additional loan creates an additional deposit (to the credit of the borrower or to the credit of those to whom he may choose to transfer it) on the other side of the balance sheet of this or some other bank. For the banking system as a whole, the " creation " of credit in this way is only "excessive" if it results in a loss of gold, which reduces the reserves of the banks and thus indicates the necessity for "reducing" the volume of credit. If, however, the supplies of gold are ample, then there need be no obstacle to the act of creation. " The ample stocks of gold in the Federal Reserve System indicate ", we commonly read in the financial press, " that the banks will have no difficulty in financing all reasonable requirements of trade and industry." Thus, if we are to believe the bankers, the amount of working capital available for industry seems to depend in some way upon the amount of gold in the Bank of England or in the Federal Reserve System.

This talk about gold, the heretics naturally retort, is surely in the nature of a bluff. It is obvious that it cannot be the gold in the Bank of England which enables industry to hum; for most of it lies there untouched from one year to another, and if it were to fade into air everything else could continue just as it did before—provided we were not told. To believe that the amount of working capital available for English industry depends on the amount of gold in the vaults of the Bank of England is to believe what is absurd.

The bankers endeavour, nevertheless, to bring the argument back to the facts, so vital to them, of their reserves—as a symptom, if not as a cause. Although it is they who create credit, the amounts of it which they create are not arbitrary and are not unlimited. The amounts are governed by the requirements of trade on the one hand, but also by the state of their reserves on the other. If they were to create credit regardless of their reserves, gold would flow out of the country and jeopardise the convertibility of the currency; or, if the gold standard is not operative, the foreign exchanges would fall and thus raise the cost of all imports. To the common-sense onlooker this seems to be true and convincing. Even the heretic begins to feel uneasy. But he is not convinced. His point has not been met. For how is it possible that the credit which the manufacturer requires can depend on how much metal lies locked up in Threadneedle Street under the ground ? He soon returns to the conviction that the bankers are duping him with a sophistry which they have invented for interested reasons. Credit is the pavement along which production travels ; and the bankers, if they knew their duty, would provide the transport facilities to just the extent that is required in order that the productive powers of the community can be employed to their full capacity.

It has been a principal object of this Treatise to give a clear answer to these perplexities. What is the true criterion of a creation of credit which shall be non-inflationary (free, that is to say, from the taint of profit inflation—income inflation is a different matter) ? We have found the answer to lie in the preservation of a balance between the rate of saving and the value of new investment. That is to say, bankers are only entitled to create credit, without laying themselves open to the charge of inflationary tendencies, if the net effect of such credit creation on the value of new investment is not to raise the value of such investment above the amount of the current savings of the public ; and, similarly, they will lay themselves open to the charge of deflationary action unless they create enough credit to prevent the value of new investment from falling below the amount of current savings. How much credit has to be created in order to preserve equilibrium is a complicated matter—because it depends upon how the credit is being used and upon what is happening to the other monetary factors. But the answer, though it is not simple, is definite ; and the test as to whether or not such equilibrium is being preserved in fact can always be found in the stability or instability of the price-level of output as a whole.

The mistake which the heretics have made is to be found, therefore, in their failure to allow for the possibility of *Profit* Inflation. They admit the nature and evils of Income Inflation ; they perceive that to advance credit to the entrepreneur, not to increase the remuneration of the factors of production, but to enable him to increase their employment and hence

their output, is not the same thing as Income Inflation, since new wealth is created to an amount
corresponding to the new Credit—which is not the
case with Income Inflation ; but they have neglected
the last term of the Fundamental Equation—they
have not allowed for the contingency of investment
outpacing savings, of the new wealth which is created
not being in consumable form simultaneously with the
new spending power allotted as their remuneration
to the factors of production. They do not perceive
that prices can rise even though the rate of remuneration of the factors of production per unit of output is
unchanged.

What, however, of the bankers' criterion of their
reserves ? We may have given a convincing answer
to the heretics ; but it does not seem, on the face of it,
to be the same answer which had been given to them by
their enemies the bankers. Nor is it the same. The
state of the bankers' reserves is, indeed, a *symptom*—
the loss of their cash-reserves is rightly regarded by
them as a symptom that the supply of buying power
is running ahead of the material means of satisfying
it within the country. This is the sole significance
of their reserves. The characteristic of this criterion,
however, lies in its being a test, not of the presence of
profit inflation, but only of whether the degree of
inflation or deflation is in the appropriate relation
to events in the outside world. A country's foreign
exchanges and gold reserves are in equilibrium under
the gold standard, not when it is free from profit
inflation or deflation, but when the degree of total
inflation or deflation leads, in the manner explained in
Chapter 21, to an equilibrium of payments due to and
from foreign countries, so that on balance there is no
tendency for gold to flow in or out. It is for this reason
that credit cycles have been commonly observed to be
international phenomena when the gold standard is
working normally, but not during the period of the

suspension of the gold standard. For the international gold standard has often operated as a means of diffusing the phenomena of profit inflation or of deflation from one country to another.

Thus the ideal of stability is not to be attained either on the principles of the heretics or on those of the bankers. The practices of the former may produce Profit Inflation; but so may the practices of the latter with the added disadvantage that they may also on other occasions produce Profit Deflation. Neither of them attends to the real criterion of stability, namely, the equilibrium between saving and investment. The banks determine how much they will lend by reference to the quantity of their reserves (though this practice is, of course, forced on them by existing currency systems); whilst the heretics would have them determine it by reference to the quantity of the factors of production available to be employed; but neither of them propose to determine it by reference to the equilibrium between saving and investment, though this is the only criterion which would preserve the stability of prices. Nevertheless the heretics are calling attention to a real defect in the present arrangements when they complain that the banks are not, and cannot be, influenced in their lending policy, under the present régime, primarily by the object of maintaining the optimum level of employment.

Thus the bankers are not even trying to preserve the stability of prices and of employment, and are not open, therefore, to accusations of failure if instability ensues; their object, under a gold standard, is to keep in step with the average behaviour of the banking systems of the world as a whole. Their idea is not to keep sober, but, in accordance with a perfect standard of manners, to enjoy just that degree of tipsiness (or sick-headache) as characterises the company as a whole.

The heretics, on the other hand, are all for strict

sobriety and a normal temperature, in the interests of the maximum activity and efficiency of the economic body. But their understanding of physiology is deficient, and they do not appreciate that the only way for a man to keep fit is to dose himself with a rate of interest which is precisely adjusted to the temperature and blood-pressure and other attendant circumstances.

A further misunderstanding—if I may continue my medical metaphors—is apt to arise after instability has actually developed and cures for it are being applied, through overlooking the fact that the remedial measures, as to the ultimate efficacy of which there is no doubt, cannot produce the required reaction except after an interval of time.

For example, a change-over in the type of production from investment-goods to consumption-goods (or *vice versa*) does not, on account of the period occupied by the process of production, produce its results in the market until after an appreciable time has elapsed. Thus, as we have seen, the price-stimulus to a change-over is apt to be continued until some time after the necessary steps have been taken. The result often is that the remedy is overdone. It is as though the family were to go on giving a child successive doses of castor-oil every ten minutes until the first dose had done its work. Or—to take a better parallel—it is as though different members of the family were to give successive doses to the child, each in ignorance of the doses given by the others. The child will be very ill. Bismuth will then be administered on the same principle. Scientists will announce that children are subject to a diarrhœa-constipation cycle, due, they will add, to the weather, or, failing that, to alternations of optimism and pessimism amongst the members of the family. If the time taken by the first dose to act is constant, they will discover that the cycle is a true one with a constant period. Perhaps they will suggest that the remedy is to be found in giving the child bismuth when it is constipated and castor-oil at the other extreme. But more probably the parents will divide into bismuth and castor-oil parties, one of which, impressed by the horrors of diarrhœa, will renounce castor-oil, and the other, moved by the depression of constipation, will abjure bismuth.

Thus it is not easy to keep to the middle path of continuous health.

CHAPTER 32

METHODS OF NATIONAL MANAGEMENT—I. THE CONTROL OF THE MEMBER BANKS

THE first necessity of a Central Bank, charged with responsibility for the management of the monetary system as a whole, is to make sure that it has an unchallengeable control over the total volume of bank-money created by its Member Banks. We have seen in Chapters 2 and 25 that the latter is determined, either rigidly or within certain defined limits, by the amount of the Member Banks' Reserve-resources. The first question, therefore, is how the Central Bank can control the amount of its Member Banks' Reserves.

It will be convenient to assume that the Central Bank is also the note-issuing authority. (Where this is not the case, it must be supposed that, for the purpose of what follows, the balance sheets of the Central Bank and of the note-issuing authority are amalgamated.) On this assumption the currency in circulation in the hands of the public, *plus* the reserve resources of the Member Banks, will be equal to the total assets of the Central Bank *minus* its own capital and reserves, and *minus* also the deposits of the Government and of any depositors of the Central Bank other than the Member Banks. Thus, broadly speaking, the Central Bank will be able to control the volume of cash and of bank-money in circulation, if it can control the volume of its own total assets. The Member Banks can only increase their own reserve-resources (unless the volume of cash in circulation is falling off) by influencing the Central Bank to increase the volume of its total assets ; and if the Central Bank can control the latter, it will control, indirectly, the total of cash and bank-money. Thus, the power of a Central Bank, to manage a representative money in such a way as to conform to an objective standard, primarily depends on its ability to determine by means of a deliberate policy the aggregate amount of its own assets ; and the first thing, therefore, is to examine the causes which determine the volume of these assets.

What are these assets ? A triple classification of a Central Bank's variable assets (*i.e.* assets other than bank premises, etc.) will be convenient, namely : (1) gold, (2) investments and (3) advances. By " gold " I mean anything which the Central Bank cannot create itself, but from or (and) into which it is bound by law to convert its legal-tender money. By " investments " I mean any asset, other than gold, which the Central Bank purchases on its own initiative ; thus it may include bills purchased in the open market. By " advances " I mean any asset, other than gold, which the Central Bank has purchased in virtue of an obligation, of law or custom, to purchase such an asset if it is tendered on specified conditions. By the " bank-rate " I mean the terms on which the Central Bank is bound or is accustomed to make such advances.[1]

The amount of the Central Bank's investments, since these are purchased and sold on its own initiative, is entirely within its own control. Action directed towards varying the amount of these is now usually called " open-market policy ". The amount of its advances is generally supposed to be at least partially (how much we will consider later) within its control by means of variations in the bank-rate, *i.e.* by raising or lowering the terms on which it will make advances.

[1] A bank may have several slightly varying rates corresponding to varieties of " eligible " assets.

The amount of gold is, in a " convertible " international system, one stage further removed from its
control ; for, directly, it depends on whether its
nationals' claims on other banking systems exceed or
fall short of foreign claims on them. Nevertheless,
this too is generally assumed to be, indirectly, at least
partially controllable—also by means of the bank-
rate, since the bank-rate, for reasons which are familiar,
influences the balance of international claims.

There are, as we shall see, various other methods
of action which are theoretically open to the Central
Bank. In practice, however, the Central Bank of
to-day, as represented by the Bank of England or the
United States Federal Reserve System—apart from
psychological pressure, veiled in the case of the Bank
of England, open in the case of the Federal Reserve
Banks, by advice, exhortations or threats—has limited
itself to these two, namely " open-market policy " and
bank-rate.

(i.) THE BRITISH SYSTEM

It has not been generally recognised that the traditional British System differs in one vital respect from
the systems in vogue elsewhere, and, in particular,
from the United States Federal Reserve System, which
was supposed by its founders to resemble the pre-war
British System more closely than is actually the case.
For the British System has contrived, what is true
of no other system, namely, that the volume of the
" advances " of the Bank of England (as defined above)
shall be normally *nil* (subject to the qualifications
mentioned below), and shall only come into existence
temporarily and for short periods to meet seasonal and
other emergencies, *e.g.* at balance-sheet dates at the
end of each half-year, or when the money market has
been taken by surprise, or to meet very temporary
conditions, or when an increase of bank-rate is anticipated in the near future. The chief qualifications to

this are, primarily, that the Bank is the banker of the Government, to whom it lends on "Ways and Means ", and secondly, that it has—on a relatively small scale —a certain number of financial and commercial customers, other than the Joint-Stock Banks, to whom it makes advances in response to their requests, just like any other bank.

This state of affairs is attributable to two peculiarities of the London system, which do not obtain elsewhere. Bank - rate is normally fixed at a level relatively to the open-market rate of discount for three months' bills, which makes it unprofitable for holders of such bills to re-discount them at the Bank of England ; and, secondly, a somewhat curious custom or convention has been tacitly established by which the Joint-Stock Banks are altogether prevented from selling their bills direct to the Bank of England. If an English Joint-Stock Bank desires to replenish its reserve-resources, there are only three ways in which it can do so : (1) by selling assets to the customers of other banks and so getting hold of a part of the balances of some other bank, which clearly does nothing to relieve the banks as a whole ; (2) by letting Treasury Bills run off and thus compelling the Treasury to borrow from the Bank of England on Ways and Means ; (3) by depleting the resources of the bill-brokers either by withdrawing funds previously lent to them at call, or by ceasing to buy bills, and so compelling the bill-brokers to borrow from the Bank of England by discounting or otherwise. The bill-broker, however, will not borrow from the Bank of England, so long as the Bank's official rate is above the market rate, except for short periods to tide over particular dates or to give himself time to rearrange his position ; but will, on the other hand, seek to replenish his resources by lowering his buying price for bills. Similarly, the Treasury will normally accept lower tenders for Treasury Bills, so as to avoid being

indebted to the Bank of England except for short
periods. So long, therefore, as the Bank of England
maintains touch with market conditions by raising
bank-rate whenever market-rate threatens to approach
or pass it, the power of the Joint-Stock Banks to
increase their aggregate reserves at the Bank of
England is virtually *nil*. An attempt to do so on
the part of any one Bank will work round to be at
the expense of the others ; and an all-round attempt
will leave none of them better off than they were
before.

But there was a further simplification in the working
of the British system in pre-war days. Not only
were the Member Banks practically precluded from
increasing their reserve-resources by discounting with
the Bank of England, but " open-market policy " in
the modern sense was virtually unknown. The Bank
of England would occasionally supplement its bank-
rate policy by the sale of Consols for " cash " and
their simultaneous repurchase for " the account "
(anything up to a month later), which was an indirect
way of relieving the money-market of the equivalent
quantity of resources for the unexpired period of the
Stock Exchange account. This expedient was re-
sorted to when market-rates were lagging too much
behind bank-rate, with possible unfavourable reactions
on the exchanges and the flow of gold. But the
practice was not very frequent, and not a very important addition to the Bank's weapons for the control
of the market. Thus, apart from certain well-
understood seasonal movements, such as the temporary
loans to the Money Market at the end of each half-year
and advances to the Treasury on Ways and Means at
certain periods of the financial year, the investments
of the Bank of England were practically constant.
Over long periods of years they slowly increased
with the general growth of the Bank's operations.
For example, for the greater part of the period between

the Boer War and the Great War, they stood, apart
from very short-period movements, somewhere about
£40,000,000 to £45,000,000.

It followed, therefore, that—the Advances being normally *nil* and the Investments practically constant—
the fluctuations in the reserve-resources of the British
Member Banks mainly depended on the fluctuations
in the amount of gold held by the Bank of England,
as determined by the flow into and out of the circulation
and into and out of the country.   This was the sweet
simplicity of the old " automatic " system to which
old-fashioned people look back with so much regret,
and the character of which new-fashioned people have
almost forgotten.   The problem of " sound " banking
had—in pre-war days—nothing whatever to do with
stabilising price-levels or with avoiding Profit Inflations and Deflations ; it consisted in the perfectly
precise technical problem of foreseeing, so far as
possible, the workings of an almost mechanical system
and of adaptation to seasonal and similar vagaries.

Looking back, it is remarkable to observe that
nothing was done by means of " open-market policy "
to mitigate the effects of the regular and well-recognised
seasonal in-flow and out-flow of gold.   Year after
year the Bank of England would gain about £10,000,000
of gold in the spring and lose an approximately corresponding amount in the autumn ; and, in the absence
of open-market policy, its deposits would also rise and
fall by a substantial percentage—sometimes approaching 20 per cent.   As often as not, the annual autumn
drain would reduce the Bank of England's reserve by
25 to 30 per cent without causing serious concern to
anyone.   The effects of these fluctuations were, however, partly offset by the consequences of the fact
that the short-term indebtedness of the Treasury was
normally at its minimum in the spring owing to the
receipt of income-tax.   Various temporary, confusing
influences might slightly obscure these processes in

individual years ; but this was, broadly, the character of what was happening.

Thus the rate of creation of credit in Great Britain was caused by a simple piece of mechanism faithfully to reflect the inward and outward movements of gold. Moreover, since the face-value of the supply of bills was sensitive to changes in the wholesale price-level, a fall of wholesale prices had a direct and immediate tendency to cheapen money, and *vice versa*. The system was, therefore, excellently adapted, by reason of the predominance of London's position in international trade and finance, both to maintain the parity of sterling with gold compatibly with comparatively small gold reserve, and also, within certain limits, to promote the stability of wholesale prices.

The new post-war element of " management " consists in the habitual employment of an " open-market " policy by which the Bank of England buys and sells investments with a view to keeping the reserve-resources of the Member Banks at the level which it desires. This method — regarded as a method—seems to me to be the ideal one. In combination with the peculiarities of the British system already described, it enables the Bank of England to maintain an absolute control over the creation of credit by the Member Banks—to a degree such as exists in no other monetary system. The Bank of England has evolved the perfect method for transferring to the Central Authority the complete control of the members of the banking system of the country. It is not an exaggeration to say that the individual Member Banks have virtually no power to influence the aggregate volume of bank-money—unless they depart from their reserve-ratio conventions, and even then the old position is restored if the Bank of England sells investments to a corresponding amount. The only weaknesses in the system are those for which remedies have been suggested above (Vol. ii. pp. 68-77), namely, that the reserve-ratios of the Member Banks, not being fixed by law, are liable to change, and that, for members of the Banking System outside the Clearing Banks, reserve practices are altogether too vague and doubtful.

The pre-war system did not do much to stabilise world prices or to ward off Credit Cycles—with such acts of God it did not consider itself in any way concerned. But it had one great advantage—everyone knew quite clearly what principles would govern the Bank of England's actions and what they would have to expect in given circumstances. The post-war system has substituted a most efficacious "management" for the old "automatic" system—which is all to the good; but, at present, no one knows exactly to what objects the "management" is directed or on what principles it proceeds. It can scarcely claim hitherto to have tried to apply scientific principles to the attainment of the economic optimum, in the light of day and with the assistance of expert discussion and criticism, but proceeds to unknown destinations by the methods described in the City as "the hidden hand". The Bank's methods are in extraordinary contrast to the full and splendid publicity of the Federal Reserve System of the United States. We know in a general way that the Bank of England, which by origin is just a Joint Stock Bank like any other, does not limit its business connections to the Member Banks, but takes private clients like any other bank, that it does important business with foreign banks, and that from time to time it transacts affairs, generally secret, with foreign governments ; also that, whilst since the war the purely private business is probably declining, the business with foreign banks is being strengthened and extended. But we have no quantitative information on these matters ; before 1928 we did not even know what part of the Bank of England's published deposits represented the balances of the Member

Banks and what part belonged to other classes of customers.

It remains true, however, that the Bank of England is in possession of the best devices hitherto evolved for the control of the creation of bank-money by the Member Banks ; and we may reasonably hope that, with the progress of knowledge, the time will come when they will be employed to the best advantage.

(ii.) THE CONTINENTAL SYSTEM

The part played by the Central Banks in most of the pre-war European monetary systems, for example in France or in Germany, was widely different from that of the Bank of England. The importance of bank-notes relatively to cheques was far greater; the resources of the Central Banks relatively to those of the Member Banks were far greater (especially if we have in mind the resources available to meet fluctuations in the demand for working capital) ; there were no obstacles in the way of increases in the Central Banks' " advances " ; and the Member Banks were not tied by law or custom to the maintenance of rigid reserve-ratios.

Since the Member Banks were not tied by reserve-ratios and were not prevented from freely re-discounting with the Central Banks whenever they wanted to expand their resources, the control exercised over them by the Central Bank was very imperfect, the main limitation on credit expansion by the Member Banks being set by their supply of bills eligible for re-discount. This weakness, however, was balanced by the fact that, if Member Banks as a whole were inclined to increase their lending, they would get back as deposits a much smaller proportion of the amount lent, because a much larger proportion of the new loans would be taken out in the shape of bank-notes. Thus the Member Banks, having much less power than in Great Britain to create credit, needed much less control. The result was that an expansion of borrowing by the business world would quickly show itself in an expansion of the Central Bank's portfolio of bills and a nearly corresponding expansion of its note-issue. Thus it was to these symptoms that the attention of the controlling authorities was primarily directed.

It is evident that a somewhat different analysis from that given above is required to explain the behaviour of a system of this kind—an adaptation which it would not be difficult to make, but from which insufficient knowledge of the particular facts involved (and considerations of space) deter me. I foresee, however, that, with the growth of the cheque-deposit system and the tendency of the European banking systems to take on rather more of the character of the British and American systems, substantial changes may be required adequately to strengthen the position of the Central Banks. The Reichsbank in particular —so far as I understand, a system which is evolving rapidly but informally—has an altogether inadequate control over its Member Banks, and would be very vulnerable to any strong pressure towards inflation on the part of the business world as a whole. The Reichsbank has to depend too much on its bank-rate, not merely to attract foreign funds, but as a deterrent to borrowing at home ; with the result that a rate, which is sufficiently high to act as a deterrent at home, may be unduly attractive to funds loanable from abroad.

(iii.) THE UNITED STATES FEDERAL RESERVE SYSTEM

When the Federal Reserve System was planned shortly before the war, it was not understood how vitally important to the control of the Central Bank was the London technique which secured that the " advances " of the Central Bank to the Member

Banks should be normally *nil*. It became accordingly a sort of blend of the British and Continental Methods. The primary importance of bank-money and the rigid reserve-ratios of the member banks resembled the corresponding features of the British system. But the full latitude allowed to the member banks to re-discount, the presumption inherent in many of its provisions that the member banks would normally avail themselves of this facility, and the maintenance of buying rates for three-month bank acceptances at or below the market-rate, were features moulded on the Continental model and vitally different from the British. For the official rates at which the Federal Reserve Banks will discount bills for their member banks or will buy bankers' acceptances commonly bear a relation to market-rates, which make it habitually profitable for some bills at any rate to be brought to the Reserve Banks, and the only question is on what scale this will be taking place at any given time. There is all the difference in the world between a system in which, to adopt London parlance, the market is habitually " in " the Bank to a certain extent as in America, and one in which it is only " in " the Bank temporarily or as a last resort when it has been taken by surprise, as in London.

At the initiation of the Federal Reserve System the point was, of course, discussed, but without a full appreciation of its fundamental importance. The question was posed in this form : " Were the Reserve Banks to function continuously, either through re-discounting bills for member banks or through open-market operations, or were their activities to be confined solely to the meeting of emergencies ? . . . The conclusion was reached that the Banks were not designed to function only in emergencies, but that the Act had created a permanent and costly organisation which should continuously occupy itself in the interests of the common good, adapting itself ' to the

needs of industry, commerce, and agriculture—with
all their seasonal fluctuations and contingencies '." [1]
So far as open-market operations are concerned, well
and good. The significance of the real question,
however, namely, whether, so far as concerned the
re-discounting facilities of the member banks on the
initiative of the latter, the Reserve Banks were to be
emergency institutions (like the Bank of England), or
whether they should be a normal and habitual source
of supply of funds, was not, I think, clearly apprehended by the founders of the Federal Reserve System,
with the result that this System, as it developed in
practice, was bound to evolve eventually on materially
different lines from the London System.

At any rate the decision went in favour of regarding
re-discounting as a facility habitually available to the
member banks. So much so, indeed, that the law
provided that the backing of the fiduciary portion of
the Reserve System's note-issue, *i.e.* that part not
covered by gold, should consist of nothing but bills ;
so that if the Reserve Banks were to follow the Bank
of England's practice, they would not always find
themselves in possession of the right kind of assets
wherewith to provide legal cover for their note-issue.
Moreover, in order to develop the New York bill
market and to encourage bill-broking, which was
thought to be a necessary preliminary to a functioning of the New York System like the London model,
it was, more especially at first, made particularly easy
and advantageous for dealers in bank acceptances to
hand on their paper to the Reserve Banks.[2]

[1] *First Annual Report of the Federal Reserve Board*, p. 17. See also
Beckhart, *Discount Policy of the Federal Reserve System*, p. 199.

[2] The fact that these are described in the Reserve Bank returns as
" bills bought in the open-market " has caused a confusion between such
purchases—which are not made on the instructions of the Reserve Banks
any more than Reserve Bank re-discounts—and the purchase of investments
which constitute " open-market " operations properly so-called. The following extracts from Governor Strong's evidence before the Stabilisation Committee (U.S. Congress, 1927) make the position clear : " The rate for the

So recently as in 1924 the Federal Reserve Board itself (in its very able Tenth Annual Report for the year 1923), in dealing with the argument " that the discount rates of the Federal Reserve Banks must be higher than current rates for commercial accommodation in order to be ' effective ' rates ", showed that it did not appreciate the real issue. The Board called attention to the facts that London banks lend to their customers at rates above bank-rate and " in the form of overdrafts and advances which do not result in negotiable instruments, and therefore cannot be converted into balances at the Bank of England ". But this is not the point. There is a plentiful floating stock of bills (not to mention Treasury Bills) which can be converted into balances at the Bank of England, and doubtless would be if these were not normally discountable in the market *below* bank-rate. The Report also pointed out that in 1923 the Federal Reserve discount rate was, as in London, above the market-rate for prime bankers' acceptances and for Treasury certificates of short maturity. But it omitted to point out that the Reserve Banks' buying rates for acceptances are normally below their discount rates, and that the market in fact sold a large volume of acceptances to the Reserve Banks in 1923. The fact that, more often than not, the Reserve Banks hold large volumes of bankers' acceptances, is in itself sufficient proof that their buying rates for this paper must frequently compare favourably with the

---

purchase of bills in the open market is changed more frequently than the re-discount rate. But we have fixed rates at which we take paper that is offered to us, almost exactly like the rate of discount. We do not on our own initiative go into the market to buy bills. In fact, it is not a voluntary purchase in the sense that the Reserve Banks' purchase of Government securities upon their own initiative is. ' Open-market purchases ' are discounted with us by member banks exactly as commercial paper is; only our rate for this type of paper is lower than the rate for commercial paper. I think to-day, if we excluded purchases which we make for account of foreign banks, that possibly 85 to 90 per cent of all bankers' acceptances which we hold comes from the Member Banks." (I have put the above together out of detached passages on pp. 315, 317, 328, 457, 458.)

market-rates. Moreover, the rate at which Member
Banks can re-discount eligible paper is invariably
lower than the rate at which these banks have them-
selves discounted such paper for their customers.
" The fact is ", to quote Goldenweiser (*Federal Reserve
System in Operation*, p. 46), " that, though the British
maxim that bank-rate should be higher than market-
rate has generally been quoted with approval in
American banking discussion, in practice, Federal
Reserve bank discount policy has been adjusted to
American conditions to which this maxim has not been
applicable."

The fundamental explanation of the different behaviour of the Federal Reserve System and the
London System is to be found, therefore, firstly, in
the ability of the Member Banks to re-discount direct
with the Reserve Banks, and secondly, in the relative
levels which prevail as a rule between call-money,
first-class bills and bank-rate. In London this is
an ascending scale, so that it usually pays to carry
first-class bills with call-money, and seldom pays to
hand on these bills to the Bank of England. In New
York, on the other hand, it may be a *descending* scale.
At the date at which I am writing these lines (end of
July 1926) the rates are as follows :

	London.	New York.
Call-Money	$3\frac{3}{4}$	4
Bank Bills	$4\frac{1}{4}$	$3\frac{3}{8}$
Central Bank's buying rate for 90-day bills	5	$3\frac{1}{4}$
„ „ re-discount rate . . .	5	$3\frac{1}{2}$

Doubtless the competition of the New York Stock
Exchange for Call-Money, which means that there
would be no profit in bill-broking unless the Reserve
Bank were to allow easy terms to dealers in bills, is a
part of the explanation. But whatever the cause,
the result is plain—the Federal Reserve Banks have
not the same control over the amount of their Member
Banks' reserve-resources that the Bank of England

has. The history of the Federal Reserve System since the war has been, first of all, a great abuse of the latitude thus accorded to the Member Banks to increase the " advances " of the Reserve Banks, and subsequently a series of efforts by the Reserve authorities to invent gadgets and conventions which shall give them a power, more nearly similar to that which the Bank of England has, without any overt alteration of the law.

The first phase, before the above flaw in the system had been discovered, was clearly seen in the great inflation of 1920. For in 1920 those responsible for the management of the Federal Reserve System had not yet realised the enormous latent possibilities of inflation resulting from its failure to imitate the Bank of England system in one essential particular, and no one seems to have noticed that the main check on which the Bank of England relies was missing from the machine. The Federal Reserve System's holdings of discounted bills, which at the end of January 1920 had already reached the enormous figure of $2,174,357,000, had risen another 30 per cent by October 1920 to $2,801,297,000 (£560,000,000). Imagine a situation in which the Money Market was borrowing even a tenth of this sum from the Bank of England ! Then, with the great deflation, by August 1922 the figure had fallen by 85 per cent to $397,448,000.

Many critics of that period have ascribed the results to the failure of the Federal Reserve Banks to raise their discount rates on the approved London model. Certainly this failure aggravated the situation. But I doubt whether any reasonable or practicable movements of the discount rate could under the American system have really stopped the avalanche—market-rates would simply have moved ahead to an appropriate extent, and so long as prices were rising no one would mind paying them. I do not see how the discount rate unaided can be expected to have the same consequences under the American System as it has under the British.

Since that time the Federal Reserve Board has been working out, largely empirically, methods of control of its own not borrowed from London. In the first place, pressure is put on the Member Banks to restrain their use of re-discounting facilities with the Federal Reserve Banks by criticising them, asking inconvenient questions, and creating a public opinion to the effect that it is not quite respectable for a Member Bank, or good for its credit, to be using the resources of the Reserve Bank more than its neighbours. At the same time the supply of bank acceptances puts a maximum limit on the amount of credit inflation which can arise from the sales of these to the Reserve Banks.[1]

The following passage from the *Annual Report of the Federal Reserve Board for 1925* (p. 15) well expresses the present practice, and also the twilight in which the Board still dwelt at that date as to how its system functions :

Throughout the latter part of 1925 the level of call-loan rates was considerably above the discount rate of the New York Reserve Bank. Recent experience has shown that in general it is not necessary to maintain a discount rate above the prevailing level of call-loan rates in order to prevent member banks from borrowing at the reserve banks for the purpose of increasing their loans on securities. Member banks generally recognise that the proper occasion for borrowing at the reserve bank is for the purpose of meeting temporary and seasonal needs of their customers in excess of funds available out of the member banks' own resources ; borrowing from the reserve bank for the purpose of enlarging their own operations is not considered a proper use of reserve bank credit either by the member banks or by the officers of the Federal reserve banks.

[1] During a part of 1929, when the Reserve Banks were desirous of tightening up credit conditions, the practice of buying Bank Acceptances at a rate below the official re-discount rate was temporarily relinquished.

In general, it is not possible to determine to what use a member bank puts the credit obtained from the reserve bank. Member banks generally borrow to make up deficiencies in their reserve balances incurred as the net result of all their operations, and it is seldom possible to trace the connection between borrowings of a member bank at the reserve bank and the specific transactions that gave rise to the necessity for borrowing. In the infrequent instances where there has been evidence that member banks have borrowed at the reserve banks and at the same time have been increasing their loans on securities, the officers of the reserve banks have pointed out to them that it was possible for them to adjust their reserve position through changes in their short-time loan accounts rather than by recourse to the reserve banks.

The Report goes on to admit that the discount rate is not very effective in its influence on the volume of borrowing, especially in country districts, " where the bulk of member bank funds is used in making loans to regular customers at rates that respond but slowly to changes in the general credit situation ". It admits also that the " rules of eligibility for paper ", in view of the large volume always in existence, " though they may in some cases be an influence on the volume of borrowing by an individual member bank, are not a considerable factor limiting the borrowing capacity of member banks as a whole ". The Report recurs, therefore, to the necessity of employing methods of individual, personal pressure and peaceful persuasion : " The reserve banks in the districts outside of the financial centres, therefore, in passing upon the loan applications of member banks consider not only the legal eligibility and soundness from the credit point of view of the paper presented for re-discount or as collateral for an advance, but also the general position of the borrowing bank, the volume and character of its outstanding loans and investments, and to some extent the character of its management ".

In short, the Federal Reserve Banks, availing themselves of the fact that no Member Bank has an absolute *right* to borrow (all the rules relating to discounts and advances by Reserve Banks for Member Banks are permissive to the Reserve Bank and not obligatory), do their best to avoid any abuse of the System by individual banks.

This point is well brought out by Goldenweiser (*Federal Reserve System in Operation*, pp. 8, 9), where he distinguishes between the " eligibility " of paper presented for discount to a Federal Reserve Bank and its " acceptability " : " *Eligibility* is a matter of law and regulation. In order to be eligible paper must comply with definite standards as to the transactions which gave it origin and as to maturity, while its *acceptability* is entirely independent of these matters and rests on the credit standing of the signers, the availability of funds, the question of whether the particular member bank has exhausted its legitimate quota of credit, whether experience has shown that the bank is using Federal reserve bank accommodation for improper or undesirable purposes, and a number of other considerations which are not definitely formulated but are entirely within the discretion of each loan committee and board of directors, subject to the legal limitation that the Federal reserve bank shall grant accommodation to each member bank with ' due regard to the rights of other member banks ', and with a view to ' accommodating commerce and business '." As Goldenweiser explains on a later page (p. 163), the reserve banks keep a record of the amount of credit to which they consider each individual member bank to be entitled ; and whilst this theoretical amount is constantly exceeded, a member bank's demands are liable to receive severer criticism when it seeks to go beyond it.[1]

---

[1] This gadget has been rendered less effective of late (1929) by the growth of a practice by which a member bank, which has not borrowed as much as it is entitled to, increases its discounts for the sole purpose of lending the reserve-resources thus obtained to other member banks, which have already borrowed from the Reserve Banks as much as they dare, at

Since 1925 the convention that Member Banks should not re-discount except for very short periods [1] has been gaining ground, especially amongst the large New York banks.[2] Whether this convention would stand the strain of a tussle between the Member Banks and the Reserve Banks with the latter trying to enforce a policy which the former resented, remains to be seen. It is clear that Member Banks are not likely to re-discount for the purpose of buying investments or of employing money on the call-market, or of lending money to their customers for Stock Exchange speculation. But measures of cajolery and mild discipline might prove inadequate against a widespread movement of expansion ascribable to the so-called " legitimate " demands of trade—which are just as inflationary as the so-called " illegitimate " demands of finance, and may be more so.

The general result is that the Federal Reserve system has approached nearer to the Bank of England system than was the case at first, and also that " open-market policy " has come to be of fundamental importance in determining the volume of bank-money.

(iv.) Will Member Banks borrow from the Central Bank at a Rate above the Market ?

We have assumed in the foregoing that if a Central Bank can make its official Bank-rate effective in the sense that it is in due relation to the market-rate, member banks will not continue to borrow from the Central Bank by discounting or otherwise, more or

---

a rate which yields it a good profit over the Federal Reserve rate which it has paid. Resources transferred in this way from one member bank to another are called " Federal funds ".

[1] The fact that the bills re-discounted do not average about eight days in length proves nothing. A good up-to-date account of the position is to be found in Riefler's *Money Rates in the United States*, pp. 30-32.

[2] Country banks feel no compunction in re-discounting to meet seasonal needs.

less regardless of the relation between the rate of interest at which they have to borrow and the rate at which they are able to lend to their customers. Some of those, however, who are sceptical about the method of Bank-rate as a means of controlling the creation of bank-money by the member banks, are disposed to deny this proposition. The ablest presentation of their case has been made by Professor J. S. Lawrence in his *Stabilization of Prices*,[1] on the ground that, the member banks being able to lend out a multiple of what they borrow from the Central Bank, an increase in the charge for the latter has to reach an impossibly high figure to outweigh the profits from the former. The essence of his argument will be made clear if I begin, not with his American instances, but with a hypothetical example of my own.[2]

Let us suppose that there is a Central Bank which does no business direct with the public, but deals only with the member banks, and that the member banks have by a process of amalgamation been reduced to *one*. Let us suppose further that this member bank is always free to discount its bills with the Central Bank at an official bank-rate fixed by the latter from time to time, but must keep a balance with the Central Bank amounting to (say) 10 per cent of its deposits. Let us suppose lastly that it is the object of the member bank to make as much profit as possible, subject to the above rules and to not laying itself open to the accusation of overcharging its customers. What would determine in this case the amount of discounting done by the member bank, and therefore at the same time the amount of the Advances of the Central Bank, on the assumption that the latter has no " open-market policy ", and depends solely on changes in bank-rate ?

---

[1] See particularly chapter xxiii.

[2] This illustration was devised before the publication of Prof. Lawrence's book, but it serves to bring out the generality of his point.

Our Bank, like other banks, may be presumed to use its assets in various typical ways at appropriately varying rates of interest—somewhat as follows (Bank-rate being taken at 5 per cent) :

50 per cent of total assets in Advances at 6 per cent.
35 per cent of total assets in Investments and Bills at $4\frac{1}{2}$ per cent.
 5 per cent of total assets at Call at 4 per cent.
10 per cent of total assets in Cash and Central Bank Balances at nil.

Average earnings, 4·775 per cent.

Against this its marginal expenses of management (after deducting receipts from customers otherwise than for interest) may be taken at $\frac{3}{4}$ per cent of any increase in its assets,[1] and we will assume that on 50 per cent of its deposits it pays interest at a rate averaging $3\frac{1}{2}$ per cent ; *i.e.* its outgoings represent 2·5 per cent on its assets. Consequently its *marginal* net profits are 2·275 on its assets.[2]

Our problem for discussion is—at what point will it no longer pay the bank to increase its scale of operations by additional discounting at the Central Bank and by additional lending on the basis of the

---

[1] Overhead expenses, as published, are much higher than this, *e.g.* 1·6 per cent in 1925 in the case of Barclay's Bank. But these figures are for *average* expenses. Since a large part of the expenses are fixed and do not fluctuate with turnover in short periods, $\frac{3}{4}$ per cent is probably a full allowance for the expenses of *additional* business.

[2] Banks do not, as a rule, make as much profit as this over the average of their whole business, partly because their average overhead expenses are perhaps 1 per cent higher than the *marginal* expenses assumed in the above, and partly because the above makes no allowance for various ways in which money can be lost—spending too much money on too many buildings, making bad debts, buying investments which depreciate, and so forth. In 1928 the disclosed profits of the Big Five represented about ·75 per cent on their deposits after paying Income Tax and making provision for bad and doubtful debts and other undisclosed reserves—which is in reasonable accordance with the above. Mr. Beaumont Pease has estimated that in the case of Lloyd's Bank on the average of the three years 1926–28, one-third of the bank's gross earnings went to its depositors by way of interest, and one-third to its staff for salaries, pensions, etc., leaving one-third to meet other expenses including rent and rates, special allocations, bad debts and net profits. These figures are reasonably consistent with the above.

reserves thus created. The bank can only lend (in
one form or another) up to the full nine times of its
additional reserves on the assumption that *all* its
loans come back to it as deposits ; that is to say, that
there are no other member banks to share the increased deposits which result from the additional
lending by the banking system as a whole, and that
the depositors do not take away any part of the new
loans in cash. We are assuming, at present, that
there are no other member banks ; but, since there is
no need to assume that all business is transacted by
cheque, let us suppose that 10 per cent is transacted
by cash, so that 10 per cent of the new advances are
taken in cash and not returned as deposits. This
means that the bank can safely lend about $5\frac{1}{4}$ times
its additional discounting at the Central Bank, and
will end up with an amount of additional deposits
equal to about $4\frac{3}{4}$ times the additional discounting.
Obviously this will pay hand over fist, so long as the
bank can continue to lend and invest at the rates
assumed above. The more the merrier.

Let us put this into a more general form, which
shows more explicitly in what way the profit is a
function of the bank-rate : Bank-rate, x ; Advances
at $1 \cdot 2\ x$; Investments and Bills at $\cdot 9\ x$; call money
at $\cdot 8\ x$; deposit rate at $\cdot 7\ x$; then profit on additional
business, before allowance for expenses, is $\cdot 6\ x$, or,
after allowance for expenses, say $\cdot 6\ x - \cdot 75$ per cent.

It is now clear not only that the more the bank
discounts the better for it, but also that so long as the
ratio of the yield on the bank's assets to the bank-
rate remains constant, the *higher* the bank-rate rises,
the *greater* is the incentive to the member bank to
increase its discounts with the Central Bank and to
increase its loans on the basis of the additional
reserves thus created. In other words, so long as the
bank-rate is " effective " in the sense that the rates
at which the bank can invest and lend its assets rise

with the bank-rate and maintain their usual relation to it, an increase in the bank-rate, so far from deterring the member bank from discounting, will be an additional incentive to it to do so.

Will an inability to find an outlet for its advances at rates of interest commensurate with bank-rate be the check preventing the member bank in its own interests from indefinitely increasing its scale of operations ? The answer is, No. An increase in market-rates far less than proportionate to the increase in the official rate will compensate the member bank for its loss in discounting bills with the Central Bank at a rate much above the market-rate at which it is buying them.[1] Even if the market-rates of interest are falling, it still pays the member bank to go on increasing its assets up to a point which can be calculated.

In short—so the argument runs—the profitableness of member-banking against a cash reserve of 10 per cent is so great that there is an inherent tendency, in the absence of checks, for member banks to increase the scale of their operations in a manner which is inflationary in its consequences ; and, further, bank-rate by itself is not, in general, an adequate check to this tendency except at too late a stage of the inflation, especially if the tendency is kept within limits sufficiently moderate not to interfere with the effectiveness of the bank-rate.

Our picture so far is, of course, quite imaginary—deliberately remote from the real facts. But it serves to introduce our minds to the important question—What in actual fact are the impediments to this inherent tendency ?

The answer is to be found in the fact of the Multi-

---

[1] Professor Lawrence calculates that, on his numerical assumptions, an increase of the Federal Reserve Bank-rate from 4½ to 9 per cent is compensated by an increase of the Member Bank-rate from 5·66 to 5·9 per cent, and if the former rises to 90 per cent the latter need only rise a little above 10 per cent. (*Op. cit.* p. 312.)

plicity of Member Banks. In our hypothetical example we assumed that there was only one member bank, so that the proceeds of its extra-lending all came back to itself in the shape of extra deposits, except for the increase in the note circulation. If there is a multiplicity of member banks, the argument is considerably altered ; particularly if, as in America, the member banks run into thousands.

A bank's coefficient of expansion on the basis of a given addition to the total banking reserves will be measured by its quota of the deposit business of the banking system as a whole ; or perhaps by a little more than this—at least for a short time—where the increased reserves come first of all into the hands of our bank, those who deal with its customers having a better chance than the average of also being its customers, since the business of a given bank is not spread evenly over the whole country. Thus a bank's coefficient will be small if there are many banks, though not so small if there are few. Accordingly a bank which borrows from the Central Bank at a cost above the market-rate pays the whole cost of expanding credit, but reaps only a proportion, and perhaps only a small proportion, of the benefit. The effect of this is to diminish, and sometimes but not necessarily to obliterate, the stimulus to an individual bank to increase its scale of business, on the basis of borrowing from the Central Bank. Nevertheless, an individual bank may still gain some advantage from an isolated act of expansion at a cost above the market-rate, where the leading member banks are reduced to five in number, as is now the case in Great Britain. And even in the United States it is possible—as Professor J. S. Lawrence argues, with what accuracy I cannot tell, against the contrary opinion held by Professor C. A. Phillips—that the increase of a member bank's own deposits as a result of its own lending is sufficiently great to make it worth while to borrow from its

Federal Reserve Bank at a rate slightly above the market-rate.[1] Moreover, if all the banks are acting in step in response to the same stimulus, the net result is as great as in the case of a single bank.

This does not give us, therefore, a complete answer to Professor Lawrence's paradox; for Professor Phillips's answer would in British conditions lack much of its force. There is, however, a further consideration —and one likely, perhaps, to have more influence in practice than it should have on the basis of strict calculation—namely, the fact that, so long as market rates are below the official rate, it will always appear to a bank, which is desirous of increasing its reserve-balances, that it will pay it better to steal away the reserve-balances of other member banks than to borrow itself from the Reserve Bank. Why—I think almost any practical banker would ask— should a member bank re-discount if it can increase its reserve-resources more cheaply by withdrawing funds from the call-market or by selling an acceptance or an investment? Accordingly, an individual bank will usually prefer to sell some asset the loss of which will not react on its deposits, *i.e.* of which the coefficient of contraction (to invent a term which shall be the inverse of Prof. Lawrence's " coefficient of expansion ") is as low as possible (*i.e.* as near unity as possible), thus increasing the reserve-balances on the basis of which it can increase those of its assets (*e.g.* loans to its own customers and neighbourhood) of which the coefficient of expansion is high, rather than to re-discount with the Central Bank above the

---

[1] Prof. Phillips (*Annals of Am. Ac. Pol. Sc.*, January 1922, pp. 195-199) contends that in the United States the coefficient of expansion (*i.e.* of the bank's own lending to the reserve it borrows) for a single bank acting by itself is about 1·25, from which " it follows that re-discount rates roughly equal to the market-rates (if the expense of carrying on the banking business is considered) will ordinarily be sufficiently high to serve as a check on borrowing member banks ". Prof. Lawrence, on the other hand, argues that the coefficient is about 1·8 (*op. cit.* p. 363). For a full development of Prof. Phillips's argument, *vide* his *Bank Credit* (p. 115 *et passim*).

market-rate.[1] Only, of course, if each member bank is doing this, no one is, on balance, any the better off.

We conclude, therefore, that, where there is a multiplicity of member banks, borrowing from the Central Bank at a rate appreciably above the rate in the market for precisely similar loans is not likely to occur ; not, that is to say, unless there is a deliberate agreement between the member banks as a whole to operate in a concerted manner contrary to the wishes of the Central Bank—and a concerted insurrection of the member banks against the deliberate policy of the Central Bank is a purely academic risk which does not materialise in practice.

But even if such concerted action were to occur, or if, for any other reason, the above deterrents were to be all of them inoperative, the Central Bank would still have weapons at its disposal in the shape of open-market policy—so long as it possesses suitable ammunition. For if the member banks start borrowing from it above the market-rate, the Central Bank can make a tiresome profit at their expense by selling all its open-market assets at the market-rate, and so forcing the member banks to borrow back from it the equivalent of these at above the market-rate.

Thus the assumption that the official rate is " effective " if it is in touch with the market-rate need not be abated.

(v.) Open-market Policy further analysed

Some writers have argued that the method of bank-rate and the method of " open-market policy " really

---

[1] The assumption of the above argument, that the " coefficient of contraction " is less in respect of some of the bank's assets than in respect of others, would not hold good if there were complete symmetry as between the particular bank's own customers and the customers of other banks. For in this case the substitution of one asset for another would have no tendency towards enabling it to increase its total assets. The assumption in the text, however, usually represents the facts.

reduce theoretically to one, namely bank-rate, the
practical limitations of " open-market policy " unaccompanied by a change of bank-rate being narrow.
According to this argument, which—as we shall see—
cannot be fully sustained, the Central Bank cannot
vary the volume of its " investments " without tending to produce an opposite and compensating variation
in the volume of its " advances ", unless it accompanies its action with an appropriate change of Bank-
rate. It is admitted that in so far as the investments
which it buys on its own initiative are a different type
of security from the advances which it makes on the
initiative of its customers, some fluctuation in the
former can be effected without an immediate or substantial reaction on the volume of advances; also
that the effect of " open-market policy ", *i.e.* of varying the amount of its investments, can produce
gradual and continuous movements *within* the range
of the more abrupt and discontinuous changes of bank-
rate. Nevertheless, according to this view, open-
market policy can only be employed by a Central
Bank, not as a substitute for, but to reinforce, its
bank-rate policy by making the latter effective ; in
other words, save in abnormal and unusual situations,
the aggregate of the Central Bank's assets is a function
of its Bank-rate, so that by appropriate variations of the
latter the whole situation can be controlled. This has
been, until lately, the orthodox doctrine in England, although it has not been accepted abroad so universally.

Now, in the last resort, it is certainly the case that
bank-rate policy and open-market policy cannot be
carried on, except within limits, along different lines.
The importance of the difference between the two
methods is not, however, affected by this. For it
arises out of the fact that the *kinds* of effect produced
by the two methods are materially different. Changes
in bank-rate may, amongst other things, affect the
volume of Central Bank " advances " ; but they do

much else besides, and their influence on Central Bank advances is an uncertain, incidental result of a much wider complex of consequences which a change in Bank-rate sets up. Open-market operations, on the other hand, produce a direct effect on the reserves of the member banks and hence on the volume of deposits and of credit generally, by their immediate consequences and apart from their indirect reactions. Moreover, changes in Bank-rate primarily affect the short-rate of interest, whereas open-market operations —so far as they relate to the Central Bank's holdings of long-dated securities—influence the long-rate of interest. The great significance which this distinction between the two may have in certain circumstances, will be the chief subject-matter of Chapter 37. We shall see there that, whilst bank-rate may be the most suitable weapon for use when the object of the Central Bank is to preserve international equilibrium, open-market sales or purchases of securities may be more effective when the object is to influence the rate of investment.

The way in which open-market operations work is not the same in England as it is in the United States. We will deal with them, therefore, separately.

In the case of England we have to distinguish between the efficacies of buying and of selling open-market operations. The efficacy of the purchase of Government securities by the Bank of England in increasing the aggregate amount of the reserves of the Joint-Stock banks is almost absolute. Since the money market normally owes the Bank of England little or nothing, the effects of market repayments to the Bank, resulting from the greater abundance of funds, are not likely to be important. Thus the first and direct effect of an increase in the Bank of England's investments is to cause an increase in the reserves of the Joint-Stock Banks and a corresponding increase in their loans and advances on the basis of this. This may react on market-rates of discount and bring the latter a little lower than they would otherwise have been. But it will often, though not always, be possible for the Joint Stock Banks to increase their loans and advances without a material weakening in the rates of interest charged. The efficacy of the sale of Government securities in decreasing the reserves of the banks is likely to be equally unqualified, so long as market-rates are below bank-rate. But if the resistance of the member banks to a restriction of credit causes market-rates to approach bank-rate, a tendency to counterbalance the open-market operation by increased discounting on the part of the money-market will set in, a tendency which cannot be stopped except by raising bank-rate. Indeed it is always easier to set in motion an inflationary than a deflationary process, because the former suits the banks and is able to arouse the inherent inflationary bias of a member-bank system, whilst the latter evokes the resistance of the banks both in their own interest and to avoid upsetting their customers. In any case, however, there is a time-lag during which the cumulative effects of the operations of the Central Bank may be able to set up a general tendency of the business and financial world in the desired direction.

The last-named consideration, namely, the tendency of any movement which may be started to propagate itself further, leads us to another important aspect of open-market policy, and one which applies even more strongly in the United States than in England. For, apart from the question whether or not deliberate changes in the volume of the " investments " of a Central Bank tend to provoke opposite changes in the volume of its " advances ", and so prove ineffective in altering the volume of bank-money, there is their effect in influencing the member banks to move in step with one another in the direction indicated and desired by the Central Bank. The

reader will recall from the preceding discussion how
the behaviour of one member bank is partly influenced
by that of the other member banks, and that a chance
event which has the effect of making many of them
move in the same direction simultaneously may confirm a durable movement of the system as a whole in
that direction, without the banks as a whole having
deliberately willed it or decided that such a movement
is in their interests. I fancy that a considerable part
of the value of open-market operations delicately
handled by the Central Bank may lie in its tacit
influence on the member banks to move in step in the
desired direction. For example, at any given moment
a particular bank may find itself with a small surplus
reserve on the basis of which it would in the ordinary
course purchase some additional asset, which purchase
would have the effect of slightly improving the reserve
positions of the other banks, and so on. If at this
moment the Central Bank snips off the small surplus
by selling some asset in the open market, the member
bank will not obstinately persist in its proposed additional purchase by re-calling funds from the money-
market for the purpose ; it will just not make the
purchase. Similarly some other bank which finds
its reserve unduly reduced by the Central Bank's
action will not make good the deficit wholly by re-
calling funds from the money-market and thus driving the money-market to borrow from the Bank of
England ; it will re-establish its equilibrium by not
replacing some of the assets which in the ordinary
course of business are daily running off. In this way
a progressive series of small deflationary open-market
sales by the Central Bank can induce the banks pro-
gressively to diminish little by little the scale of their
operations. Certainly there can be no doubt that a
progressive series of small inflationary open-market
purchases by the Central Bank (whether in the form
of additional lending to the Government or otherwise)

are potently, and almost invariably, effective in inducing the member banks to follow suit. In this way much can be achieved without changing the bank-rate. A member of the public, who, as a result of the credit restriction, is unable to borrow from his bank, generally has no facilities—at least in England —for obtaining the funds he requires by bidding up the price of loans in the open market, even though he is quite willing to pay more than the market price. In short, open-market operations give the Central Bank a means of using the inherent instability of the system for its own purposes. Especially is this the case where there is a great multiplicity of member banks, as in the United States.

Open-market operations by the U.S. Federal Reserve Banks date, as a fact, on an important scale, from the spring of 1922, and as a systematised policy from April 1923.[1] They began, not with the idea of controlling or influencing the behaviour of the member banks, but to prevent the earning assets of the Reserve Banks themselves from falling any further. The net imports of gold into the United States during 1921 amounted to about $660,000,000. The proceeds were paid into the Reserve Banks and were largely employed to repay the indebtedness of the member banks, with the result that by the spring of 1922 the Reserve Banks found their interest-earning assets falling to a level below what would meet their expenses and their dividend requirements. Accordingly, during 1922 the Reserve Banks, acting each for itself and with no co-ordinated policy or far-reaching intentions, bought on the open market what was in the aggregate a very large volume of U.S. Government securities. The inflationary possibilities of these pro-

---

[1] The best account of the genesis of open-market policy is to be found in the *Tenth Annual Report of the Federal Reserve Board for the Year 1923* (published in 1924), of which I have made use in what follows. See also Governor Strong's *Evidence before the Stabilisation Committee* (U.S. Congress, 1927), pp. 207-332, and for statistics of open-market operations, p. 426.

ceedings on the top of the heavy imports of gold soon
became obvious, and in April 1923 the Federal Reserve Board took the matter in hand—probably just
in time to prevent a repetition of the 1920 boom.
The principle publicly laid down by the Board was as
follows : " That the time, manner, character and
volume of open-market investments purchased by
the Federal reserve banks be governed with primary
regard to the accommodation of commerce and business and to the effect of such purchases or sales on
the general credit situation ". This is studiously
vague, but it does at least prescribe that securities
must not be purchased merely to increase the earnings
of the reserve banks. More important, however, than
this abstract statement of intention was the appoint-
ment of a " Committee of reserve bank officers to act
under the general supervision of the Board in handling
open-market problems and operations ". From this
point we may date the empirical discovery by the
Federal Reserve Board that the London method of
relying on discount policy for the management of the
national monetary system was not adequate by itself
to control a system built on the American lines, but
that open-market policy, by going straight to the root
of the matter and affecting directly the volume of
member bank reserves, furnished them with an instrument more adequate to their task.

So long as the object of open-market operations
was neither to modify the existing equilibrium nor
to thwart the tendencies of the member banks away
therefrom, but to protect the existing equilibrium
from disturbance, this expedient was perfectly adapted
to the purpose. Nevertheless, when it became a
question of inducing the member banks to modify
the scale of their operations, it was inevitably more
exposed than in London, by reason of the nature of
the American system already described, to counteraction by a movement of the " advances " in the

opposite direction. Since the American banks as a whole are normally indebted to the Reserve Banks, it is easy and natural for them to repay some part of this indebtedness if they find their balances with the Reserve Banks increased beyond their needs. Contrariwise, the rates of the Reserve Banks for re-discounting and the purchase of acceptances are not so prohibitive or even punitive in relation to market rates as to deter the member banks from replenishing their balances with the Reserve Banks when they find these falling below their requirements.

For these reasons some authorities, in the early days of open-market policy, were inclined to doubt whether, in spite of appearances to the contrary, the policy was really of much use. In March 1925, Dr. Chandler wrote in the *Journal of the New York National Bank of Commerce* as follows :

As the reserve banks have sold their investments, the volume of re-discounts of member banks with the System has tended correspondingly to increase. So long as member banks may borrow freely from the reserve banks, therefore, it would appear that the open-market operations of the reserve banks may have little effect upon the volume of credit at the disposal of the member banks. It is true that, in so far as the withdrawing of funds from the market through the process of selling reserve bank open-market investments forces the member banks to borrow, there may be created a certain reluctance on the part of member banks to extend credits. . . . This is quite different, however, from saying that the net effect of the open-market operations over an extended period has any permanent influence upon the volume of credit available.

Dr. Burgess also (*The Reserve Banks and the Money Market*, chap. xii.) says that " increases or decreases in holdings of government securities purchased outright (voluntary) have been accompanied by almost corresponding changes in bills discounted, bankers' acceptances held, etc. (involuntary) ". But his statistics do not really show more than that where the movements of the former are large they are apt to be partially offset by movements of the latter. Moreover, movements in the former have sometimes been *intended* to compensate movements in the latter.

Governor Strong, who—more than anyone else—was responsible for the development of open-market policy, expressed his philosophy of the subject as follows :

> The operations in the open market are designed, I should say, to prepare the way for a change in rates. Unfortunately, it has always seemed to me that the country has given exaggerated importance to change of the discount rate sentimentally. The danger is that an advance of rate will operate as a sort of sledge-hammer blow to the feeling of confidence and security of the country as to credit, and that reaction has been somewhat modified by these open-market operations. . . . If considerations move the Reserve Banks to tighten up a bit on the use of their credit, it is a more effective programme, we find by actual experience, to begin to sell our Government securities. . . . The effect is less dramatic and less alarming to the country.[1]

These authorities under-estimate, in my opinion, the efficacy of open-market policy. But Governor Strong shows, in the above quotation, that he was partly aware of the qualitative difference between open-market policy and bank-rate policy. Later experience has shown that open-market operations can be so handled as to be quite extraordinarily effective in managing the currency. The successful management of the dollar by the Federal Reserve Board from 1923 to 1928 was a triumph—mitigated, however, by the events of 1929-30—for the view that currency management is feasible, in conditions which are virtually independent of the movements of gold.

Nevertheless the policy of these years might not have been feasible but for the fact that the Federal Reserve Board was not seriously embarrassed during this period by the movements of gold. For the

---

[1] *Report of Stabilisation Committee* (U.S. Congress, 1927), pp. 307, 332.

success of open-market policy depends on the Central
Bank always having in hand adequate ammunition
in the shape of open-market securities available
for sale. The reserve banks can only fire off against
an incipient boom such ammunition as they have
been able to pick up whilst resisting the slump.
If, however, there is a continuous large influx of gold,
this steadily steals their ammunition from them,
and by the substitution in their reserves of non-
marketable gold in place of marketable securities,
they must sooner or later find their stock of ammunition reduced to a level below what they require
to fight the next boom. Under a gold standard no
system of management can stand up indefinitely
before a continued influx of gold of an amount
far greater in proportion than the growth of balances
required by the banking system at large. Sooner
or later the influx must produce an inflation. The
influx of gold into the United States in 1921 and subsequent years was on so great a scale that it might
have been expected to exhaust so much of the reserve
banks' ammunition in avoiding its otherwise inflationary results that not enough would be left to fight the
incipient credit boom in 1923 and subsequently. Indeed most observers at the time expected that this
would be the case. That it was not so was attributable to the remarkable growth during the same period
in the volume of bank-money required by the American
public. For, to the extent that more bank-money is
required at the existing price-level, new gold can be
absorbed into the reserves without any inflationary
consequences to prices, and without the use of the
reserve banks' ammunition being necessary. The test
of the adequacy of the reserve banks' ammunition in
the shape of saleable securities for the management
of the dollar will come in the event of an influx of
gold coinciding with diminishing, instead of with
expanding, requirements of bank-money.

If the course of monetary events in the United
States from 1922 to 1928 is an example of successful
management, the inflation of 1920 was an example
of singularly ineffective management.   Open-market
operations were not attempted, because the principles of this policy had not been discovered at that
date.   At the same time the statistics of that period
raise a doubt how far in 1919 and 1920 adequate
ammunition would have been at the disposal of the
reserve banks.

(vi.) Method of varying Member Bank Reserve-ratios

The possibility of an inadequacy of ammunition
interfering in exceptional circumstances with the
efficacy of open-market operations makes it worth
while to mention a further expedient which has never
yet been put into practice, namely, a discretion to the
Central Bank to vary with due notice and by small
degrees the proportion of legal reserves which the
member banks are required to hold.

The Federal Reserve Board made a proposal on
these lines in 1917.   The increases in the reserve
requirements of member banks were not to exceed 20
per cent of the member bank's reserve with its Reserve Bank, and were not to be in force for more than
thirty days.   The Federal Advisory Council opposed
the proposal on the ground that it did not apply to
non-member banks, and it was never carried out.   In
any case, it would have made a very trifling difference
to the reserve requirements.[1]   Dr. Chandler [2] has
commented :   " Unquestionably such power would
have enabled the System effectively to sterilize

---

[1] See Beckhart, *Discount Policy of the Federal Reserve System*, p. 190,
and *Federal Reserve Bulletin*, 1917.

[2] In his article " International Aspects of Federal Reserve Policy ",
American Economic Review (Supplement), March 1926.

excess gold, but the suggestion was so revolutionary that its adoption was out of the question ".

Though it may seem revolutionary now, nevertheless some such provision, duly safeguarded, should, I think, be added to the powers of the ideal Central Bank of the future. It goes straight to the root of the matter, instead of relying on the indirect and roundabout influences which our empirical systems of monetary management have evolved for themselves. If the member banks are lending too much and increasing cash balances without due regard to the requirements of their customers in the existing equilibrium, or if, on the other hand, they are lending too little, the variation in their reserve proportions puts on them the directest possible pressure to move in the desired direction. I have proposed accordingly (see Vol. ii. p. 77) the introduction of this feature into the British System.

CHAPTER 33

METHODS OF NATIONAL MANAGEMENT—II. THE REGULATION OF THE CENTRAL RESERVES

WE have been concerned in the preceding chapter with the various methods by which a Central Bank can control the amount of the reserve-resources of its Member Banks. We there concentrated on the regulation of the amount of the " advances " and " investments " of the Central Bank, arguing that, if these were under effective control, the aggregate reserve-resources of the Member Banks, resulting from the aggregate " gold ", " advances " and " investments " held by the Central Bank *minus* the notes held by the public, could also be controlled. In this chapter we must deal with a matter which might have been, and perhaps ought to be, non-existent, namely, the regulations to which the Central Bank is itself subject, and within the limitations of which it has to perform its functions.

One might have supposed that in any well-contrived monetary system the member banks, who operate in isolation and without special regard to the general interests, would be put under the discipline of the Central Bank, and that the element of discretion in the system would mainly inhere in the management of the latter. Nor would one expect that the rules of wise behaviour by a Central Bank could be conveniently laid down—having regard to the immense complexity of its problems and their varying character in varying circumstances—by Act of Parliament. But for historical reasons—reasons which were never very good and are now obsolete in their application—we find that in most modern monetary systems exactly the opposite is the case. The regulation of the member banks is usually somewhat indefinite, whilst that of the Central Bank is very precise—very precise, that is, in one particular, namely, the relationship between one item from amongst its liabilities, *i.e.* its note-issue, and one item from amongst its assets, *i.e.* its gold.

These regulations, the character of which we shall examine in detail in a moment, derive from two influences. The first is historical. In the early days of representative money, such money mainly took the form, not of bank-deposits but of bank-notes. A hundred years ago in Great Britain, twenty-five years ago in Germany, and even to-day, probably, in some countries, anyone who wished to control the quantity of representative money would reasonably concentrate on the regulation of bank-notes. Moreover in most countries, up to so recently as 1914, bank-notes generally circulated alongside of gold coins, so that the total amount of circulating money other than bank-money depended, not on the amount of bank-notes, but on this amount *plus* the amount of circulating gold ; which required, as a condition of the stability of the total currency in circulation, that changes in the quantity of gold circulating should be balanced by opposite changes in the quantity of notes circulating. The method of regulation was designed, therefore, to secure this result.

The second influence was political. It has been thought desirable to limit the discretionary power of the Central Bank on account of the risk of the latter proving subservient to the imprudent demands of the Government, and consequently making advances to the Treasury which must involve an inflation of the note-issue. Doubtless in some countries and in some circumstances there is force in this consideration. But unfortunately an Act of Parliament is a very ineffective method of curtailing the powers of a government ; and in almost every known case of stress and strain, in which the Note Regulations interfere with the wishes of the Government of the day, it is the former which have given way.

So far as the historical influences apply, the conditions which explain them have, of course, almost entirely passed away—especially in Great Britain. To regulate the volume of bank-notes is a very clumsy, slow, indirect and inefficient method of regulating the volume of bank-money. For while it may be true that the volume of the bank-notes bears, at any time, a more or less determined relationship to the volume of bank-money, the relationship has been steadily changing, quantitatively speaking, over long periods as a result of changes of monetary habits and customs ; whilst over short periods there is a serious time-lag, the volume of bank-money generally changing *first*, so that a control over the volume of notes operates too late—after the evil has been done by a change in the volume of bank-money which may have taken place some months earlier.

But apart from the obsolescence of the principle of attempting to regulate the volume of Central Bank Notes instead of the volume of Central Bank Deposits (or Central Bank Notes *plus* Deposits),[1] the methods of regulation in general use have lost any meaning they may ever have had, since the general disuse of actual gold in circulation which has followed the war. For these regulations usually provide that the Central Bank shall always hold a minimum quantity of gold, the amount of which is determined by the

---

[1] We shall see, below, that in several countries the Central Bank must now keep reserves against Notes *plus* Deposits, and no longer against Notes alone. But in these cases also, the objection to the method of regulation adopted still remains.

amount of notes in circulation. Since the central gold reserve is no longer required, as it used to be in part, to meet a drain of gold into the internal circulation—a loss which it would often be reasonable to balance by a decrease of the note circulation—the effect of such provisions is merely to lock away a large part, and sometimes the major part, of the gold reserve so that it can *never* be used, leaving the effective reserves of the Central Bank actually available against contingencies at so low a figure as seriously to hamper it in the reasonable exercise of its discretion. To illustrate all this, we will now give a short summary of the existing provisions of the law in various countries.

(i.) Existing Methods of Regulating Note-issues

Broadly speaking, four methods have been applied in practice :

(*a*) Up to the year 1928 there was in France no prescribed relationship between the note circulation and the amount of the gold (and silver) reserves. The method of regulation adopted was to prescribe a maximum which the note circulation should not exceed irrespective of the amount of the reserves. This maximum was generally in excess of what the note circulation was expected to be in normal circumstances, and it was revised upwards from time to time. As a part of the Currency Reform of 1928, however, this regulation was abandoned in favour of the popular percentage method (*c*) below.

The method of a fixed maximum has the great advantage of allowing as much discretion as possible to the Central Bank, and, in particular, of rendering the whole of the reserves available for use in case of need (a liberty of which, however, the Bank of France almost never availed itself), whilst interposing a legislative safeguard against any serious measure of inflation. If the volume of the note-issue is to be regulated by law, this is perhaps the best system.

(b) The British Bank Act of 1844 prescribed a method of regulation which had some logic behind it at the time when it was introduced—the method (as it is called) of the " fixed fiduciary issue ". It requires that the amount of the note-issue shall not exceed the amount of the gold reserves by more than a stated amount fixed by law (but capable of revision, of course, from time to time). The idea was to cover the fluctuating margin of the note-issue with gold, so that there would always be gold available to redeem all the notes that were at all likely to be presented in any normal circumstances ; and it also secured that, once the note-issue exceeded its normal minimum, no further expansion should be possible unless there was a margin of gold-cover available against it. It dates from a period of gold and notes circulating side by side, and of recently experienced abuses due to an unjustified increase in the internal currency through the Bank of England having allowed additional gold and additional notes both to go out into circulation at the same time.

In modern times the " fixed fiduciary issue " method may work fairly well, if the fiduciary issue is fixed high enough to leave the Central Bank in unfettered control of the bulk of its gold reserves. In this case its provisions operate as a check only on extreme measures of expansion by the Central Bank. Otherwise it has the effect of locking up too much gold in a fashion which has lost its *raison d'être* in countries where gold coins no longer circulate.

This system now obtains in Great Britain (where the amount of the fiduciary issue was re-settled in 1928, though at a figure so low as to fetter unreasonably the discretion of the bank), Norway and Japan. The Swedish System is similar, except that the gold reserve may not fall below a minimum figure, whilst the reserve against notes in excess of the fiduciary issue need be only 50 per cent instead of 100 per cent. In all these countries there exist emergency powers to increase the fiduciary issue in extraordinary circumstances.

(c) The most fashionable system at the present day is the "percentage" system, which prescribes that the gold reserve shall not fall below a fixed percentage of the note-issue, which percentage lies as a rule between 30 and 40 per cent. The percentage system sometimes applies to Central Bank Deposits as well as to notes (though not always the same percentage for both)—which in modern conditions would have more logic in it if this method had any logic at all. The following table summarises the present position :

	Against Notes.	Against Deposits.
	Per cent.	Per cent.
Australia	25	..
Belgium	30	30
Denmark	30	..
France	35	35
Germany	40 [1]	..
Holland and Java . .	40	40
Poland	30	30
South Africa . . .	40	40
Spain	37 [2]	..
Switzerland	40	..
United States . . .	40 [3]	35
Uruguay	40	..

In one or two of the above cases a part of the legal reserves may consist of silver.

[1] Of which up to a quarter may be in the form of foreign exchange.

[2] The Spanish system is complicated, the required percentage rising to 47 when the note-issue exceeds a given figure.

[3] Federal Reserve Notes. The further complications of the American system, due to historical survivals, are familiar and need not be mentioned here.

The " percentage " method possesses—it seems to me—no sound foundations in logic or common-sense. In spite of its inclusion in the quite modern United States Federal Reserve System and in most of the recent Currency Reforms in Europe associated with the restoration of the gold standard, I have never seen in print a reasoned defence of its provisions. It appears to combine all the possible defects of systems of note regulation. For it is very extravagant in locking away gold and does not even exempt—as the " Fixed fiduciary issue " system does—the irreducible minimum of the note-issue. It allows the influx of new gold to produce a disproportionate relaxation of the credit position,[1] unless the Central Bank exercises an extra degree of prudence not required by the law— whereas if the prudence of the Central Bank can be relied on, the law itself is unnecessary and probably hampering. And, finally, in emergencies and difficult moments when the gold reserves are falling, it requires so drastic a curtailment of money proportionately to the loss of gold as to be exceedingly dangerous. Indeed a country having the percentage system is not safe from the liability to severe currency disorders, unless it normally maintains a reserve largely in excess of the prescribed minimum—as has been the case in the United States since the war—so that the Central Bank has no need in practice seriously to consider the question of its legal reserves. But this, of course, involves a still more extravagant lock-up of gold. This, in fact, is a law which is highly dangerous, unless a country is rich enough in reserves (like France and the United States) to make the law entirely in-effective in influencing the policy of the Bank. It is, therefore, a great misfortune that at the time of the Gold Standard Restorations, when most currency

---

[1] If the Central Bank's percentage reserve is 33 per cent and the Member Banks' reserve-ratios 10 per cent, an influx of new gold allows an increase of Bank-money equal to 30 times the amount of the new gold.

laws were in the melting-pot, this system should have been the fashionable and respectable thing.

(d) The fourth method, which—according to the definitions of Chapter 1 (Vol. i. p. 18)—amounts to Exchange Management, but not, generally speaking, to an Exchange Standard, is a variant of the third, by which all or some part of the percentage reserve required against the note-issue may be held, not in actual gold, but in bills or cash at some foreign bank. The adoption of this method, which is usual in the case of those countries which have restored the gold standard with the assistance of the Financial Committee of the League of Nations, is in accordance with the recommendations of the Genoa Conference of 1922, and has been made, in many cases, under their influence.

The countries which—so far as the law goes—are entitled to hold the *whole* of their reserves in foreign balances and bills, include the following : Albania, Austria, Chile, Czechoslovakia, Danzig, Ecuador, Egypt, Estonia, Greece, Hungary, Italy, Latvia, Peru and Russia ; certain other countries—Belgium, Colombia, Denmark, Germany, Poland, Spain and Uruguay—are allowed, as we have seen above, to maintain a *proportion* of their reserves in foreign exchange as an alternative to gold.

This method has the great advantage of economising gold—subject to the considerations which have been discussed in Chapter 21 (Vol. i. pp. 350-356) ; but, as a means of regulating the volume of notes or of bank-money, it is open in other respects to the same objections as the " percentage " method. The economy of gold is, moreover, optional, and there is a danger that considerations of fashion and prestige —for Italy is the only major Power which has adopted this method—may lead some of the countries in the above list not to exercise their option but to hold actual gold. For example, at the end of 1929 the

Austrian National Bank held in gold about two-fifths of its legal reserves, the Bank of Italy more than half, the Czechoslovak National Bank about two-fifths, the Bank of Poland three-quarters, and the National Bank of Hungary almost the whole.

Two countries of first-rate importance—France and Japan—hold, at present, a large part of their *excess* reserves in foreign bills and balances. In the case of Japan this is an old-standing practice, dating back to pre-war days. But in the case of France it is probably an accident—a survival of the transition to gold—on the continuance of which we cannot rely. The adequacy of the gold supply in the near future largely turns, indeed, on how far France decides to convert her reserves in the shape of foreign balances into reserves in the shape of actual gold.

The result of these various methods is to make the release of a portion of a Central Bank's reserves conditional on a decrease (and in the case of the " percentage " method a severe decrease) in the volume of notes circulating within the country. But since in modern conditions notes are chiefly used for wage payments and petty cash, their volume is governed by the level of wages and the volume of employment. Since it is evident that a reduction in the level of wages cannot be effected quickly and is only likely to come as the result of unemployment, the note-issue cannot be rapidly reduced except by reducing employment. Moreover, a 10 per cent reduction of the normal note-issue would be a very violent measure ; yet even this would, under the " percentage " method, release an amount of gold equal to only 3 per cent of the Bank's note-issue.

Thus in effect a Central Bank's gold reserves are divided into two parts—its legal minimum reserve, which for practical purposes is locked up and useless, and cannot be taken into its calculations by a prudent

Central Bank; and its excess reserve, which is alone available to meet emergencies.

Now the risk of a long period of a shortage of gold leading to tight credit conditions and a sagging price-level depends not on the total volume of gold held by Central Banks, which is very substantial, but on their excess reserves, which are uncomfortably small. How large a proportion of the world's monetary gold has been sterilised by belonging to the legal minimum reserves of Central Banks is shown by the following table :

(£1,000,000)

	Date of Return.	Legal Reserves.	Excess Reserves.	Per cent of Excess Reserves to Total Reserves.
	1928			
Great Britain .	October 24	108	59	35
United States [1] .	,, 25	311	233	43
France . .	,, 19	222	26	10
Germany . .	,, 15	63	60	49
Spain [2] . .	,, 20	55	32	37
Holland . .	,, 22[3]	14	22	61
Java . . .	,, 20	6	9	60
Sweden . .	,, 20	10	3	23
South Africa .	September 28	6	2	25
		795	446	36

This list is not, of course, complete, but it covers the countries which hold about three-quarters of the gold reserves of the world. It shows that nearly two-thirds of the world's monetary gold is locked away out of use, and is not available either to meet the actual requirements of Central Banks or to assuage their fears. The effects of the new French Currency Law stand out with special prominence.

[1] Excluding gold certificates.
[2] Since this date, Holland has doubled her legal reserves—thus restoring the pre-war proportion.
[3] Peseta taken at 30 to £1.

(ii.) The Right Principles of Regulation

I believe that, in any civilised country to-day with a responsible government and a powerful Central Bank, it would be much better to leave the management of the reserves of the Central Bank to its own unfettered discretion than to attempt to lay down by law what it should do or within what limits it should act. What the law—or, failing the law, the force of a binding convention—should attend to is the regulation of the reserves of the Member Banks, so as to ensure that the decision as to the total volume of bank-money outstanding shall be centralised in the hands of a body whose duty it is to be guided by considerations of the general social and economic advantage and not of pecuniary profit. Moreover, a legal reserve laid down for the Member Banks is likely to be effective in the sense that the actual reserve will approximate to it, since the Member Banks have in any well-devised system emergency facilities from the Central Bank ; whereas a Central Bank, which has no such facilities on which in its turn it can rely, must maintain an excess over its legal reserve to meet contingencies. The legal reserves of Member Banks are, also, a means of making them contribute to the expense of the maintenance of the Central reserves. But the legal reserves of the Central Bank merely lock away resources where they are useless, and the effective strength of a Central Bank entirely depends in practice on the amount of its *excess* reserves. Thus we have the paradox that the more strictly and conservatively the gold reserves of a Central Bank are prescribed by law, the weaker it is and the more utterly exposed to disastrous disturbances from every wind which blows. A Central Bank which was compelled to keep 100 per cent of its assets in gold would be not much better off than one which had no reserves at all.

But even if the principle of a percentage reserve or a fiduciary maximum were to be conceded, it would be better to apply it to the Central Bank-Money held by the Member Banks, and not to the amount of notes circulating in the pockets of the public. For in the event of an inflation developing, the note-issue is in modern conditions the *latest* phenomenon in point of time to exhibit symptoms of the disorder which is at work in the economic system. To attempt to maintain monetary health by regulating the volume of the note-issue is like attempting to maintain physical health by ordering a drastic operation or amputation after the affection has run its full course and mortification is setting in. For, generally speaking, the note-issue will not expand—for reasons other than an increase in the volume of employment—until the inflationary influences have had time to raise the money-rates of remuneration of the factors of production, which, once raised, it will be difficult to bring down again without injurious reactions.

There are, therefore—I suggest—only two respects in which the law can usefully limit the discretion of the Central Bank. It may be prudent in a precarious world deliberately to set aside a certain amount of gold which it is not intended to use in any ordinary circumstances, and which is to be held as a reserve against ultimate emergencies. Accordingly, a country's gold reserve should be divided into two portions, one of which is, so to speak, a war-chest, and the other to meet ordinary contingencies and fluctuations. But there is no reason why the first portion need bear any rigid relationship to the volume of notes or the volume of bank-money. The law might, then, reasonably require that the gold reserves shall not fall below a stated minimum figure—which should certainly be much lower in most cases than the present legal reserves.

Secondly, it might be an aid to psychological confidence, and also prove at least a delaying safeguard in emergencies, if the law were to fix a maximum which the note-issue shall not exceed, on the lines of the former French law. Since there is no reason why the note-issue should suffer sudden or violent changes, it would be sufficient if the maximum were to exceed by a comfortable, but not excessive, margin the anti-cipated circulation in times of good trade at its seasonal maximum.

If the law were to fix a minimum absolute figure for the gold reserve and a maximum absolute figure for the note circulation, both these figures being subject to reasonable revision from time to time and so chosen as to allow a wide discretion to the Central Bank in its day-to-day and year-to-year policies, I do not believe that there is any further safeguard which—however much it may be intended in the interests of prudence—will not render the country's currency system more, rather than less, precarious, sometimes compelling the Central Bank to take steps which are, in its own judgment, unwise and possibly dangerous.

One other matter, which is properly one of law, may be mentioned at this point—namely, the form of the circulating cash other than bank-money. There is to-day a fair consensus of opinion as to what is best. In the first place, in view of the risks of a shortage of monetary gold, gold coins, or their equiva-lent in the shape of gold certificates, should certainly not be allowed to circulate, and should be kept solely for the purpose of settling international indebted-ness. In the second place, there should be only one form of note, which should be managed by the Central Bank—Treasury notes and private bank notes being eliminated.

The world is fast approximating to this state of affairs. In only two countries are reforms desirable. In the United States a variety of notes, including gold certificates, and even gold coins, still circulate. It would be a good example to the rest of the world if the notes of the Federal Reserve Banks were to supersede all other forms of currency. In France the law has made provision for the possible reintroduction of gold coins in the active circulation, and there are well-founded fears that the intention exists in some quarters to take advantage of this provision at a later date. If this were to be so, it would be, both in itself and as an example, a real misfortune.

The law aside, on what general principles should a Central Bank decide the appropriate amount of its free reserves ? What is the object of a gold reserve ? Partly, to provide liquid resources for use in ultimate emergencies—for this we would provide by our fixed minimum : partly, for merely psychological reasons, to promote confidence—though this object is easily exaggerated, since public opinion is always content with what it is used to, as, for example, in pre-war days the very small reserves of the Bank of England promoted just as much confidence as the very large reserves of the Bank of France, so that it is, indeed, a source of weakness to get the public into the habit of expecting the permanent and continuous maintenance of large free reserves : but mainly, to meet short-period fluctuations in the international balance of indebtedness, or, as it used to be called, the external drain.

It is, therefore, the criteria determining the amount appropriate to be held against the external drain to which we must address ourselves. In the long run, of course, an adverse balance of international indebtedness can only be redressed by the Central Bank taking measures to influence the volume of foreign lending and the volume of the foreign balance, on the lines discussed in Chapter 21. But such measures, unless they are undesirably drastic, take time to produce their effects. Moreover, there is often a temporary adverse balance, for seasonal or other passing reasons, which will redress itself in due course, and for which, therefore, provision should be made without upsetting the fundamental economic factors. Finally—if anything is to come of projects for the supernational regulation of the monetary situation— there are times when it is in the general interest that gold should be released and reserves reduced below their previous figure.

Thus a Central Bank must, in determining the normal level of its free reserves, consider the probable maximum amount of (a) the *sudden* fluctuations in the balance of international indebtedness which may occur before there is time to bring other safeguards into operation, and (b) the *temporary* fluctuations against which it ought to be unnecessary to make any fundamental readjustments. Neither of these things is likely to bear any stable relationship to the volume of money within the country, which will depend partly on the national income and partly on the national habits. They are governed, rather, by the magnitude and variability of the country's international business as traders, investors and financiers.

The classical investigations directed to determining on these lines the appropriate amount of a country's free reserves to meet an external drain are those which, twenty years ago, were the subject of memoranda by Sir Lionel Abrahams, the Financial Secretary of the India Office, who, faced with the difficult technical problems of preserving the exchange-stability of the rupee, was led by hard experience to the true theoretical solution. He caused to be established the Gold Standard Reserve, which was held separately from the Currency Note Reserve in order that it might be at the unfettered disposal of the authorities to meet exchange emergencies. In deciding the right amount for this reserve he endeavoured to arrive at a reasoned estimate of the magnitude of the drain which India might have to meet through the sudden withdrawal of foreign funds, or through a sudden drop in the value of Indian exports (particularly jute and, secondarily, wheat) as a result of bad harvests or poor prices.[1]

This is the sort of calculation which every Central Bank ought to make. The Bank of a country the exports of which are largely dependent on a small variety of crops highly variable in price and quantity —Brazil, for example—needs a larger free reserve than a country of varied trade, the aggregate volume of the exports and imports of which are fairly stable. The Bank of a country doing a large international financial and banking business—Great Britain, for example—needs a larger free reserve than a country which is little concerned with such business, say, Spain.

Prima facie the Bank of England needs a larger free reserve in proportion to the volume of money within the country than the Bank of France or the United States Federal Reserve System. In fact the Bank of England's free reserve is startlingly small. Formerly this state of affairs was justified by the consideration that the City of London was acting as a lender in the international bill market on a larger scale than as a borrower of foreign deposits, so that it was always within its power to redress the situation at short notice by revising the terms on which it would lend. Since the war foreign deposits in London have increased in magnitude very greatly, so that it is doubtful whether London is not sometimes borrowing on short term internationally more than she is lending. But the former justification for a narrow margin of reserves might, perhaps, be re-written to the effect that it is within the power of the City to redress a situation at short notice by revising the terms on which it will borrow.

It is, however, no part of my object in this chapter to discuss the practical problems of particular countries.

[1] *Vide* my *Indian Currency and Finance*, pp. 157 *et seq.*

The conclusion is that a country now holds a reserve in gold and foreign currency for no other purposes than as a war-chest and as a safeguard against being unduly sensitive to unexpected or temporary fluctuations in its immediate international indebtedness ; that the part of the reserve which is held for the latter purpose should be at the free disposal of the Central Bank ; and that its normal amount should be determined by reference to the probable magnitude, generously estimated, of the requirements it may have to meet—which are not likely to be measured by a proportion, such as 35 per cent, of that part of the note-issue which it would be practicable to withdraw from circulation at short notice.

CHAPTER 34

PROBLEMS OF INTERNATIONAL MANAGEMENT—I. THE RELATIONS OF CENTRAL BANKS TO ONE ANOTHER

In Chapters 2 and 25 we considered the limitations on the discretion of a member bank in a monetary system to " create " bank-money. We found that any individual bank is compelled—unless it is prepared to allow its reserve-ratio to be modified (up or down)—to " keep step " with the other banks of the system, including the Central Bank. They can all march forward together and they can all march backward together. A tentative movement in one direction or the other on the part of a single bank may confirm, strengthen or stimulate a tendency on the part of the other banks to move in the same direction. But a single bank cannot move far unless the others move too ; for otherwise its loss or gain of reserve-resources will rupture its reserve-ratio. Accordingly the total quantity of bank-money created is closely governed by whatever causes determine the aggregate of reserve-resources for the member banks as a whole.

Now the behaviour of an international system, made up of several national systems of member banks each clustering round its central bank, with a uniform currency standard, is essentially the same in principle as that of a closed national system. The discretion of the Central Banks in respect of their lending policies is limited by the effect of these policies on their reserves —on whether these policies are causing them to draw reserve-resources from, or to lose reserve-resources to, their neighbour Central Banks ; and there is a similar pressure on them to "keep step"—unless they are prepared to see their reserve - ratios modified. For since—by reason of our hypothesis of an international system—the customers of our Central Bank are in buying and selling, and in borrowing and lending, relations with the customers of other Central Banks, a "creation" of credit by the former bank will lead to a certain proportion of the claims against itself, which are thus brought into existence, falling into the hands of the customers of the other banks.

The laws and conventions subject to which Central Banks manage their reserves differ in practice in several important respects, as we shall see below, from those which we have assumed in dealing with Member Banks. But let us begin by considering what would happen if they were in all respects the same (except that there is no Bankers' Bank for Central Banks, so that they have to keep all their reserves in cash in their own vaults). In this case each Central Bank would have its rigid reserve-ratio, so that the aggregate quantity of Central Bank-Money in the world would be rigidly determined—assuming a gold standard—by the aggregate quantity of gold in the reserves of the Central Banks. If no gold was used in circulation, any variations would solely depend on the annual difference between the amount of new gold mined and the amount of gold consumed in the arts. If, on the other hand, gold circulated, there would be some ratio, more or less stable in the long run, between the amount of gold in circulation and the amount in reserve, the ratio being the weighted average for all the countries concerned of the various national ratios, such as that one which Governor Strong worked out for the United States (see p. 51).

Let us suppose, however, that so far as concerns new supplies of gold into the aggregate reserves the position is stable, in the sense that the annual increment of new gold approximately corresponds to the annual increment of the world's output of goods and services. Our Fundamental Equation shows that, even so, this would certainly not secure a stable price-level. The world's monetary system as a whole would still feel the effect of every inequality which might arise between the value of new investment throughout the world and the volume of saving throughout the world. Thus an appropriate regulation of the new supplies of gold would leave us still exposed to the full blasts of every Credit Cycle which blew, unless some further mitigating action were taken by the Central Bank acting in unison and with well-directed purpose. One or two Central Banks acting alone would not, unless they were very preponderant in size, be able to change the weather or direct the storm—any more than a single member bank can control the behaviour of a national system. If a single Central Bank lags behind in a boom it will be overwhelmed by excess reserve-resources, and if it steps ahead in a depression it will have its reserve-resources quickly drawn from it. The limit to its power, even granted its willingness to break away from its own normal reserve-ratio, will depend upon what proportion its surplus reserves bear to the aggregate surplus reserves of all the Central Banks.

The pre-war international gold standard did not, indeed, function very differently from a rigid-ratio system of member banks, subject to a gradual modification of the prevailing ratio (as suggested in Chapter 30, p. 205 above) under the influence of the relative scarcity or abundance of gold. The long-period price-level depended—after allowing for secular changes in other monetary factors—on whether the new gold available for the reserves was increasing faster or slower than the trade of gold-standard countries, which, in its turn, depended on the rate of the discovery of gold mines, the proportionate use of gold in circulation and the number of gold-standard countries, as well as on the growth of population and of trade per head; whilst the short-period price-level depended on whether the fluctuations in the second term of the Fundamental Equation were set in the direction of inflation or of deflation.

Nevertheless the behaviour of the pre-war system varied from this norm in numerous important particulars; and much more so the behaviour of the post-war system. We must, therefore, analyse those *differentiae* of Central Banks behaving as members of an international system, which do not exist or are not important when we are analysing the behaviour of member banks belonging to a national system. The principal points to notice are the three following:

(i.) The reserve-ratios of the Central Banks are not so rigid as we have found them to be in the case of Member Banks; for the conditions are not fulfilled which enable or induce the latter to keep their actual reserves in the near neighbourhood of their legal or conventional minimum. In the first place the Central Bank has not, generally speaking, a resort open to it for the rapid replenishment of its reserves corresponding to the Member Banks' facility for discounting (directly or indirectly) with the Central Bank. To the extent that Central Banks maintain balances abroad or interest-bearing assets other than gold, which are of such a character that they can be quickly sold to other Central Banks, the analogy between the position of Central Bank and that of a Member Bank is somewhat closer. This point we shall consider later, but it does not operate in most cases so as greatly to affect the validity of our generalisation.

In the second place a Central Bank is not aiming at maximum profit, as we have assumed that a Member Bank is. Thus all kinds of considerations of public policy and national advantage may influence it to keep a reserve in excess of the minimum required by law and even in excess of that required by reasonable prudence.

It follows that the reserve-ratios of Central Banks are capable of wide fluctuations. Some statistics showing how wide will be given below (p. 297).

(ii.) We assumed in the case of Member Banks that an individual bank could not rely, when it " created " bank-money, on a substantial proportion of this new money coming back to itself as increased deposits. Even when the number of leading banks is reduced so low as five, the proportion so returned is still a very moderate one. But in the case of a Central Bank, whose customers are primarily the Member Banks of its own national system and indirectly the individual citizens of its own national area, the proportion to be returned in this way may be, in the first instance, more substantial. Some part of the new money is sure to be spent or lent, directly or indirectly, abroad, and will therefore set up a tendency for the Central Bank to lose reserve-resources to other Central Banks. But how much gets transferred to the customers of other Central Banks will depend on the relative importance to local consumers of goods entering into foreign trade, on the extent to which tariffs interfere with the equalisation of the price-level at home and abroad, and on whether our country is a sensitive centre of international finance. Some Central Banks may have a considerable short-period latitude for independent action; others, as for example the Bank of England, much less.

(iii.) Between Central Banks there is a form of competition which we were able to ignore when we were discussing Member Banks. There is, of course, intense competition of various kinds between Member Banks to attract and retain depositors. But this does not as a rule take the form—at any rate in Great Britain —of the offer of competitive rates of interest at which an individual bank will lend or borrow. There is generally an agreement or understanding between the Banks as to the rate of interest which they will allow on deposits of a given type or will charge for loans of a given type. Undoubtedly there is a fringe of competitive bidding or price-cutting to attract or retain particular customers, generally *sub rosâ* and not disclosed to the bank's other customers. But there is no frank competition between their published interest-rates. There is the excellent reason for this, that, since it costs nothing to transfer funds from one bank to another, this form of competition might have a devastating effect on the profits of the banks all round. If it were not for a conventional abstention from this form of competition, an individual bank, finding that it was losing reserve-resources, might seek to protect its position by bidding for the transfer of savings-deposits from other banks or by driving its own borrowing customers away to other banks by its relatively high rates for accommodation (this latter course is, indeed, sometimes taken).

But however this may be as between the Member Banks of a national system, the practice of announcing competitive or deterrent interest-rates, in order to attract depositors or drive away borrowers from its own national banking system to those of other systems, is in regular use as between Central Banks—being one of the objects of Bank-rate policy. Changes in the relative bank-rates of different national systems will not, of course, easily move the vast mass of ordinary depositors or borrowers belonging to either system ; for they have no facilities for transferring their banking business at short notice from one country to another. But there is an important fringe of international financial business which can flow easily from one place to another according to the rates obtainable. Here, therefore, is a floating body of claims on international reserve-resources which any individual Central Bank is able to bid for when it is suffering an excessive loss of its own reserves. On the other hand, there are certain obstacles and expenses in the way of moving

even this body of claims from one international centre
to another—such as do not exist in the case of transfers
between Member Banks—which prevent the international movement of funds from being *too* sensitive
to differences of interest-rates, and constitute a certain
protection against too rapid or too excessive movements—a point which, as we shall see below (Section
(iii.) of Chapter 36), is of great importance to the
satisfactory working of the international system.

We can now see in broad outline how the position
and behaviour of Central Banks relatively to one
another differs from those of Member Banks within a
national system. Over short periods a Central Bank
has a greater discretion in the amount of bank-money
which it " creates " than a Member Bank has : firstly,
because it is more willing to vary its reserve-ratio ;
secondly, because, in some cases, more of its "creations"
come back to itself and go on doing so for a longer
period ; and thirdly, because the offer of competitive
rates of interest, wherewith to divert financial business
as between itself and other Central Banks, is available
to it as a regular and open expedient for the protection
of its reserve-resources. Since, however, the latitude
of a Central Bank is limited in each of these directions,
there are three things which it has to watch if it is to
be secure of being always able to meet claims maturing
against it in the hands of foreign monetary systems,
namely—(1) its reserve-ratio, (2) the effect of its
lending policy on the balance of trade on income
account, (3) the effect of its lending policy on the
movements both of long-term and of short-term international loans.

In a closed system a Central Bank could safely pursue
that lending policy which would achieve whatever it
might fix on as representing the economic optimum.
But in an international system it can only pursue this
policy within narrow limits and for short periods.
Where larger changes and longer periods are concerned,

its policy is necessarily governed by the policies of all
the other Central Banks. If a change of policy by one
Central Bank influences the other Banks in the same
direction, so that they follow suit, or, as I have expressed it above, keep step, well and good. But apart
from small movements and short periods, each Bank
is necessarily governed by the *average* policy of the
Banks as a whole. If our Bank is a large Bank, it
will contribute more to the average and so will get
more of its own way than a small Bank can. If our
Bank is ready to allow wide variations in the amount
of its reserve-resources, this greatly increases its power
to influence other Central Banks to keep step with it;
for it increases the length of time during which it can
persist with its own independent policy and the extent
by which it can increase or decrease the reserve-ratios
of the other Banks by decreasing or increasing its own.
Even in the case of a small Bank, the degree of its
short-period independence is much affected by the
hindrances—the nature of which will be discussed in
Chapter 36 (iii.) below—which it puts (or does not put)
on the movements of international short-loan funds in
and out of its system.

It is evident that the main effect of an international
gold standard (or any other international standard) is
to secure *uniformity* of movement in different countries
—everyone must conform to the average behaviour
of everyone else. The advantage of this is that it
prevents individual follies and eccentricities. The disadvantage is that it hampers each Central Bank in
tackling its own national problems, interferes with
pioneer improvements of policy the wisdom of which
is ahead of average wisdom, and does nothing to
secure either the short-period or the long-period optimum if the average behaviour is governed by blind
forces such as the total quantity of gold, or is hap-
hazard and without any concerted or deliberate policy
behind it on the part of the Central Banks as a body.

It has been observed that, when the gold standard is fully operative, Credit Cycles generally have an international character. We are now able to see that this must necessarily be so. No individual Central Bank can go very far either in the direction of Inflation or in that of Deflation unless the other Central Banks are moving, faster or slower, the same way. The International Gold Standard has no views on Inflation or Deflation as such. Its business is to ensure that no Central Bank shall inflate or deflate at a pace very different from that of its neighbours. By the law of average behaviour this may obviate major disturbances, but by the complexity it introduces and its lack of central direction it multiplies disturbances of intermediate magnitude.

An international system works particularly badly if the Central Banks, which are strong enough to dominate for a time the general *tempo* and to set the pace for the others, use this power to promote national policies which are out of keeping with the requirements of the international position as a whole. For this may bring about very violent disequilibria in the position of other Central Banks. The behaviour of the United States Federal Reserve System in 1929 and that of the Bank of France in 1930 were thought by some to be open to criticism from this point of view. So, I am sure, was the behaviour of the Bank of England at certain critical dates in the nineteenth century. Nevertheless we should, I think, be somewhat cautious in criticising a Central Bank for exercising in the interests of its own nationals powers which every Central Bank would like to possess and have an unfettered discretion to exercise if it chose. If the Bank of England had believed itself to have the power in 1928–29 to satisfy its domestic critics by pursuing a more liberal credit policy, would it have refrained from doing so for fear of adding fuel to the flames of a potential inflation in the United States ?

Would it have been prepared, that is to say, to keep the volume of employment in Great Britain below the optimum in order to promote stability in the United States ? Or when the Bank was pursuing a policy of deflation in the years preceding Great Britain's return to the gold standard, could it be expected—believing, as it did, that a return to gold on the pre-war parity at the earliest possible date was vital to the interests of Great Britain—to be much influenced by the fact that this policy was aggravating the problems of the rest of Europe ?

We must recognise, I think, that there can be a real divergence of interest; and we must not expect of Central Banks a degree of international disinterestedness far in advance of national sentiment and of the behaviour of the other organs of national government.

In the following chapters I shall seek, therefore, for a solution which is reasonably compatible with separate national interests.

CHAPTER 35

(i.) AURI SACRA FAMES

THE choice of gold as a standard of value is chiefly based on tradition. In the days before the evolution of Representative Money, it was natural, for reasons which have been many times told, to choose one or more of the metals as the most suitable commodity for holding a store of value or a command of purchasing power.

Some four or five thousand years ago the civilised world settled down to the use of gold, silver and copper for pounds, shillings and pence, but with silver in the first place of importance and copper in the second. The Mycenaeans put gold in the first place. Next, under Celtic or Dorian influences, came a brief invasion of iron in place of copper over Europe and the northern shores of the Mediterranean. With the Achaemenid Persian Empire, which maintained a bimetallic standard of gold and silver at a fixed ratio (until Alexander overturned them), the world settled down again to gold, silver and copper, with silver once more of predominant importance ; and there followed silver's long hegemony (except for a certain revival of the influence of gold in Roman Constantinople), chequered by imperfectly successful attempts at gold - and - silver bimetallism, especially in the eighteenth century and the first half of the nineteenth, and only concluded by the final victory of gold during the fifty years before the war.

Dr. Freud relates that there are peculiar reasons deep in our subconsciousness why gold in particular should satisfy strong instincts and serve as a symbol.[1] The magical properties, with which Egyptian priest-craft anciently imbued the yellow metal, it has never altogether lost. Yet, whilst gold as a store of value has always had devoted patrons, it is, as the sole standard of purchasing power, almost a parvenu. In 1914 gold had held this position in Great Britain *de jure* over less than a hundred years (though *de facto* for more than two hundred), and in most other countries over less than sixty. For except during rather brief intervals gold has been too scarce to serve the needs of the world's principal medium of currency. Gold is, and always has been, an extraordinarily scarce commodity. A modern liner could convey across the Atlantic in a single voyage all the gold which has been dredged or mined in seven thousand years. At intervals of five hundred or a thousand years a new source of supply has been discovered—the latter half of the nineteenth century was one of these epochs—and a temporary abundance has ensued. But as a rule, generally speaking, there has been not enough.

Of late years the *auri sacra fames* has sought to envelop itself in a garment of respectability as densely respectable as was ever met with, even in the realms of sex or religion. Whether this was first put on as a necessary armour to win the hard-won fight against bimetallism and is still worn, as the gold-advocates allege, because gold is the sole prophylactic against the

---

[1] For the Freudian theory of the love of money, and of gold in particular, *vide* Freud, *Collected Papers*, vol. ii., Clinical Paper No. IV. ; Ferenczi, *Bausteine zur Psychoanalyse*, vol. i., " Zur Ontogenie des Geldinteresses ", p. 109 *et seq.* ; and Ernest Jones, *Papers on Psycho-analysis*, chap. vii., " The Theory of Symbolism ", also chap. xl. The following prophecy, written by Dr. Jones in 1917, may be reckoned, perhaps, a success for the psycho-analytic method : " The ideas of possession and wealth, therefore, obstinately adhere to the idea of ' money ' and gold for definite psychological reasons. This superstitious attitude will cost England in particular many sacrifices after the war, when efforts will probably be made at all costs to reintroduce a gold currency " (*op. cit.* p. 172).

plague of fiat moneys, or whether it is a furtive Freudian cloak, we need not be curious to inquire. But before we proceed with a scientific and would-be unbiassed examination of its claims, we had better remind the reader of what he well knows—namely, that gold has become part of the apparatus of conservatism and is one of the matters which we cannot expect to see handled without prejudice.

One great change, nevertheless—probably, in the end, a fatal change — has been effected by our generation. During the war individuals threw their little stocks into the national melting-pots. Wars have sometimes served to disperse gold, as when Alexander scattered the temple hoards of Persia [1] or Pizarro those of the Incas.[2] But on this occasion war concentrated gold in the vaults of the Central Banks ; and these Banks have not released it. Thus, almost throughout the world, gold has been withdrawn from circulation. It no longer passes from hand to hand, and the touch of the metal has been taken away from men's greedy palms. The little household gods, who dwelt in purses and stockings and tin boxes, have been swallowed by a single golden image in each country, which lives underground and is not seen. Gold is out of sight—gone back again into the soil. But when gods are no longer seen in a yellow panoply walking the earth, we begin to rationalise them ; and it is not long before there is nothing left.

[1] The gold and silver reserves of the Persian Empire have been estimated at as much as £43,000,000 (this is the figure of E. Meyer, confirmed by Andréadès and other authorities). It was with these funds that Alexander waged his later campaigns (cf. Andréadès, " Les Finances de Guerre d'Alexander ", *Annales d'histoire économique*, July 1929), and it is no wonder that the release of this enormous sum into the active circulation should have had a catastrophic effect on the price-level. (When Alexander had set out a few years before to cross the Hellespont, he had less than £20,000 in his treasury !)

[2] Recent researches, however—by Mr. E. J. Hamilton (" Imports of American Gold and Silver into Spain, 1503–1660 ", *Quarterly Journal of Economics*, May 1929, p. 436)—seem to show that tradition has much exaggerated the quantity of such gold which reached Spain from South America.

Thus the long age of Commodity Money has at last passed finally away before the age of Representative Money. Gold has ceased to be a coin, a hoard, a tangible claim to wealth, of which the value cannot slip away so long as the hand of the individual clutches the material stuff. It has become a much more abstract thing—just a standard of value ; and it only keeps this nominal status by being handed round from time to time in quite small quantities amongst a group of Central Banks, on the occasions when one of them has been inflating or deflating its managed representative money in a different degree from what is appropriate to the behaviour of its neighbours. Even the handing round is becoming a little old-fashioned, being the occasion of unnecessary travelling expenses, and the most modern way, called " ear-marking ", is to change the ownership without shifting the location.[1] It is not a far step from this to the beginning of arrangements between Central Banks by which, without ever formally renouncing the rule of gold, the quantity of metal actually buried in their vaults may come to stand, by a modern alchemy, for what they please, and its value for what they choose. Thus gold, originally stationed in heaven with his consort silver, as Sun and Moon, having first doffed his sacred attributes and come to earth as an autocrat, may next descend to the sober status of a constitutional king with a cabinet of Banks ; and it may never be necessary to proclaim a Republic. But this is not yet—the evolution may be quite otherwise. The friends of gold will have to be extremely wise and moderate if they are to avoid a Revolution.

---

[1] The earliest example of " ear-marking " is in the case of the stone money of Rossel Island, which, being too heavy to move without difficulty, could be conveniently dealt with in no other way. One of the largest and most valuable of these stones lay at the bottom of the sea, the boat which was importing it having been capsized. But there being no doubt that the stone was there, these civilised islanders saw no objection to including it as a part of their stock of currency—its lawful owner at any time being, in fact, thereby established as the richest man in the island—or to changing its ownership by " ear-marking ".

(ii.) THE CASE FOR THE GOLD STANDARD

What is the case for gold in modern conditions and in the light of recent experience ?

(1) It is claimed for gold that it has been fairly successful over longish periods in maintaining a reasonable stability of purchasing power. I have briefly examined, and partially conceded, this claim in my *Tract on Monetary Reform* (pp. 164 *et seq.*). But this is certainly not to be attributed to any inherent tendency on the part of the supplies of the metal to keep step with the demand for it. As we have pointed out above, the periods prior to the development of Representative Money, during which the rate of supply of gold was such as to make it capable of serving the needs of the world's principal medium of currency, have been rare and intermittent. If any metal is to make this claim on the basis of long historical experience, it must be silver and not gold. The modern rule of gold is contemporary with the development of Representative Money. Such stability of price-levels—which was nothing to be proud of, far from it—which the gold standard can claim to have secured for the fifty years before the war, is certainly to be attributed in large measure to management on the part of the users of gold. During the first half of this period the various countries of the world were gradually adopting the gold standard, and the rate at which they did so was influenced by the relative abundance of the new supplies of gold ; and during the second half, when the use of Representative Money was rapidly becoming dominant, the rate of development of methods of " economising " the use of actual gold and the gold-basis of the Representative Money was influenced in the same way.

Thus I think it is an illusion to suppose that there are any special characteristics governing the supply of gold which make it likely to furnish automatically a stable standard of value, except the characteristic which it shares with all durable goods—namely, that the increment of the total supply in any year is likely to be very small. Apart from this, gold has depended, and will continue to depend, for its stability of value, not so much on the conditions of its supply, as on deliberate regulation of the demand.

Nevertheless, it may be useful to interpolate at this point the latest available data as to the present and prospective supply in relation to the world's requirements on the basis of existing practices.

Mr. Kitchin's estimate of the output of gold since the war and its distribution between different uses is shown in the table on the page opposite.[1]

The only respect in which these figures are open to possible criticism is in the estimate for the present annual consumption in the industrial arts. It may be that Mr. Kitchin has under-estimated the amount of gold, used in this way since the war, which has been supplied out of gold coins previously in circulation and gradually surrendered by their owners. It is arguable that the concealed supplies, which have thus come into the market from European countries, particularly France and Russia, have allowed a larger industrial consumption than Mr. Kitchin estimates—say £20,000,000 to £25,000,000 in place of £15,000,000.[2] If this is the case, the balance available for monetary purposes in the next ensuing years, as the above source of supply for the arts becomes steadily exhausted, may fall below Mr. Kitchin's figure of £50,000,000.

[1] This table is taken from the latest of Mr. Joseph Kitchin's very valuable estimates of gold statistics (*Review of Economic Statistics*, May 1929, pp. 64-67), with the exception of the figures for gold held by the Central Banks and Governments of forty countries, which have been compiled by the *Federal Reserve Bulletin*, June 1929, p. 396.

[2] Prof. Edie in his *Capital, the Money Market and Gold* (1929) has criticised Mr. Kitchin's conclusions along these lines. Prof. Edie's own figure—about £35,000,000 a year on the average of the fifteen years 1913 to 1928—may err, however, in the opposite direction. All estimates of the amount of gold coin in active circulation in 1913 must be open to a wide margin of error.

Unit: Millions of £ Sterling at 85 Shillings per Fine Ounce.

	1919.	1920.	1921.	1922.	1923.	1924.	1925.	1926.	1927.	1928.
I. OUTPUT:										
Transvaal	35·4	34·7	34·5	29·8	38·9	40·7	40·8	42·3	43·0	44·0
United States	12·4	10·5	10·3	9·7	10·4	10·4	9·9	9·5	9·0	9·3
Canada	3·3	3·3	3·9	5·4	5·2	6·5	7·4	7·5	7·8	7·9
Australasia	5·5	4·7	3·8	3·9	3·8	3·4	2·9	2·8	2·7	2·7
Other countries	18·4	15·8	15·5	16·7	17·2	20·0	20·0	19·9	20·0	20·1
Total World output	75·0	69·0	68·0	65·5	75·5	81·0	81·0	82·0	82·5	84·0
II. CONSUMPTION:										
Industrial arts [1]	23·0	22·0	15·0	17·0	17·0	16·0	15·0	16·0	15·0	15·0
India [2]	27·9	3·5	0·7	26·6	20·1	52·4	28·0	16·1	15·1	18·0
China and Egypt	11·5	−3·0	−2·2	1·2	1·5	0·2	1·3	−0·4	0·4	0·5
Consumed in arts and Orient	62·4	22·5	13·5	44·8	38·6	68·6	44·3	31·7	30·5	33·5
Balance available for money	12·6	46·5	54·5	20·7	36·9	12·4	36·7	50·3	52·0	50·5
Total World supply	75·0	69·0	68·0	65·5	75·5	81·0	81·0	82·0	82·5	84·0
III. WORLD'S STOCK OF GOLD MONEY: [3]										
Held by Central Banks and Governments of forty countries	..	..	..	1716	1769	1837	1832	1888	1960	2055
Elsewhere (including all gold in circulation)	..	..	..	327	311	256	297	292	272	227
Total	1922	1968	2023	2043	2080	2093	2129	2180	2232	2282

[1] Europe and America. [2] Year to March 31 following. [3] Dec. 31 of each year.

As regards future output, Mr. Kitchin estimates that, for the coming quinquennium, the output will be maintained at about its present figure, the increase in the New Rand about balancing the exhaustion of the Old Rand so as to leave the total output of the Transvaal unchanged, and moderate increases in Canada and Russia balancing declines in the rest of the world. After 1940 he expects a sharp decline.[1]   On this basis the past and prospective changes in the world's stock of monetary gold can be calculated as follows :

(£1,000,000)

World's Stock of Monetary Gold.   Increase in the Interval.

1867	£519	
		£255 in 26 years = 1·5% p.a.
1893	£774	
		£1135 in 25 years = 3·7% p.a.
1918	£1909	
		£373 in 10 years = 1·8% p.a.
1928	£2282	
		£290 in 6 years = 2·0% p.a.
1934	£2572	

The most usual guess as to the rate of the general economic development of the world is 3 per cent per annum—I think that it was Professor Cassel who made himself responsible for this guess.   If this is roughly right,[2] the new supply of gold will not be adequate,

[1] Now that the world's supplies of alluvial gold have been almost exhausted, there is a very long time-lag between the discovery of new sources and actual supply ;—a modern mine in the Rand costs nearly £2,000,000 and takes six or seven years to sink before commencing output. Moreover, it would need a large change in the costs of production to prolong materially the life of existing mines. Thus forecasts for five, and even ten, years ahead can be made with some accuracy.

[2] For the output of raw materials and the volume of trade which get into the statistics, it seems about right. But it may be much too high if we include the vastly greater volume of unrecorded activities. The population of the world is increasing by about 1 per cent. Surely it is not plausible to maintain that the average standard of life of the human race, including Asia and Africa, is rising at the rate of 2 per cent cumulative. On the other hand, it is the statistically recorded activities which are most relevant to the demand for money.

assuming unchanged monetary practices, to maintain the price-level, and there will be a long-period downward trend of 1 per cent per annum (cumulative). But we need not, in my judgment, attach so much importance to this as to the fact that more than 90 per cent of the monetary gold of the world is now held by Central Banks and Governments, and that the distribution of this sum between different countries is exceedingly uneven and bears no steady proportion to the volume of their economic activities, as is shown in the following table : [1]

(£1,000,000)

	Gold in Banks and Treasuries and in circulation. End 1913.	Gold in Central Banks and Treasuries.				
		End 1913.	End 1919.	End 1927.	End 1928.	End 1929.
United States . .	392	266	520	818	770	800
France . .	304	140	143	196	258	336
Great Britain . .	150	35	120	152	153	146
Germany . . .	184	57	54	92	134	112
Japan . . .	17	13	72	111	111	109
Spain . . .	19	19	97	103	102	102
Argentine . .	59	53	69	109	125	91
Italy . . .	55	55	41	49	55	56
Netherlands . .	13	12	53	33	36	37
Belgium . . .	16	12	11	20	26	34
Russia . . .	211	162	?	20	19	31
Switzerland . .	9	7	20	20	21	24
Australia . .	15	4	24	22	22	18
Poland . . .	..	..	..	12	14	16
Java . . .	2	2	14	15	14	14
Sweden . . .	6	6	15	13	13	13
Austria and Hungary .	52	52	9	9	12	11
Denmark . . .	4	4	13	10	9	10
South Africa . .	8	8	7	8	8	8
Czechoslovakia . .	..	..	..	6	7	8
Norway . . .	2	2	8	103	8	7
Other countries . .	61	56	65	103	105	85
Total . .	1579	965	1355	1929	2022	2078

[1] From the *Economist*, Feb. 15, 1930, the figures being extracted from the *Federal Reserve Bulletin* and other sources.

The percentage distribution of gold between the leading countries at end of each year was as follows :

Country.	1913. (a)	1913. (b)	1919.	1927.	1928.	1929.
United Kingdom	9·5%	3·6%	8·9%	7·9%	7·6%	7·0%
France	19·5	14·5	10·5	10·2	12·7	16·2
Germany	11·7	5·9	4·0	4·8	6·6	5·4
United States	24·8	27·6	38·4	42·4	38·0	38·5
Argentine	3·7	5·5	5·1	5·7	6·2	4·4
Japan	1·1	1·3	5·3	5·8	5·5	5·2
Other countries	29·7	41·6	27·8	23·2	23·4	23·3

1913 : (a) Gold in banks and treasuries and in circulation.
(b) Gold in central banks and treasuries.

It appears from these tables that more than half of the total monetary gold in the world is in the United States and France. Moreover, during the last three and a half years France alone has absorbed considerably more than the whole of the new monetary gold becoming available. On the other hand, for six and a half years (*i.e.* since December 1923) the gold holdings of the United States and Great Britain have remained practically stationary. If we consider only the near future, say the next five years, it is evident that the policy of individual Central Banks towards increasing or decreasing their own reserves is likely to be the decisive factor. The new gold will be enough or not enough, according to the decisions taken by the Central Institutions of the United States and France.

I do not, however, attribute decisive importance to the statistical outlook, one way or the other. The most disastrous price fluctuations of modern times have been those associated with Profit (or Commodity) Inflations and Deflations ; and these, whilst they may have been indirectly connected with fluctuations in the supply of the metal gold, have directly depended on the combined effect of the policies of the world's Central Banks taken as a whole on the market-rate of interest in relation to the natural-rate. The long-period tendency of price-levels up or down, which is more likely than the short-period movements to be influenced, even with Representative Money, by the long-period supply of the metal, is of secondary importance to economic welfare compared with the Profit Inflations and Deflations which mark the short and intermediate periods. Thus the International Gold Standard must stand or fall rather by its capacity for dealing with these disturbances—a matter which we shall take up in more detail in subsequent chapters.

(2) It is claimed for gold that it keeps slovenly currency systems up to the mark. It limits the discretion and fetters the independent action of the Government or Central Bank of any country which has bound itself to the international gold standard. It may not be the ideal system, but—the argument runs —it maintains a certain standard of efficiency and avoids violent disturbances and gross aberrations of policy.

So long as a country continues to adhere to the gold standard, there is force in this. But experience —an experience covering much ground and subject to scarcely any exceptions—shows that, when severe stress comes, the gold standard is usually suspended. There is little evidence to support the view that authorities who cannot be trusted to run a nationally managed standard, can be trusted to run an international gold standard. Indeed the presumption— there can be no evidence as yet of something which has never, so far, been tried—is rather to the contrary. For a nationally managed standard would not subject the country's internal economy to such violent strains as those to which the attempt to continue to conform to an international standard may subject it ; so that the inherent difficulty and the necessary sacrifice will be less in the former case than in the latter.

Moreover, even if an international gold standard does serve to keep slovenly countries up to the mark, it may also keep progressive countries below the standard of monetary management which they might otherwise attain.　Thus the gold standard is, as I have said above, part of the apparatus of Conservatism. For Conservatism is always more concerned to prevent backsliding from that degree of progress which human institutions have already attained, than to promote progress in those quarters which are ready for progress, at the risk of " upsetting the ideas " of the weaker brethren and bringing into question precarious and hard-won conventions which have the merit that they do at least preserve a certain modicum of decent behaviour.

(3) In the main, however, the case for an international gold standard—or some intelligent and scientific modification of it which can still claim the name—must stand or fall, I think, by the answer we give to the question whether the ideal standard of value—whatever it may be in other respects—should be of an international character.　For if we attach great importance to our standard of value being an international one, then it is improbable for many years to come that we could secure international adhesion to any standard which was not in some way linked to gold.　Moreover, if we could once overcome the many obstacles in the way of a scientifically managed world system, it would not add much to our difficulties to give it a gold camouflage.　Provided that the world's currency system is managed with plenary wisdom by a supernational body, and provided that, as a part of this scheme, gold is everywhere excluded from the active circulation, then—since we can make the gold standard worth what we choose— the ideal standard of value, whatever that may be, is compatible with the forms of a gold standard of value ; —it is only necessary for the Supernational Authority so to manage gold as to conform to the ideal standard. The formal homage and the courtesy title which we

offer to gold may involve a certain annual expenditure on purchasing the current output of the mines ; but this is the worst that can happen.

But is it certain that the ideal standard is an international standard ? It has been usual to assume that the answer is so obviously in the affirmative as to need no argument. I do not know where it has been questioned, except in my own *Tract on Monetary Reform*, Chapter iv. The conveniences and facilities which an international standard offers to foreign trade and foreign investment is thought sufficient to clinch the matter. The lack of an international standard of value is assumed to be just one more of these foolish hindrances to international mobility, such as tariffs, which can only serve to impoverish the whole world in the misguided attempt to benefit some separate part of it.

To the considerations which can be advanced on the other side, but which are commonly overlooked, we must attempt to do justice in our next chapter.

CHAPTER 36

PROBLEMS OF INTERNATIONAL MANAGEMENT— III. THE PROBLEM OF NATIONAL AUTONOMY

(i.) THE DILEMMA OF AN INTERNATIONAL SYSTEM

WE have seen that the Management of Money, national or international, always presents a dual aspect. There are the long-period movements in the equilibrium price-level, *i.e.* in the level of efficiency-earnings, due to permanent changes in the quantities of the monetary factors relatively to the volume of output. And there are the short-period movements round the long-period trend of the equilibrium price-level due to the temporary disequilibrium of the investment factors, which we have summed up in brief as the Credit Cycle.

Now, so far as the first aspect is concerned, membership of an international system necessarily binds the long-period value of the local money to the long-period value of the international standard. This must be accepted as inevitable, and also, if one believes in the virtues of an international standard, as desirable. But, as regards the second aspect, each country naturally wishes to save itself from temporary disturbances as much as it possibly can. When investment disequilibria are being initiated within its own borders, it will endeavour to counteract them, whatever may be happening abroad ; and when investment disequilibria are arising outside its own borders, it will endeavour not to share them. Since, therefore, investment disequilibria do not arise everywhere in the same degree at the same time, a given national system may be under an incentive to take measures to preserve its own investment equilibrium, which may not suit other members of the same international system.

The natural desire thus arising for short-period independence presents great difficulties. For it is, as we have seen, of the essence of membership of an international system that international equilibrium ($i.e.$ $G = 0$), in the sense of equality between a country's foreign lending and its foreign balance, requires that the main criterion of the banking policy of each member should be the average behaviour of all the other members, its own voluntary and independent contribution to the final result being a modest one. If any country departs from this criterion, then it is inevitable that there must be movements of gold.

Perhaps the difficulty can be made vivid by assuming a perfectly mobile international monetary system, in the sense that the rate of every foreign exchange is rigidly fixed, so that there is no expense in remitting funds from one country to another, and that the financiers of every country are completely indifferent as to where they lend their money, merely seeking the highest rate of interest. It is evident that in such conditions the rate of interest would have to be the same throughout the world. If any country tried to maintain a higher rate than its neighbours, gold would flow towards it until either it gave way or the international system broke down by its having absorbed all the gold in the world. And if it tried to maintain a lower rate, gold would flow out until either it gave way or had to leave the international system through having lost all its gold. Thus the degree of its power of independent action would have no relation to its local needs.

Yet, as we have seen previously, circumstances may exist in which, if a country's rate of interest is fixed for it by outside circumstances, it is impracticable for it to reach investment equilibrium at home. This will happen if its foreign balance is inelastic, and if, at the same time, it is unable to absorb the whole of its savings in new investment at the world rate of interest. It will also tend to happen even where the foreign balance is elastic, if its money costs of production are sticky. There are, moreover, all sorts of other reasons why the day-to-day preservation of local investment equilibrium may require some departure of the local rate of interest from the international rate.

This, then, is the dilemma of an international monetary system — to preserve the advantages of the stability of the local currencies of the various members of the system in terms of the international standard, and to preserve at the same time an adequate local autonomy for each member over its domestic rate of interest and its volume of foreign lending.

I fancy that some advocates of the general return to gold after the war did not fully foresee how great the urge would be towards local autonomy and independent action. They conceived that a sort of automatic stability would be attained by everyone voluntarily agreeing, or being practically compelled, to govern his behaviour in conformity with the average behaviour of the system as a whole. The ideal working of the gold standard from this point of view would be one in which there was never a necessity for any movement of gold (apart from the distribution of the newly mined gold in appropriate proportions). For the maximum degree of automatic action along these lines would be attained if every Central Bank were to surrender its right of independent action to the extent of agreeing that it would always so regulate its credit policy that no appreciable quantity of gold would ever flow either into or out of its vaults—a result which would be sufficiently attained in practice if every Central Bank were to cause or to allow the inflow or outflow of gold to produce as much effect as possible on its terms of credit, *e.g.* by causing it to move its bank-rate up or down, as the case might be, to whatever extent might be necessary to reverse the movement of gold.

Governor Strong, for example, before the United States Committee of Congress on Stabilisation in 1927, testified as follows :

" In course of time, when the return to the Gold Standard by former gold standard countries begins to be felt upon prices throughout the world, and there is the readjustment of bank reserves resulting from that, then I think a very important step towards stabilisation of prices will have been taken.[1] . . . Under conditions such as have existed since the war, where there is not a free movement of gold between the nations, you cannot expect to bring about that more or less automatic stability which comes by readjustments of domestic and world prices.   Until we get back to the automatic flow of gold which affects bank reserves and brings into play the automatic reactions from loss of reserves, I do not believe we are going to have all the satisfaction from the Federal Reserve System that we will have after that time comes.[2] . . . I have great confidence that when the time comes to conduct these things as they were in former years, a lot of the need for the type of management which has to be applied in the present situation will be eliminated.   It will be more automatic.   We won't have to depend so much on judgment, and we can rely more upon the play of natural forces and their reaction on prices such as I have very roughly and inadequately described." [3]

Something of the same philosophy and the same expectations lay, perhaps, behind Dr. Miller's evidence on the same occasion :

" The gold standard means more than a legal undertaking to redeem the currency and credit of a nation in gold.   The gold standard, to my mind, means a device which acts as a kind of regulating and levelling influence, so as to keep the price level, credit conditions, and the currency situation in all countries that are of the group that have the gold standard in some sort of proper alignment to one another.   To me, the

[1] Report of Commissioners, p. 306.   [2] *Op. cit.* p. 378.
[3] *Op. cit.* p. 379.

gold standard means a set of practices, a system of procedure, never formulated, never consciously thought out, not invented by anybody, but the growth of experience of the great commercial countries of the world, rather than merely the employment of gold to redeem all forms of obligations." [1]

It is on some such assumptions as these as to what the International Gold Standard ought to mean, that accusations are sometimes made against the United States or against France, that they are breaking the rules of the " Gold Standard game ", when in recent times they have, for purely local and domestic reasons, chosen to pursue a credit policy which attracted large quantities of gold to their vaults without allowing this influx materially to modify their policy. Yet it may be too much to expect that these countries will voluntarily sacrifice what they believe to be their own interests, in order to pursue a credit policy which would suit certain other countries better. I shall argue, therefore, in what follows, that the solution is to be sought, not by making such demands, but by arranging some compromise in virtue of which adherence to an international standard is combined in a regular and legitimate way with a reasonable measure of local autonomy over the rate of foreign lending. To this objective—which is one that each country must work out in detail for itself—we will now direct our attention.

(ii.) Methods of Regulating the Rate of Foreign Lending

The dilemma which I have presented in the previous section is a novel one only, perhaps, to Great Britain. During the latter half of the nineteenth century the influence of London on credit conditions throughout the world was so predominant that the Bank of England could almost have claimed to be

---

[1] *Op. cit.* p. 693.

the conductor of the international orchestra. By modifying the terms on which she was prepared to lend, aided by her own readiness to vary the volume of her gold reserves and the unreadiness of other Central Banks to vary the volume of theirs, she could to a large extent determine the credit conditions prevailing elsewhere.

This power to call the tune, coupled with certain other characteristics of the period which we have examined in Chapter 21, put Great Britain in a position to afford a degree of *laissez-faire* towards foreign lending which other countries could not imitate. Thus for her it was a rare event for the dilemma to present itself in an acute form—sufficiently rare for her to be able to ignore it as a general problem of policy. Indeed her economists were scarcely aware of its existence either for herself or for others. They attributed the actual success of her *laissez-faire* policy, not to the transitory peculiarities of her position, but to the sovereign virtues of *laissez-faire* as such. That other countries did not follow her example was deemed—like their bias towards protective tariffs—to be an indication of their inferior political wisdom.

But to-day, unfortunately, the position is considerably changed. The United States has successfully established the Federal Reserve System, and has used her rapidly growing wealth to convert herself from a debtor to a creditor nation and to accumulate at the same time a large proportion of the world's stock of gold. The magnanimity of Great Britain and her readiness to make sacrifices to promote the pacification of post-war Europe (and also to satisfy her own financial pride) have ended in making France and the United States the main creditors in the financial settlements arising out of the war to the total exclusion of herself, although her financial efforts during the war were

the greatest of all.   Even though London still remains
the most influential financial centre in the world,
even though Great Britain still (I speak of 1929)
has a surplus for new foreign investment half as
great again as that possessed by any other country,
including the United States, her relative importance
in influencing credit conditions throughout the world
is, inevitably, not what it was.

Thus she too must now face the dilemma.   Moreover, her rash act, in returning to the gold standard
in such conditions that her existing level of incomes
in terms of gold was out of equilibrium with the
levels of gold incomes in other countries as fixed by
the terms on which they respectively were to return
to the gold standard, has presented her with it in a
form much more acute, for the time being, than was
ever likely to have arisen if all the countries concerned
had maintained the same international standard continuously over a period of years.

Yet her traditional belief in *laissez-faire* in such
matters, and the established forms of her financial
organisation, make it extraordinarily difficult for
her to face it.   The mentality of the City is deeply
impregnated with simple-minded maxims, such as one
still reads in old-fashioned financial weeklies, to the
effect that foreign lending generates almost automatically a corresponding increase in the foreign balance.

Let us consider the various devices which are
available for preventing the fluctuations in the rate
of a country's foreign lending (or borrowing), imposed
on it by the mobility consequent on its adhering
to an international monetary standard, from interfering unduly with its own domestic equilibrium.
But let me preface this with a restatement of the
nature of the problem.

An international monetary standard greatly facili-
tates the lending of money between one country and
another, by minimising the expenses and the risks.

In modern times, when large reserves are held by capitalists in a liquid form, comparatively small changes in the rate of interest in one centre relatively to the rate in others may swing a large volume of lending from one to the other. That is to say, the amount of foreign lending is highly sensitive to small changes. The amount of the foreign balance, on the other hand, is by no means so sensitive. It is not easy for a country suddenly to contract its imports or suddenly to expand its markets even by a sharp reduction of prices. The prevalence of high protective tariffs aggravates the difficulty. It is, therefore, impracticable to bring about a change in the foreign balance great enough to balance the change in foreign lending which even a small stimulus may provoke. This high degree of short-period mobility of international lending, combined with a low degree of short-period mobility of international trade, means—failing steps to deal with the former—that even a small and temporary divergence in the local rate of interest from the international rate may be dangerous. In this way adherence to an international standard tends to limit unduly the power of a Central Bank to deal with its own domestic situation so as to maintain internal stability and the optimum of employment.

The problem presents itself in different forms to debtor and to creditor nations respectively. It is likely to prove more severe and intractable in the case of a debtor nation than in the case of a creditor nation, because it is easier to lend less in an emergency than to borrow more. Indeed, when the crisis comes to a debtor nation it results nine times out of ten in its temporarily abandoning its international standard. One of the few " tenth " cases has been, so far, India, which has got through difficult moments partly through the advantages arising out of the official position of the India Office in London, and

partly because she has built up a large foreign reserve
for the express purpose of tiding over short-period
differences between the debit foreign balance and
foreign borrowing. In what follows, however, we
shall treat the problem primarily from the standpoint of a creditor nation.

The possible remedies may be divided into—(i.)
those whereby the authorities *offset* the action of
the market, and (ii.) those whereby the authorities
influence the action of the market.

(i.) The first class comprises the various ways
by which a Central Bank can fortify itself with a
command over liquid foreign resources, so that it
can vary the amount of these on a large scale and
thus offset inconvenient fluctuations in the rate of
foreign lending (short-term or long-term) by the
market, namely :

(*a*) By holding gold reserves largely in excess of
its legal minimum and *being willing to allow this
excess to suffer wide fluctuations*. Most Central Banks
have, as we have already seen, far too much of their
stock of gold locked up by legal restrictions, so that
the free portion is not adequate ; and many banks
are not even willing to use that free portion with
any readiness. The only institution which has
made full use hitherto of this particular expedient,
namely, large excess reserves freely used, is the
Federal Reserve Board of the United States—to the
great advantage of its domestic stability. Since
there is not enough gold available for all Central
Banks to increase their free stock to a figure greatly
in excess of their present legal requirements, there
is no all-round remedy along these lines—except
by a general reduction of the legal requirements.
We have discussed this matter in Chapter 33. There
may be a sound reason for keeping a certain quantity
of gold as a last resort. But the amounts actually
locked up have probably been fixed, not as the result

of a careful calculation of need, but on considerations of fashion and respectability. We need an edict by the arbiters of fashion, who are none other than the Central Banks themselves (and their governments) acting in agreement, that legal reserves may now be fixed lower.

(b) By holding large liquid balances in foreign centres, i.e. by gold - exchange management, and being willing to allow these balances to suffer wide fluctuations. This expedient is in fact employed to-day on a large scale. We have discussed certain aspects of it in Chapter 21 (v.) above.

(c) By arranging over-draft facilities with other Central Banks. This expedient was adopted when Great Britain returned to the gold standard, such facilities to cover a period of two years being arranged with Messrs. J. P. Morgan of New York and with the Federal Reserve Bank of New York. Other countries have made corresponding arrangements on similar occasions. This resource always lies in the background, but it is probably one which Central Banks will be slow and reluctant to use save on quite exceptional occasions.

(d) By borrowing and lending arrangements between Central Banks and a Supernational Bank. There may be great hopes in this for the future. I return to the question in Chapter 38 below.

(ii.) The second class comprises the ways by which the market can be influenced to regulate the rate of its net foreign lending in accordance with the wishes and the policy of the Central Bank, namely :

(a) The established organisation of a country's securities market should obviously be adapted to its normal capacity for foreign lending. In steady times a process of evolution will have brought this about. But when changes are taking place, there may be an interval of maladjustment. To-day the London securities market may be excessively orientated towards foreign issues—as a consequence of the past experience and connections of the large issue houses and the habits of the large professional investors such as Insurance Companies and Investment Trusts ; so that there is a bias towards an excessive volume of foreign lending relatively to Great Britain's present foreign balance. In the United States, on the other hand, and especially in France, as a result partly of her unfortunate pre-war experiences in the foreign field and partly of a deliberate prohibition of foreign investment during the collapse of the franc, the opposite is the case. For habit and organisation play a large part—as large a part, perhaps, as intrinsic merit—in determining the direction of lending.

(b) Under present conditions of high direct taxation, the relative attractions of home and foreign securities may be materially affected by discriminatory taxation. This has played an important part in France. It may be necessary in Great Britain as a counterweight to the existing bias of habit and organisation towards foreign securities.

And it may also be necessary as a counterweight to another tendency. *Laissez-faire* towards foreign investment means that the net rate of interest will tend to the same level everywhere, apart from risks, etc. Consequently, quantities of labour of equal efficiency must be combined with equal quantities of capital in all countries, with the result that the marginal efficiency of labour will be the same everywhere, and hence labour's share of the product. Thus if lending is mobile internationally and the risks the same, efficiency-wages must tend to the same level everywhere. Otherwise, foreign lending by the country where efficiency-wages are relatively high will tend to exceed its foreign balance, thus requiring a Profit Deflation to preserve its stock of gold, until by the pressure of unemployment an Income Deflation ensues and wages are eventually brought down to the same level as elsewhere. This means that the workers in an old country cannot obtain directly the benefit of its large capital accumulation, in the shape of higher wages, ahead of the workers in the rest of the world— except in so far as there is a drag on foreign lending due to the unfamiliarity of its investors with foreign outlets, to the risks, real or supposed, of lending abroad, or to discriminatory taxation (and the like) against such lending. Unrestricted foreign lending may lead to the more rapid growth of a country's wealth, but it does this by putting off the day at which the workers in the country can enjoy, in the shape of higher wages, the advantages of this growing accumulation of capital. Nineteenth-century philosophy was wont to assume that the future is always to be preferred to the present. But modern communities are more inclined to claim the right to decide for themselves in what measure they shall subscribe to this austere doctrine.

(c) The two factors just considered are of a long-period character. What is more important, as a means of meeting the essential problem which we are discussing in this chapter, is a method of regulating the rate of foreign lending day by day in the interests of domestic short-period equilibrium. I offer, therefore, the following suggestions to this end.

(a) There is, first of all, the control of the rate of long-term foreign lending, i.e. the rate of purchase of foreign securities of the type which is held by investors. So far as the public issue of new foreign securities on the domestic market is concerned, there is already a formal or informal control in the chief lending countries. In France the official control, which is exercised both by the Treasury and by the Foreign Office, has been in recent years so tight as, in combination with punitive taxation, to strangle the new issue market altogether; and there are proposals for relaxing it. In the United States there is now an established custom by which the acquiescence of the Treasury is obtained before the offer of any new foreign issue. In London the Bank of England has on several occasions since the war —I am not aware that such a thing ever occurred before the war—imposed, without the aid of legislation and solely by the exercise of its authority with the issue houses, an effective embargo on the public issue of new foreign loans ; and, apart from these embargoes directed to the almost complete cessation of foreign lending for the time being, a practice has gradually grown up by which the Bank of England is regularly consulted beforehand about new foreign issues of any magnitude, and uses this opportunity to regulate the rate at which they are offered.

Whilst this informal method is quite effective within its own field of operation, *i.e.* in regulating the rate at which foreign issues are publicly offered in the London market, it is unpopular, and also incompletely effective, for the wider and more important purpose of regulating the rate of Great Britain's *total* foreign lending, because it does not apply to the purchase by the public or by investment institutions of securities on foreign Stock Exchanges, particularly Wall Street, which have never been issued in London. In actual recent experience a very large volume of foreign bonds issued in New York have been purchased, sooner or later, by London. It is evident that in so far as an embargo, total or partial, merely causes a diversion of the channels through which securities are purchased, it is harmful to the financial centre imposing it—since its financiers lose the valuable profits of issue and its Treasury the valuable receipts from stamp duties on issue and transfer.

Just dissatisfaction at such results joins with the tradition of *laissez-faire* to deprecate altogether the

machinery of control. But it would be wiser, I
believe, to perfect the control than to abandon it.
I suggest that this might be done by prescribing that
in future foreign bonds (meaning by this the fixed-
interest securities of overseas governments and
public authorities and of companies or corporations
which are not registered as British companies) should
not be dealt in on any Stock Exchange except with
the prior approval of the Bank of England ; [1] and
that British holders of securities which have not
received the *imprimatur* of the Bank of England
should pay an additional income-tax of (say) two
shillings in the £ on income received from such
securities. Such a tax would be justifiable, quite
apart from the object of improving the Bank of
England's control over the rate of foreign lending,
to balance the avoidance of stamp duties when bonds
are purchased abroad ;—for it is an anomaly that
foreign bonds purchased by Englishmen in New
York should escape taxation levied on similar transactions carried out in London.

(β) Secondly, there is the control of the rate of
short - term foreign lending. This has, of course,
always been a matter of first-rate importance. But
it presents to-day a far more difficult problem than
formerly. There are now two centres of equal importance for international short-term funds, namely,
London and New York, instead of London alone in
a position of unchallenged predominance, so that there
is an ever-present possibility of large movements
between the two centres. In the second place, the
character of the international short-loan market
has—so one gathers—undergone a change. An international centre to-day, whether it be London or New
York, is at least as much a debtor as a creditor
(probably more so), *vis-à-vis* the rest of the world.

---

[1] Such approval should, of course, convey no opinion as to the merit of the
security offered.

I fancy that even in the nineteenth century London's position in this respect was a more balanced one than we were then taught to believe, and that foreign short-term funds employed in London were not far short of the volume of foreign business financed through British holdings of sterling bills drawn in respect of trade which was not specifically British. To-day, it is certain that an international short-term market is a depository of funds, which foreigners wish to keep liquid, on a much greater scale than that on which it is a source of short-term borrowing by foreigners through its acceptances for them. Thus it is very much at the mercy of the initiative of its foreign clients, according as they wish to change between long-term and short-term assets, between short-term assets and gold, and between one international centre and another. It is a sort of banking business, which requires on the part of those who carry it on both an ability and a willingness to see substantial fluctuations from time to time in their stock of gold and other liquid reserves. Those who carry it on will also find it advisable, in my judgment, to segregate it so far as they can from the operations of their domestic industry and trade.

In the third place, the scale of the international short-loan fund has been vastly increased. There are no exact statistics. But I should estimate its magnitude at the end of 1929 as being not less than £1,000,000,000, of which £600,000,000 was in New York, £300,000,000 in London and £100,000,000 elsewhere ; though there is, of course, a fair amount of duplication in this, in the sense that country A will hold balances in country B, and at the same time country B will hold balances in country A. Only in the case of the United States has there been any attempt to compile the statistics of a country's gross and net short-loan position. The results, as published by the Department of Commerce (Trade

Information Bulletin, No. 698, by Ray Hall), are so instructive as to deserve reproduction :

DUE FROM " FOREIGNERS " TO " AMERICANS "[1]

$1000.

	Dec. 31, 1928.	Dec. 31, 1929.
American deposits with foreigners .	198,588	189,740
Liabilities of American banks for un-matured bills, drawn by foreigners and accepted by American banks .	508,822	768,942
Overdrafts by foreigners . .	255,373	202,348
Other short-term loans and advances	318,762	285,460
American short-term funds put out in foreign money markets . .	24,077	37,357
Total short-term funds due from abroad	1,305,622	1,483,847

DUE TO " FOREIGNERS " FROM " AMERICANS "

$1000.

	Dec. 31, 1928.	Dec. 31, 1929.
Foreign deposits with Americans .	1,580,481	1,652,858
Unmatured bills drawn by Americans, accepted abroad and discounted there	93,356	72,238
Foreign funds put out in American market into American acceptances	564,601	891,132
Foreign funds put out in American market into brokers' loans . .	332,888	270,627
Foreign funds put out in American market into Treasury certificates .	166,319	61,827
Foreign funds put out in American market into other short-term loans	12,176	8,817
Undiscounted foreign-drawn accept-ances held for collection by Ameri-can banks [2]	99,247	104,938
Sundry	47,152	24,844
Total short-term funds due to foreigners	2,896,220	3,087,281
Net short-term indebtedness to foreigners on banking account .	1,590,598	1,603,434

[1] The foreign branch of an American bank is a " foreigner " ; an American branch of a foreign bank is an " American ".

[2] A corrective entry offsetting the second item of the table of sums due from foreigners.

It is evident that a movement of (say) 10 per cent of the gross debt of the New York money market to foreigners is a formidable affair, both for the payer-out and for the recipient, and represents what is absolutely a large sum relatively to any possible short-period change in the foreign balance. But if movements of short-term funds cannot be offset by corresponding changes in the foreign balances of the countries concerned, it follows that the rate of interest must be so fixed that the movements are not greater than can be offset by opposite movements of other short-term funds or of long-term funds or of gold. Yet it may well be the case that the rate of interest determined by the resultant of these forces is not the optimum rate for maintaining the equilibrium of domestic industry.

In the case of Great Britain two reforms seem to be necessary. Exact information, compiled monthly on the same lines as the American statement quoted above, as to the magnitude and movements of London's international banking position is essential. At present no one knows the amount of London's short-term liabilities to foreigners, either net or gross, or whether they are increasing or diminishing. Yet, it must be impossible for the Bank of England to manage its bank-rate policy and its open-market operations efficiently without this information. It is —literally—as though the head office of a bank, with branches doing business all over the country, were to manage its policy and maintain its reserves without any regular source of information as to the volume of its deposits or whether they were increasing or decreasing.

The second reform would consist in some device whereby London's international deposit business and the means of controlling it could be, in some measure, segregated from the domestic business arising out of British trade and industry, so that every change in the terms offered with a view to regulating the former need not react to its full extent on the terms asked for credit applicable to the latter. This objective presents a severe technical problem. Credit is like water ;—whilst it may be used for a multiplicity of purposes, it is in itself undifferentiated, can drip through crannies, and will remorselessly seek its own level over the whole field unless the parts of the field are rendered uncompromisingly water-tight,—which in the case of credit is scarcely possible. I have, however, a suggestion to make which I reckon of sufficient importance to deserve a separate section.

(iii.) The Significance of the Gold Points

We have seen that, if rates of exchange were absolutely fixed, so that it cost nothing to exchange the money of one country into the money of another, exactly the same rate of interest would always prevail in both countries for loans of the same type and believed to offer the same security. If such conditions were to prevail between all countries, each change occurring anywhere in the conditions of borrowing and lending would be reflected by a change in the Bank-rate and Bond-rate everywhere. Every puff of wind, that is to say, would travel round the world without resistance. If its force were spread over a large area, it would, of course, be less than if it were boxed up within a small area. If, on the other hand, most countries were to erect wind-screens of greater or less effectiveness, then any country which remained exposed would, unless it were large relatively to the rest of the world, be subjected to perpetual instability.

If, therefore, a country adopts an international standard, it is a question just how international it wishes to be—just how sensitive to every international change. The device which we have now to consider is expressly directed towards damping down this sensitiveness without departing from effective conformity with an international standard.

A loan in terms of one currency is not *identical* with a loan in terms of another, even when both broadly conform to the same international standard, unless the currencies are interchangeable without cost and at a rate which is known for certain beforehand. If there is an element of expense or an element of doubt in the conditions of exchange of one currency for another, then the rate of interest on loans in terms of the first can fluctuate, within limits set by the amount of the cost and the degree of the doubt, independently of the rate of interest on loans in terms of the second. The possible range, between the terms on which one currency can be exchanged for another and the terms on which the exchange can be reversed at a later date, is determined by what is called, in the technical language of the foreign exchanges, the distance between the gold points. The greater the distance between the gold points, the less sensitive to short-period external changes a country's rate of foreign lending will be.

Thus the degree of separation of the gold points is a vital factor in the problem of managing a country's currency and ought to be the subject of very careful decision. It has not, however, been treated as such hitherto, but has been governed by influences some of them historical and some of them purely fortuitous, though, doubtless, there has been over extended periods a sort of empirical survival of the fittest.

One of the most effective means of keeping short-term foreign lending insensitive is to allow an element of *doubt* as to the future terms of exchange between currencies. This was the traditional method of the Bank of France for many decades before the war. Silver five-franc pieces remained legal tender, and the Bank of France gave no guarantee that they would always exchange them for gold at their legal parity.

It was not necessary for the efficacy of the method that the threat should be exercised often or at all, its mere existence being enough to hinder the activities of the arbitrageur, who is essentially concerned with certainties and narrow margins. In many other European countries besides France doubt used to exist, for one reason or another,[1] as to whether gold would be freely obtainable for export in all circumstances ; whilst in the United States the fact that there was no Central Bank imported an element of uncertainty into the atmosphere. Even since the post-war restorations of the Gold Standard there are several countries which protect themselves, in one way or another, from their obligation to redeem their notes, gold being of too absolute a character.

In Great Britain, however, this form of protection has never been used[2] (apart from the war and post-war period of the suspension of gold convertibility) ; nor is it in use in the United States since the foundation of the Federal Reserve System. These countries depend, not on an element of doubt, but on an element of cost ; though—it should be added—the element of cost is also present, as an additional protection, in all other countries. In what follows I will take Great Britain as typical, the practices of most other countries being the same in principle though quantitatively different.

The element of cost is made up of two factors, both of which are familiar enough. The first is the difference between the Bank of England's buying and selling prices for gold,[3] *i.e.* the difference between the rate at which the Bank will give notes for gold and

---

[1] *E.g.* the possibility of the Central Bank meeting its legal obligations by paying out light-weight gold coins.

[2] The option to the Bank of England to pay in fine gold or in standard gold will be dealt with below.

[3] To which must be added, to get the extreme limits of fluctuation, the corresponding charge made by the other country whose currency is being exchanged.

the rate at which it will give gold for notes. Historic-
ally this difference was based on the convenience and
economy of getting notes for gold *at once* instead of
taking gold to the Mint and waiting for it to be coined ;
and before the war the effective difference was in fact
tied down to the actual measure of this convenience,
since holders of gold had an option between selling it
to the Bank at the Bank's price or taking it to the
Mint and waiting. The Currency Act of 1928, however,
abolished this option, and the precise amount of the
difference between the Bank's buying and selling prices
(namely the difference between £3 : 17 : 10½ per oz.
and £3 : 17 : 9, which amounts to 0·16 per cent) is
nothing but an historical survival.[1]

The second factor represents the actual cost, in
freight-charges, insurance and loss of interest, of transporting gold from one place to another. The amount
of this is variable, not only because some destinations
are nearer than others, but also in accordance with
the varying rates of interest and insurance charges
and the time occupied by different means of transport.
On balance, however, the amount of this second factor
tends in modern conditions to be reduced.[2] As
between London and New York, the extreme variation
between the best and worst terms on which dollars
and sterling can be exchanged is about ¾ per cent.
As between London and Paris, on the other hand,

---

[1] In 1929 the Bank of England revived a practice, which had existed up
to 1912, of paying *more* than its statutory minimum price whenever it is
specially anxious to secure gold.

[2] Some interesting calculations, bearing on this, have been published
by Dr. P. Einzig in articles published in the *Economic Journal*, March 1927,
September 1927 and December 1928. Dr. Einzig calls attention to the
narrowing of the gold points made possible by air transport. The most
up-to-date calculations are to be found in Dr. Einzig's *International Gold
Movements*, Appendix I. For example, in 1913 the dollar-sterling gold
points were $4·89 and $4·8509, or 0·81 per cent ; they widened in 1925 to
$4·8949 and $4·8491, or 0·96 per cent ; and they narrowed in 1928 to $4·8884
and $4·8515, or 0·76 per cent. If the rate of interest was to fall to 3 per cent
(as against 5 per cent assumed in the above) the difference between the gold
points would narrow to 0·7 per cent.

the variation is obviously smaller.[1]   But in the case
of India I calculated (before the war) that the range
was nearly $1\frac{1}{2}$ per cent.[2]   Generally speaking, the
maximum extent of the range for different pairs of
countries varies from $\frac{1}{2}$ to $1\frac{1}{2}$ per cent.

Whilst these are the extreme limits, the organisation of the "forward exchanges" usually enables
borrowers to make a better bargain than this as to the
terms on which they will be able to exchange one
currency for another three months ahead.[3]   But even
in the most favourable circumstances some cost will be
incurred or some risk will have to be run, which an
owner of one currency who wishes to effect a loan in
terms of another will have to take into consideration
in calculating whether a given transaction offers a
profit ; and, as the pressure of transactions in one
direction drives the rate of exchange towards one of
the gold points, the prospective cost of a further transaction in the same direction will probably increase.

Let us, for the sake of illustration, assume that
the anticipated cost is $\frac{1}{2}$ per cent.   Now in the case of
a loan of long duration this does not appreciably affect
the net rate of interest obtainable after allowing for the
exchange of one currency into another.   For example,
with a loan for ten years, the factor only reduces the
rate obtainable by $\frac{1}{20}$ per cent per annum. But in the
case of a short-period loan the position is materially
different.   For example, with a loan for three months,
the cost of exchange would, on the above hypothesis,
reduce the rate obtainable by 2 per cent per annum.

Thus this factor enables a substantial inequality

---

[1] The range between London and Amsterdam is about 0·8 per cent,
between London and Berlin about 0·7 per cent, and between London and
Paris about 0·5 per cent (reckoning interest at 5 per cent in each case).   Cf.
Einzig, *op. cit.*

[2] For a detailed examination of this point in the particular case of India
see my *Indian Currency and Finance*, Chapter 5.

[3] I have described in detail the machinery of the "forward exchange"
market, and have analysed the factors which determine the rates quoted, in
my *Tract on Monetary Reform*, Chapter 3, § 4.

to exist between the rates of interest obtainable in two different currencies respectively if the rate of exchange existing at the moment cannot be relied on to last for more than a short period. For example, if the dollar-sterling exchange stands at the gold-export point for sterling, an interest-rate in London higher than the New York rate for comparable loans will attract lending from New York to London, since loans can be remitted from New York to London with a certainty that they can at any future date be brought home again without exchange loss ; that is to say, the dollar-sterling exchange can always be kept above gold-export point for sterling, and the flow of gold from London to New York thereby prevented, by keeping interest-rates in London higher than in New York. The same, of course, is also true in the opposite direction. But if, on the other hand, the rate of exchange lies somewhere intermediate between the gold points, then there is no necessity for interest-rates to be equal in the two centres, though there are still limits beyond which the inequality cannot go ; if, for example, the gold points are $\frac{3}{4}$ per cent apart, the rate for three months' loans in New York could conceivably be 3 per cent per annum higher in New York than in London with the exchange at the gold-export point for sterling, or—equally well—the three-month rate could be 3 per cent per annum higher in London than in New York with the exchange at the gold-export points for dollars. The mathematical expectation, however, or probable cost of reversing a remittance three months hence, will seldom, or never, equal its maximum possible value. The market's estimation of this probability is given by the " forward exchange " quotations, so that in equilibrium :

Three months' interest at the London rate, plus (or minus) an allowance for the discount (or premium) on forward dollars

= Three months' interest at the New York rate.

Thus if there is a fair distance between the gold points, there is a fair margin of difference which can exist between short-money rates in two centres—provided always that the money-market cannot rely on a long continuance of this margin of difference. It is this distance, therefore, which protects the money-market of one country from being upset by every puff of wind which blows in the money-markets of other countries.

It follows that the magnitude of the difference is a matter of great importance for the stability of a country's internal economy. One might have supposed, therefore, that it would have been fixed after careful consideration at a safe amount. But this has not been the case hitherto. Moreover, the amount of the difference is liable to be upset by air-transport, or, for example, by a bank being willing to forgo interest on gold during transit.

I believe that there is room here for a reform of real importance.[1] I suggest that the difference between a Central Bank's obligatory buying and selling prices of gold should be made somewhat greater than hitherto, say 2 per cent, so that there would be at least this difference between the gold points irrespective of the actual costs of transporting gold (double the amount of which would have to be added on to the 2 per cent to give the difference between the gold points). But a Central Bank would be free at any time, if it wished to encourage the movement of gold inwards or outwards, to quote closer prices within the legal limits. Further, a Central Bank should be in a position to control when necessary, within the limits set by the gold points and the relative rates of interest at home and abroad, the premium or discount of the forward exchange on the spot exchange ; whereby short-period interest-rates at home could stand *temporarily* in such

---

[1] The proposal which follows is substantially the same in principle as that which I made in my *Tract on Monetary Reform*, pp. 189-191.

relation (within limits) to similar rates abroad as the Central Bank might deem to be advisable.

The object of this reform is to enable a Central Bank to protect the credit structure of its own country from the repercussions of purely temporary disturbances abroad, whilst the laws of long-period equilibrium would remain as before. Let us give an example where the proposed arrangements would have been useful. In the autumn of 1928 local conditions in the United States convinced the Federal Reserve Board that the short-period interest-rate should be raised in the interests of business stability ; but local conditions in Great Britain were of a precisely opposite character, and the Bank of England was anxious to keep money as cheap as possible. The Federal Reserve Board did not desire that its high rates should attract gold from Great Britain ; for this, if it occurred, would have tended to defeat its efforts. Nor did the Bank of England desire to impose high rates in Great Britain —to which it might be driven—in order to prevent its gold from flowing out. Such a situation could be handled by the above plan. The Federal Reserve Banks would reduce their buying price for gold to a figure nearer to their legal minimum, whilst the Bank of England would raise its selling price for gold nearer to its legal maximum.[1] If the Central Banks had also the practice, as suggested above, of influencing the rates for forward exchange, then these rates too would have to be moved correspondingly. This would permit *temporarily* the maintenance of materially different short-money rates in the two centres. It would not, of course, permit a *permanent* difference, since it is the expectation or the possibility of fluctuations between the gold points within a short period which permits the difference to exist. Thus a lasting

---

[1] Owing to the absence of any such provisions, the Bank of England was, in the middle of 1929, resorting to the unsatisfactory expedient of putting moral pressure on banks and finance houses to forgo the small profit which would have been obtainable by exporting gold.

divergence in interest-rates in favour of New York
would cause the dollar-sterling exchange to reach the
gold point corresponding to the Bank of England's
legal maximum selling price for gold and so cause
gold to flow.

I would propose, therefore, to furnish Central
Banks with a trident for the control of the rate of
short-term foreign lending — their bank-rate, their
forward-exchange rate, and their buying and selling
rates for gold (within the limits of the lawful gold
points). I conceive of them as fixing week by week,
not only their official rate of discount, but also the
terms on which they are prepared to buy or sell forward exchange on one or two leading foreign centres
and the terms on which they are prepared to buy or
sell gold within the gold points. This would have the
effect of putting Central Banks in the same short-
period position as that in which they would be in if
they were to feel themselves able to suffer larger
fluctuations in their stock of gold without inconvenience. The reader must also notice in particular that
a Central Bank would be able, by fixing appropriately
its forward-exchange rates relatively to the spot rates
prevailing in the market, to fix in effect different short-
term rates of interest for foreign funds and for domestic
funds respectively.

The anomalies of the present situation and the
instinctive striving of Central Banks to widen the
gold points are well illustrated by two events which
occurred during 1929–30, whilst these pages were being
passed through the press.

The reader will have perceived that the distance
between the gold points is narrower for a pair of
countries which are geographical neighbours than for
a pair which are more distant from one another. It
follows that the gold points are particularly narrow as
between Paris and London. Thus, unless the sterling
rate is (e.g.) well above its parity on New York, the

gold export point to Paris, when France is on the point of importing gold, will be reached sooner in London than in New York; so that the mere propinquity of London to Paris will tend to throw on her more of the short-period burden of the French gold requirements than on New York.   Under pressure of such circumstances, however, the Bank of England and the Bank of France found a roundabout way within the letter of the existing law for making the cost of transporting gold from New York to Paris more nearly equal to the cost of transporting it from London to Paris.   The Bank of England exercised its statutory right to deliver only standard gold and the Bank of France exercised its statutory right to accept only fine gold, which had the effect of widening the gold points by the addition of the expenses of refining and of the consequent delay ;   and at the same time ways were found of minimising the loss of interest during the period occupied in transporting gold from New York to Paris. The result was to transfer the bulk of the gold exports from London which was an unwilling exporter, to New York which was a willing one, *without* the change in the relative short-money rates in the two centres, which would have been required otherwise as a necessary accompaniment of the movement of the sterling-dollar exchange towards the gold export point from New York to London.   This is an excellent example of the technique the habitual use of which I am advocating ; but it is somewhat absurd that the possibility of employing it on the above occasion should have depended on an accidental feature of the existing statutes in the two countries concerned.[1]

The other recent example is supplied by Canada.

---

[1] The technical details of this episode have been described by Dr. Paul Einzig in the *Economic Journal*, Sept. 1930.   Since some Central Banks, *e.g.* the Reichsbank, were prepared to accept standard gold and pay out fine gold (at the usual margin between their buying and selling prices), the theoretical limit to the movement of the franc-sterling exchange was set temporarily by the cost of a triangular transaction over some third country.

The gold points between Canada and the United States are—for geographical reasons as in the previous case—particularly narrow, with the result that gold movements between the two countries are frequently brought about by transient causes. In September 1929, the combined effects of a slow movement of the Canadian wheat crop out of the country and of the high rates for short-term loans in Wall Street, led to a tendency for gold to leave Canada on a greater scale than was convenient. The position was dealt with by lowering the gold-export point in virtue of an informal agreement between the Minister of Finance and the ten Chartered Banks not to export gold for the sake of a small arbitrage profit. The rate of exchange inevitably went outside the lower gold point presumed by the terms of Canada's adherence to the gold standard ; but the expedient was justified by the event, since the high rates for short-term loans in New York proved to be temporary, and by the summer of 1930, when they had evaporated, the Canadian exchange had not only recovered to parity but had gone beyond it to the gold-import point. Thus this informal widening of the gold points was probably the wisest way of preventing the abnormal position in Wall Street from reacting unduly on the domestic credit conditions in Canada.

The objections likely to be raised against the proposals of this section are two. It is likely to be urged that the extra latitude which it would allow might be abused and become the occasion and the excuse for a Central Bank to omit to take measures to remedy what was not a passing phase but a cause of persisting disequilibrium. It is true, of course, that every increase in the discretion allowed to a Central Bank, so as to increase its power of intelligent management, is liable to abuse. But in this case the risk is slight. For the effect on any element in the situation, other than the international short-loan position, would be insignificant, and the effect on this would be strictly limited and incapable of cumulative repetition.

Or it may be urged that an expedient of this kind, whilst well enough for a country which is not a depository of part of the international short-loan fund, is against the interests of a financial centre which aspires to be an important depository of such funds. Some force must be allowed to this. It is a question of how high a price in the shape of domestic instability it is worth while to pay in order to secure international banking business. From the standpoint of the latter the ideal would be to narrow the gold points until they were identical. It is a matter of finding a just and advantageous compromise between the competing interests. But there are also reasons for not attaching much importance to this objection. For I have coupled with this proposal a further suggestion by which the Central Bank would quote rates of forward exchange ; and by this means the foreign depositor can always be accorded, for three-monthly periods at a time, such degree of security and economy in the movement of his funds, backwards and forwards, as the Central Bank deems it safe and advantageous to accord to him. That is to say, we should only be loosening the tightness of the legal obligation laid on the Central Bank ;—we should not be preventing or hindering it from working the system, in practice and as a rule, exactly as at present.

Moreover, London could overcome the awkwardness due to geographical propinquity without weakening her competitive position against New York as a depository of foreign funds, if she were to fix her new gold points on any third country no wider than New York's.

The ideal system, however—and one which would entirely overcome the competitive argument—would be an arrangement for uniform action by all the leading countries. It would be better to supplant the existing haphazard and fluctuating gold points, different between every pair of countries and open to all kinds of minor uncertainties, with a fixed and uniform system between every pair of countries. There is a way in which, in the ideal international currency system of the future, we could ensure this, namely, by every country substituting, for its Central Bank's existing legal obligation to buy and sell its local money on prescribed terms in exchange for gold, an obligation to buy and sell its local money on prescribed terms in exchange for balances at a Supernational Bank. A reasonable measure of domestic autonomy could then be obtained by every country's buying rate being fixed 1 per cent below the parity of its local money and its selling rate 1 per cent above. This would not be incompatible with the maintenance of a gold standard, provided that balances at the Supernational Bank were encashable in gold ;—it would merely mean that there would be no movements of gold between pairs of individual countries, but only between individual countries and the Supernational Bank. We shall return in Chapter 38 to the contribution which such a Bank might make to the solution of the currency problems of the world.

At any rate, we may conclude, the precise magnitude of the stretch between the gold points deserves more scientific consideration than it has yet received. The present system of an international gold standard, in combination with separate national systems of Central Banks and domestic money, would be unworkable if the gold points coincided (as they do, in practice, within a country) ; and if this is agreed, it follows that the degree of their separation should not be a matter of material costs of transport or historical survivals.

(iv.) Should Standards of Value be International ?

Everyone agrees that there are many fields of human activity in which it is only common-sense to establish international standards. If there are arguments to the contrary, they are generally of a non-economic character. We may dislike the idea of adopting the metric system or a universal language ; but, if so, our objections are not likely to depend on economic advantage. Now, in the case of a currency system, it is obvious that advantages of variety, idiosyncrasy or tradition, which might well be held of overwhelming force in the case of a language, can scarcely weigh against economic well - being. In determining our currency system, therefore, we need be influenced by nothing but economic benefit—including in this political expediency and justice.

It has been common to conclude from this that it goes without saying that the ideal currency system and the ideal standard of value should be international in character. But the analogy is false ; and for reasons already given the answer is not so easy. For one thing, as we have seen in Book II., Purchasing Power does not and cannot *mean* the same thing in different parts of the world. If the force of gravity was materially different in different countries, the same might apply to the standard of weight. But in the case of the standard of purchasing power this difficulty does necessarily arise. It is certain that the fluctuations in the purchasing power of money in the United States will not be the same as its fluctuations in India in terms of a uniform standard, whatever that standard may be. Moreover, there are, as we shall see, other considerations also which must be taken into account.

What, then, should be our final conclusion in the

choice between an international and a national standard of value ?

Let us first make sure that the claims of the International Standard—namely, the conveniences and facilities secured to foreign trade and foreign lending —do not receive *more* than justice.

So far as foreign trade is concerned, I think that the advantage of fixing the maximum fluctuations of the foreign exchanges within quite narrow limits is usually much over-estimated. It is, indeed, little more than a convenience. It is important for anyone engaged in foreign trade that he should know for certain, at the same time as he enters into a transaction, the rate of foreign exchange at which he can cover himself ; but this can be satisfactorily secured to him by a free and reliable market in forward exchange.[1] It is not important that the rate of exchange at which he covers himself this year should be exactly the same as the rate at which he covered himself for a similar transaction last year. Moreover, there can be *moderate* fluctuations in the exchanges which will still be small relatively to the normal fluctuations in the prices of the individual commodities in which the trader is interested, and the exchange fluctuations will be as likely—perhaps more likely— to compensate these individual fluctuations as to aggravate them. Thus—provided our Central Bank offers adequate facilities for dealing in the Forward Exchanges—I do not consider that a fixity of the foreign exchanges is necessary in the interests of foreign traders. Moderate fluctuations, if they are desirable on other grounds, will not be seriously inconvenient.

When we come to Foreign Lending, however, the advantages of a fixed exchange must, as we have already seen, be estimated much higher. In this case the contracts between borrower and lender may cover

---

[1] Cf. my *Tract on Monetary Reform*, p. 133.

a far longer period than would be contemplated by any practicable dealings in forward exchange. This uncertainty as to the future rate of foreign exchange would inevitably introduce an element of doubt into the transaction which would certainly have some deterrent effect on the international mobility of loan-capital.

We must, however, distinguish sharply in this respect between long-period and short-period loans; particularly if some outside limit is set to the amplitude of the possible fluctuation in the exchange. Suppose, for example, that the limit to the fluctuation of exchange has been fixed at 5 per cent on either side of par, then a 5 per cent loan in terms of the lender's money remitted at the par of exchange may cost in future years anything between $4\frac{3}{4}$ per cent and $5\frac{1}{4}$ per cent interest, and when it is paid off the redemption may cost anything between 95 and 105, in terms of the borrower's money. In the case of a long-period loan these possibilities are not very serious; but in the case of a short-period loan the exact cost of paying off the loan at maturity may have a decisive effect on the total net cost of the loan reckoned *per annum*. This leads us to the heart of our argument. If we deliberately desire that there should be a high degree of mobility for international lending, both for long and for short periods, then this is, admittedly, a strong argument for a fixed rate of exchange and a rigid international standard.

What, then, is the reason for hesitating before we commit ourselves to such a system? Primarily a doubt whether it is wise to have a Currency System with a much wider ambit than our Banking System, our Tariff System and our Wage System. Can we afford to allow a disproportionate degree of mobility to a single element in an economic system which we leave extremely rigid in several other respects? If there was the same mobility internationally in all

other respects as there is nationally, it might be a
different matter. But to introduce a mobile element,
highly sensitive to outside influences, as a connected
part of a machine of which the other parts are much
more rigid, may invite breakages.

Therefore this is not a question to be answered
lightly. The belief in an extreme mobility of international lending and a policy of unmitigated *laissez-
faire* towards foreign loans, on which most Englishmen
have been brought up, has been based, as I have re-
peatedly urged above, on too simple a view of the
causal relations between foreign lending and foreign
investment. Because—apart from gold movements—
net foreign lending and *net* foreign investment must
always exactly balance, it has been assumed that
no serious problem presents itself. Since lending
and investment must be equal, an increase of lending must cause an increase of investment—so the
argument runs—and a decrease of lending must cause
a decrease of investment; in short, the prosperity of
our export industries is bound up with the volume of
our foreign lending. Indeed, the argument sometimes
goes further, and—instead of being limited to *net*
foreign lending—even maintains that the making of
an individual foreign loan has in itself the effect of
increasing our exports. All this, however, neglects
the painful, and perhaps violent, reactions of the
mechanism which has to be brought into play in order
to force *net* foreign lending and *net* foreign investment
into equality.

I do not know why this should not be considered
obvious. If English investors, not liking the outlook
at home, fearing labour disputes or nervous about a
change of government, begin to buy more American
securities than before, why should it be supposed that
this will be naturally balanced by increased British
exports ? For, of course, it will not. It will, in the
first instance, set up a serious instability of the domestic

credit system—the ultimate working out of which it is difficult or impossible to predict. Or, if American investors take a fancy to British ordinary shares, is this going, in any direct way, to decrease British exports ?

It is, therefore, a serious question whether it is right to adopt an international standard, which will allow an extreme mobility and sensitiveness of foreign lending, whilst the remaining elements of the economic complex remain exceedingly rigid. If it were as easy to put wages up and down as it is to put bank-rate up and down, well and good. But this is not the actual situation. A change in international financial conditions or in the wind and weather of speculative sentiment may alter the volume of foreign lending, if nothing is done to counteract it, by tens of millions in a few weeks. Yet there is no possibility of rapidly altering the balance of imports and exports to correspond.

Nor are short-period considerations of this character the only ground for hesitation before plumping for an international standard. The monetary development of different countries is at many different stages ; and the education of the public in monetary principles is also along differing lines. I should say, for example, that the present attitude towards gold on the part of the Bank of England or of the Reichsbank is fundamentally different from that of the Bank of France or of the Bank of Spain, and that changes for which the former may be ripe in the course of the next five or ten years might still prove too novel for the latter.

There is, moreover, a further obstacle—namely, the attitude of the United States. Owing to her immensely large holdings of gold, the United States is able to obtain, to a great extent, the combined advantages of a local and of an international standard ; and she is, besides, exceedingly jealous of surrendering any of her own autonomous powers to an international body. Thus, to overcome the obstacles to an international agreement—the conservatism of France and the independence of the United States—might cause serious and perhaps intolerable delays.

Assuming, however, that these practical and probably temporary, even if prolonged, difficulties are out of the way, there still remains an objection to an international standard, in that it commits the world to one particular type of standard of value as governing the long-period norm.

For our long-period standard of value we have to choose, broadly speaking, between three general types. The first of these is the Purchasing Power of Money or Consumption Standard, or something of that type. The second is the Earnings Standard, the ratio of which to the Consumption Standard rises in proportion to any increase in the efficiency of the factors of production. The third is some version of the International Standard, *i.e.* a standard based on the prices of the principal commodities which enter into international trade weighted in proportion to their importance in world commerce, which in practice might not be very different from a wholesale standard of raw materials.

The first two of these are necessarily local standards, since they do not move in the same way in different countries. Thus, if our standard is to be the same for all countries, we are tied down to choosing the third type of standard.

I do not attach first-rate importance to this objection ; for the long-period variability of local Consumption Standards or Earnings Standards in terms of a stable International Standard is not likely to be so large as to matter much to economic well-being. Nevertheless, it is right to take some account of the fact that an International Standard of this type is not likely to be the *ideal* standard for any individual country.

On a balance of these various considerations, it seemed, before the *de facto* return to the Gold Standard, that there were better prospects for the management of a national currency on progressive lines, if it were to be freed from the inconvenient and sometimes dangerous obligation of being tied to an unmanaged international system; that the evolution of independent national systems with fluctuating exchange rates would be the next step to work for; and that the linking up of these again into a managed international system would probably come as the last stage of all.

To-day the reasons seem stronger—in spite of the disastrous inefficiency which the international gold standard has worked since its restoration five years ago (fulfilling the worst fears and gloomiest prognostications of its opponents), and the economic losses, second only in amount to those of a great war, which it has brought upon the world—to reverse the order of procedure; to accept, substantially, the *fait accompli* of an international standard; and to hope for progress from that starting-point towards a scientific management of the central controls—for that is what our monetary system surely is—of our economic life. For to seek the ultimate good *viâ* an autonomous national system would mean not only a frontal attack on the forces of conservatism, entrenched with all the advantages of possession, but it would divide the forces of intelligence and goodwill and separate the interests of nations.

I am disposed to conclude, therefore, that if the various difficulties in the way of an internationally managed Gold Standard—to which the Resolutions of the Genoa Conference of 1922 first pointed the way —could be overcome within a reasonable period of time, then the best practical objective might be the management of the value of gold by a Supernational Authority, with a number of national monetary systems clustering round it, each with a discretion to vary the value of its local money in terms of gold within a range of (say) 2 per cent.

CHAPTER 37

PROBLEMS OF NATIONAL MANAGEMENT—III. THE CONTROL OF THE RATE OF INVESTMENT

(i.) CAN THE BANKING SYSTEM CONTROL THE PRICE-LEVEL ?

I REACH at last the crux of the whole matter. We have endeavoured to analyse and to classify the multifarious factors which determine the price-level and the means by which the Central Bank in a Closed System, or the aggregate behaviour of Central Banks throughout the world, can influence and dominate the behaviour of the banking and monetary system as a whole. But when all is said and done, does it lie within the power of a Central Bank in actual practice to pursue a policy which will have the effect of fixing the value of money at any prescribed level ? If, for example, the duty of preserving the stability of the purchasing power of money within narrow limits were to be laid upon a Central Bank by law, would it be possible for the Central Bank to fulfil this obligation in all circumstances ?

Those who attribute sovereign power to the monetary authority in the governance of prices do not, of course, claim that the terms on which money is supplied is the *only* influence affecting the price-level. To maintain that the supplies in a reservoir can be maintained at any required level by pouring enough water into it, is not inconsistent with admitting that the level of the reservoir depends on many other

factors besides how much water is poured in,—for
example, the natural rainfall, evaporation, leakage
and the habits of the users of the system. Such a
claim would only be unjustified if the amount of
evaporation or leakage or other source of loss, or the
consumption of those using the system, were a direct
function of the amount of water poured in, of such
a character that the more poured in the greater for
that reason the consumption or the diminution in the
natural rainfall or other occasion of loss, so that no
amount of inflow would raise the supplies in the
reservoir above a certain level. Which of these alternatives is the true analogy for the effect on the price-
level of the creation of additional supplies of money
by the banking system ?

I have more sympathy to-day than I had a few
years ago with some of the doubts and hesitations such
as were expressed in 1927 by Governor Strong and
other witnesses before the Committee of the United
States Congress on Stabilisation. This Committee was
appointed to examine the wisdom of a proposed
amendment to the Federal Reserve Act, the effect of
which would have been to lay upon the Federal Reserve Board the duty of using all the powers at its
disposal to " promote a stable price-level for commodities in general ". The reasonable doubts of
practical men, towards the idea that " the Federal
Reserve System has the power to raise or lower the
price-level by some automatic method, by some magic
mathematical formula ",[1] are well expressed in the
following extracts :

Governor Strong [2]

I believe there is a tendency to look at the price-level
as though it operated up and down against a counter-

---

[1] Governor Strong before the Stabilisation Committee, p. 295.

[2] I have pieced the following into a continuous narrative from scattered
passages in Governor Strong's evidence before the Stabilisation Committee
—pp. 295, 359, 550, 577.

weight of credit, and as if you could open a spigot when prices are declining and put a little more credit in the counter-weight and raise prices, and if prices are going up you could drain a little credit out of the counter-weight and let prices go down. But I am afraid the price problem is much more complicated than that.

I would like to describe to you a situation which is very recent, to show how the relation of a price movement to other elements that we take into consideration presents a real practical puzzle of management. Two months ago there was some concern felt in the country as to the extent of speculation in stocks and the amount of credit which was being employed in support of that speculation. At the same time, our studies of the price structure showed very clearly that there was taking place, and had for some little time taken place, a decline in the wholesale price-level, and when we came to analyse that decline we found that it was almost entirely due to a decline in the prices of cotton and grains. Assume that we here are the directors of the Federal Reserve Bank trying to determine what to do about the discount rate. We have this feeling that there is a growth of speculation; possibly a feeling that it ought to be curbed by the Federal Reserve System in some way. On the other hand, we are faced with a clear indication of some decline in the price of farm commodities. Now, if very great concern had been felt about the price of farm commodities, and we felt that the introduction of credit into the market or lowering interest rate might correct the prices of those individual commodities, what might the consequences be in speculation? There you are between the devil and the deep sea.

I believe that administration of credit such as is afforded by the Federal Reserve System is capable of exerting an influence upon the volume of credit employed by the country and upon the cost of that credit. Within the limitations which the volume and the cost of credit exert an influence upon the price-level, and only within that limitation, can the operations of the Federal Reserve System influence prices. But there will be times when even the power to somewhat regulate the volume of credit and its cost will fail of complete or anything like complete regulation of the price-level, because there are many other things, far beyond the influence of the volume and cost of credit, such as the mood of the people. Therefore, if any expression is contained in the Federal Reserve Act which appears to represent to the people that the Federal Reserve System can do more in stabilising the price-level than the limited control of credit is capable of performing, I am afraid that disappointment will come when there are fluctuations of prices which cannot be controlled within the strict limitations I have described.

When the Federal Reserve System has an adequate volume of earning assets, it has a very considerable capacity to control a runaway movement of prices. But when you get to a decline in prices, one of those insidious periods of liquidation, and not a sharp movement like in 1921—one of these very difficult slow price movements, possibly not attributable to credit operations at all— what is the Federal Reserve System to do ?   There is a present decline of prices.   Possibly the spirit of optimism of last year has resulted in all merchants contracting for goods which they expected to sell, but are unable to sell when delivered ; in other words, there is an overstock of goods beyond what the trade will consume or the people will consume.   If there is a margin of goods for sale beyond the capacity of consumption, the introduction of more credit into the credit system will not correct that until the goods are consumed, and that situation arises in the form of contracts long before it can be detected in any reports on volume of business, inventories, or anything of that sort.   The amount of goods being transported over the railroads will be just the same ; the amount of employment will be just the same.   Everything will be marching along with all outward evidence of a sound business situation, but when the public, for one or another reason, slows down in buying and consuming goods, which starts a declining price movement, I don't see how we can correct it.

If we had such a severe decline in the value of cotton and all the commodities that are influenced by world market prices as to cause a decline in the general price-level, and we should attempt to remedy it just by buying securities and making cheap money, it would not cause an advance, certainly not immediately, in the prices of those

commodities whose prices are fixed by world markets and
world competition.   It would have an inflationary effect
which might indeed affect price-levels of purely domestic
commodities ; and if it did, it would be thereby advancing
the price of everything the farmer consumed, at the
same time that the selling price for what he produces
was being reduced.

Take the situation at the present time and for quite a
period past.   We have had a remarkably stable level of
prices for general commodities, with the exception in the
last few months of a decline in grain and cotton prices.
Prices of cattle and hogs have remained pretty steady.
There has been a decline in agricultural prices sufficient
to bring about a gradual reduction in the index number
of general prices.   Now, take the problem of to-day.   Is
the Federal Reserve System to step in and attempt to
regulate this movement which seems to have started ;
and if so, how ?   That is the practical thing that the price
regulator would face from time to time.

Mr. Williamson

Do you think that the Federal Reserve Board could,
as a matter of fact, stabilise price-levels to a greater extent
than they have in the past, by giving greater expansion
to market operations and restriction or extension of credit
facilities ?

Governor Strong

I personally think that the administration of the
Federal Reserve System since the reaction of 1921 has
been just as nearly directed as reasonable human wisdom
could direct it toward that very object.

Then there is another possibility that has always
struck me as inherent in any recognition of a power
resting anywhere to regulate prices, and that is in the
everlasting contest that takes place with all humanity
between the producer and the consumer. . . . It seems
to me that if the Federal Reserve System is recognised
as a price regulator, it is going to be somewhat in the
position of the poor man who tried to stop a row between
an Irishman and his wife.   They both turned in and beat
him.

Mr. Wingo

And you are afraid that without giving you any power that you do not already possess, or without making it possible for you to have any greater desire or ability to serve the common good, the country will be led to believe that by mere legislative declaration the capacity to remove all the economic evils incident to fluctuations of credit will be lodged in this super-wise Board.

Governor Strong

Thank you, Mr. Wingo. You express it better than I could.

The following from Dr. Stewart's evidence on the same occasion is also instructive :

Dr. Walter Stewart [1]

Let us assume that there is a recession of building activity, that this carries with it some unemployment in the production of automobiles; let us further assume that the crops turn out sufficiently large to enable us to make large exports, but because of certain disturbances in Europe and the lack of foreign confidence in investments there develops a sagging tendency in the general level of commodity prices. What is there that the Federal Reserve System can do ? Suppose, for instance, these prices move off 5 per cent. As I understand it, those who favour the proposal before the Committee believe that by a change of the discount rate, or by open market operations, the international price-level will be given stability. We are not talking about the price-level in the United States, for when we speak of the gold price-level we are talking about the international price-level. I believe that in such a situation an increase or decrease of a small percentage in the discount rates will have little bearing on the price situation.

To what extent, by an addition to credits at a time when prices are declining, not as an aftermath of war inflation but of maladjustments in business, can you cure the causes which lie back of declining prices ? My point is that in such circumstances you take a chance of aggravating the very causes which are responsible for

---

[1] Pieced together from passages *op. cit.*—pp. 769-775.

the declining prices. If stocks are accumulating and the
mood of the community is speculative, then an attempt
to use credit for the purpose of stabilising prices is more
likely to aggravate the causes responsible for the movement in prices.

To assume that declining prices, which are after all
largely a readjustment to take care of the mistakes made
previously, can be overcome by an additional extension
of credit is more likely to add to the difficulties in the
situation rather than to cure it.

Ease in the money market will be reflected in the
demand for certain investment securities, and possibly in
a bidding up of speculative securities. But we have had
in this country periods when money has remained very
easy for more than a year, as in 1908, and yet business
remained depressed, not because money was not available
at easy rates, but because business was going through a
readjustment. Business will continue to go through such
readjustments as long as human judgment has to be used
and mistakes are made, and to say you can save business
from the risks it necessarily assumes by a credit policy
which is exercised by the Reserve Banks is an unwarranted
assumption.

I think we meet periods in which credit is inflated in
the sense of being extended beyond the capacity of
industry to use it for productive purposes, even on a
declining price-level.

These are reasonable doubts expressed by persons
of great experience. They cannot be dispelled merely
by pointing to the truism of a Quantity Equation.
In a sense they can only be dispelled by the prolonged
success of an actual attempt at scientific control. But
I should like to try to show that the prospects of such
an attempt are sufficiently promising for it to be worth
a trial.

We have claimed to prove in this Treatise that the
price-level of output depends on the level of money-
incomes relatively to efficiency, on the volume of
investment (measured in cost of production) relatively
to saving, and on the " bearish " or " bullish " senti-

ment of capitalists relatively to the supply of savings-deposits available in the banking system. We have claimed, further, that the banking system can control the supply of savings-deposits, and hence the third factor; that it can by the terms of credit influence to any required extent the volume of investment, and hence the second factor; and that the indirect effects of its influence on the value and the volume of investment determine the money offers which entrepreneurs make to the factors of production, and hence the third factor. But we have *not* claimed that the banking system can produce any of these effects instantaneously; or that it can be expected always to foresee the operation of non-monetary factors in time to take measures in advance to counteract their influence on prices; or that it can avoid violent fluctuations in the prices of different classes of commodities relatively to one another; or that a Central Bank, which is a member of an international system, can preserve domestic stability irrespective of the behaviour of other Central Banks.

Some of the occasions of doubt expressed by Governor Strong and Dr. Stewart are conceded by these qualifications. Dr. Stewart's evidence, in particular, emphasised the interdependence of American prices and world prices. But putting aside for the moment the question of international complications, to which we will return in a later section of this chapter, how far are we prepared to attribute to a Central Bank a greater degree of influence on the price-level than these authorities believed it to have?

I think that in one fundamental respect they have mistaken the character of the problem and have underestimated the possibilities of control. For they have not perceived the vital difference between the production of consumption-goods and the production of investment-goods, and have not allowed, in consequence, for the effect of an increased production of

investment-goods on the state of demand for, and
hence the price-level of, consumption-goods.

This is partly the result, perhaps, of the traditional
view which the banking system has always taken of
its own functions. In actual fact the banking system
has a dual function—the direction of the supply of
resources for working capital through the loans which
it makes to producers to cover their outgoings during
the period of production (and no longer), and of the
supply *pari passu* of the current cash required for use
in the Industrial Circulation ; and, on the other hand,
the direction of the supply of resources which determines the value of securities through the investments which it purchases directly and the loans which
it makes to the Stock Exchange and to other persons
who are prepared to carry securities with borrowed
bank-money, and of the supply *pari passu* of the
savings-deposits required for use in the Financial
Circulation to satisfy the bullishness or bearishness of
financial sentiment, so as to prevent its reacting on
the value and the volume of new investment.   The
statistical proportion of a bank's financial activities to
its industrial activities varies widely, but, in the
modern world, it will seldom be less than one-half, and
may sometimes rise to equality.   Yet there is a notion
kept up amongst respectable bankers (I am speaking
of London—perhaps this is not true of New York) that
the first function is the *proper* function of banking,
that its needs must always have the first claim on their
resources, and that the second function (particularly
in so far as it relates to loans for the purpose of
carrying securities or other fixed assets) is something
to be apologetic about, the importance of which is to be
minimised, something which the bankers would like
to avoid altogether if they could.   The reasons given
for this are that the second category of business,
namely the financial business, is not self-liquidating
and savours of " speculation ".

Yet it is doubtful whether these reasons are as valid as they seem. Any given financial loan is probably more liquid than any given industrial loan, and financial loans, which are seldom made except on good security, probably lead to fewer bad debts than industrial loans ; whilst the whole body of financial loans and the whole body of industrial loans are equally non-liquid in the sense that no material reduction in the aggregate of either can be made quickly without disaster, the former—if there is anything to choose between them—being probably the easier to curtail of the two, since the assets will be taken over at a price by the holders of savings-deposits. As for "speculation", it is probably true that the banks have to be more on the look-out against ill-informed and reckless borrowers in the case of financial loans than in the case of industrial loans. But, apart from this, the supply of increased credit for providing working capital ought sometimes to be encouraged and sometimes to be discouraged, just as much as the supply of increased credit for carrying fixed capital ; and in both cases the pressure of borrowers is likely to be greatest at times when it is least desirable to satisfy it in full, and smallest at times when it is most to be encouraged.

At any rate, when we are considering the *regulative* powers and functions of the banking system, we must study its influence over the rate of investment in fixed capital at least as much as its influence over the rate of investment in working capital; indeed it is probably true that it cannot, in most cases, exert an effective influence over the latter except through its influence over the former. Therefore we shall not understand the full measure of control which the banking system is capable of exerting on the price-level unless we take account of all the ways in which it can influence the rate of investment as a whole.

A further quotation from Dr. Stewart's evidence

before the U.S. Stabilisation Committee [1] may help to elucidate my point :

> There seems to be in this proposal the suggestion that the aim of Federal Reserve policy should be to stabilise the general level of commodity prices. I would be inclined to state the aim and responsibility of the Federal Reserve System somewhat differently. I would say that the responsibility that rests upon Central Banks abroad and the Federal Reserve System in this country is primarily one of maintenance of sound credit conditions. I realise that the term " sound credit conditions " is a vague one. What is meant depends on what one regards sound functions of credit to be. The function of commercial uses of credit is simply to facilitate the production and the marketing of commodities with the maintenance of adequate stocks of commodities in order that the marketing may be orderly. . . . I can see a situation where prices may be declining, yet inventories of commodities were accumulating, and where, if additional credit were granted, it would be used for the purpose of adding to the stock and would mean simply encouraging the accumulation of additional stocks . . . so that, rather than use the price index as a test, I would prefer to know what the inventories were and whether or not production was moving promptly into distribution.

For reasons which I have given fully in Chapter 29 above, I should not expect the cheapness and abundance of credit to have much effect, by itself, in over-encouraging the market to carry redundant stocks. The market is never eager to carry redundant stocks, and the degree of its willingness to do so chiefly depends on its expectations of the future course of prices. At the best the·existence of such stocks will keep prices below the normal cost of production of the commodities concerned and will act as an effective drag on the volume of current output.

But, in any case, this definition of " sound credit conditions " is, to my way of thinking, too narrow.

---

[1] *Op. cit.* p. 763.

It does not allow for the fact that, if the inability to sell current output at the current cost of production is *general* and not confined to a few special commodities, this is an indication of a maladjustment on the side of *demand* rather than of supply, that the only way of influencing demand is by increasing investment relatively to saving, and that this ought to lead the thoughts of the controllers of the banking system away from the " commercial uses of credit " to its financial uses. To refrain from lowering the rate of interest during a slump for fear of increasing the accumulation of stocks could only have the effect of accentuating the violence of the Credit Cycle ; though —I should admit—in conceivable circumstances, and as compared with conceivable alternatives, of perhaps shortening its duration.

According to my own definition " sound credit conditions " would, of course, be those in which the market-rate of interest was equal to the natural-rate, and both the value and the cost of new investment were equal to the volume of current savings. If we take this as our criterion, many of Governor Strong's perplexities will become much less formidable. We could, I think, in each case tell him—in general terms —what he ought to do to preserve the stability of the general price-level.

Granted, however, that the Banking System can control the price-level if it can control the value and volume of current investment, certain limitations which we have not yet removed are suggested by doubts whether in practice it does always lie within the power of the Banking System to control the rate of investment. To this question we will now address ourselves. But it may be convenient that I should summarise forthwith my final conclusions as to the limitations, which must be ultimately conceded, on the actual power of the Banking System to control the price-level :

(*a*) It is much easier to preserve stability than to restore it quickly, after a serious state of disequilibrium has been allowed to set in. Thus, if we are asked to start control operations in a situation which is already unstable, we may find that the position has got, for the time being, beyond effective control.

(*b*) Granted all reasonable intelligence and foresight on the part of the managers of the monetary system, non-monetary causes of instability may sometimes arise so suddenly that it is impossible to counteract them in time. In this event it may be inevitable that an interval should elapse before stability can be restored.

(*c*) If there are strong social or political forces causing spontaneous changes in the money-rates of efficiency-wages, the control of the price-level may pass beyond the power of the banking system. The effective power of the latter is primarily to prevent forces from operating which tend towards induced changes. It can, of course, provoke induced changes to balance spontaneous changes; but it may not be able, in that case, to control the pace or the route of the journey towards the new position of equilibrium.

(*d*) If a country adheres to an international standard and that standard is itself unstable, it is, of course, impossible to preserve the stability of the domestic price-level in face of this. But even if the international standard is itself stable, it may still be impossible to keep the domestic price-level stable if the changes in the demand schedule for capital in terms of the rate of interest are different at home from what they are abroad.

(*e*) Even where the banking system is strong enough to preserve the *stability* of the price-level, it does not follow that it is strong enough both to *alter* the price-level and to establish equilibrium at the new level without long delays and frictions.

In short, I should attribute to the banking system much greater power to *preserve* investment equilibrium than to force the prevailing rate of money-incomes away from the existing level or from the level produced by spontaneous changes, to a new and changed level imposed by conditions abroad or by arbitrary decree at home.

It follows that our existing currency system, in which we frequently impose on our Central Banks the duty of altering their domestic price-levels and rates of money-incomes as the necessary condition of maintaining the convertibility of their domestic currencies in terms of the international standard, puts on them a much more onerous and technically difficult task than that which would confront a Supernational Currency Authority charged with the duty of maintaining stability and armed with full powers and the firm confidence of its constituents.

(ii.) Short-term Rates of Interest and Long-term Rates

The main, direct influence of the Banking System is over the short-term rate of interest. But when it is a question of controlling the rate of investment, not in working capital but in fixed capital, it is the long-term rate of interest which chiefly matters. How can we be sure that the long-term rate of interest will respond to the wishes of a Currency Authority which will be exerting its direct influence, as it must, mainly on the short-term rate ? For whilst it is reasonable that long-term rates should bear a definite relation to the prospective short-term rates, quarter by quarter, over the years to come, the contribution of the current three-monthly period to this aggregate expectation should be insignificant in amount—so one might suppose. It may, therefore, seem illogical that the rate of interest fixed for a period of three months should have any noticeable effect on the terms asked for loans of twenty years or more.

In fact, however, experience shows that, as a rule, the influence of the short-term rate of interest on the long-term rate is much greater than anyone who argued on the above lines would have expected. We shall find, moreover, that there are some sound reasons, based on the technical character of the market, why it is not unnatural that this should be so.

The statistics have been worked up in a much more exact and convenient form for the United States than for Great Britain ; and up-to-date material has lately become available in Mr. W. W. Riefler's *Money Rates and Money Markets in the United States*, which is based on work done in the Division of Research and Statistics of the Federal Reserve Board. Unfortunately Mr. Riefler presents his results in the form of a chart only, without tables of the figures on which he has based them. The conclusion of the charts, which are reproduced on the following page, is, however, unmistakeable.

The long-term rates are measured by the average yield of sixty high-grade bonds, and the short-term rates by a weighted average of various typical short-term rates. Mr. Riefler concludes that " as indexes they can be used without question to indicate the direction of change of money rates in each market, and as fairly accurate indicators of the amount of change ". The generalisations which he draws from his results (which I prefer to give rather than my own, since he is merely interpreting the statistics and is not concerned to lead up to any particular conclusion) are as follows :

(1) " With the exception of the years 1921 and 1926, all the important movements in short-term rates from 1919 to 1928 were reflected in bond yields. Minor fluctuations in short-term rates were also frequently reflected in bond yields, even in the years 1921 and 1926." Moreover, it is shown subsequently that

SHORT and LONG-TERM RATES

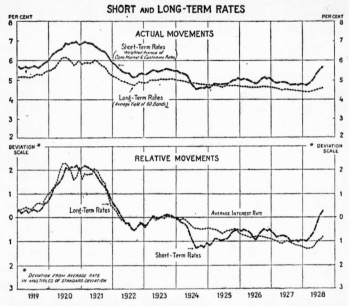

The lower section of the chart compares relative rather than actual movements of the two series. Each series is shown in relation to its own average fluctuations over the period charted. In order to obtain comparability between the relative fluctuations in the series, deviations from each average were divided by the standard deviation for the period. The zero line on the chart represents the average of the individual items in each series. When actual figures fall below this average they appear below the zero line, and *vice versa*.

" the fall of bond yields at that time, despite the fact that short-term rates were rising, was not entirely unconnected with the general credit situation ".[1]

(2) " Short-term rates moved over a wider actual range than long-term rates, although there was little difference of general levels as between the two series." But, as is brought out in the lower section of the chart, " current changes in each series relative to its general range of fluctuation are in nearly equal amounts as compared with corresponding changes in the other series ".[2]

(3) " The surprising fact is not that bond yields

[1] *Op. cit.* p. 117.   [2] *Op. cit.* p. 9.

are relatively stable in comparison with short-term rates, but rather that they have reflected fluctuations in short-term rates so strikingly and to such a considerable extent."[1]

In the case of Great Britain no statistics comparable to the above have been worked out, though the data are, of course, available. I have had to be content, for the corroboration of a general impression gained from watching the data as they have occurred during the last ten years, with a comparison between Bank-rate and the yield on Consols. The great advantage of the figures for the period 1919–1929 is that—as it happens—no correction is necessary for the general trend in the rate of interest, since both Bank-rate and the yield on Consols at the end of this period were approximately the same as at the beginning. These figures are given below, together with a third column, to guide the eye, based on the assumption that short-period fluctuations in Bank-rate are four times as wide as those in the yield on Consols (i.e. a 4 per cent fluctuation in the former corresponds to a 1 per cent fluctuation in the latter) :

	Average Bank-rate for the Year.	Average Price of Consols.	Index 1924=100.		
			Bank-rate.	Ditto with Fluctuations reduced by Three-quarters.	Yield on Consols at Average Price of the Year.
1919	5·166	$54\frac{1}{12}$	129	107	105
1920	6·71	$47\frac{1}{60}$	168	117	121
1921	6·092	$47\frac{29}{30}$	152	113	119
1922	3·692	$56\frac{15}{32}$	92	98	100
1923	3·496	$57\frac{63}{64}$	87	97	98
1924	4·0	$56\frac{63}{64}$	100	100	100
1925	4·575	$56\frac{3}{8}$	114	103	101
1926	5·0	$54\frac{29}{30}$	125	106	104
1927	4·650	$54\frac{39}{48}$	116	104	104
1928	4·5	$55\frac{12}{15}$	112	103	102
1929	5·508	$54\frac{5}{16}$	138	109	105

[1] Op. cit. p. 123.

The last two columns of this table, though by no means an entirely satisfactory index of what we are seeking, show results broadly similar to those found by Mr. Riefler for the United States.[1]

As a measure of the degree in which the terms of new long-term borrowing for current investment are responsible to the short-term rate, the above very much under-states, of course, the sensitiveness of the former. For we have been compelled to take the *least* sensitive of established long-term bonds. If the fluctuations in the yield on Consols are a quarter of those in Bank-rate, we might find that those in the yield of new long-term borrowing for fixed investment are nearly as much as a half, averaged over yearly periods. This means that a change of 2 per cent in Bank-rate, if continued for a year, may be capable of effecting a change in the cost of long-term borrowing (assuming fluctuations round 5 per cent as the basic rate) of as much as 10 to 20 per cent.

Indeed the facts are undoubted. The effect of " cheap money " on the price of bonds is a commonplace of the investment market. What is the ex-

---

[1] So far as pre-war British statistics are concerned, a chart by Mr. E. G. Peake will be found in the *Bankers' Magazine* (May 1928, p. 720), showing the rate of interest on floating money against the yield on L. and N.W. Railway Debentures plotted year by year for the period 1882-1913. For the period before (say) 1894 the extreme insensitiveness of Consols—there was no year between 1867 and 1924 in which the yield on the average price of Consols varied more than 1s. 6d. per cent from one year to another—disqualifies it as an index of the price at which current long-term borrowing could be arranged. For the twenty years before the war, the results corrected for trend would not, I think, be very different from those quoted above for the post-war period. The index for the eight years before the war (taking 1909 = 100), corrected for trend and with the fluctuations of Bank-rate damped down to a quarter as above, is as follows :

Year.	Bank-rate.	Yield on Consols.	Year.	Bank-rate.	Yield on Consols.
1906	110	104	1910	104	102
1907	113	105	1911	102	103
1908	100	100	1912	103	104
1909	100	100	1913	109	104

planation ? There are several reasons, I think, why we need not be surprised at the above results.

(*a*) If the running yield on bonds is greater than the rate payable on short-term loans, a profit is obtainable by borrowing short in order to carry long-term securities, so long as the latter do not actually fall in value during the currency of the loan. Thus the pressure of transactions of this kind will initiate an upward trend, and this, for a time at least, will confirm the investor in a " bullish " feeling towards the bond market. Moreover, firms, which need to utilise in their business some part of their liquid reserves which they have been keeping in high-grade bonds, will tend to borrow on the security of these bonds when the cost of such borrowing is less than the running yield on the bonds; whilst they will sell the bonds outright when the contrary is the case.[1]

Thus it is a matter of significance when the short-term open-market rate crosses the running yield on bonds. It is rarely the case that bond yields will fail to rise (or fall) if the short-term rate remains at an absolutely higher (or lower) level than the bond yield even for a few weeks.

(*b*) There are a number of financial institutions— amongst which the banks themselves are the most important, but also including Insurance Offices, Investment Trusts, Finance Houses, etc.—which vary from time to time the proportionate division of their assets between long-term and short-term securities respectively. Where short-term yields are high, the safety and liquidity of short-term securities appear extremely attractive. But when short-term yields are

---

[1] Cf. Riefler (*op. cit.* p. 119) : " Securities are widely used as collateral for loans and are carried in large volume on the basis of bank-credit. . . . The continued availability of short-term credit, the level of short-term rates and the relation of these rates to the yield of the securities is naturally a factor with all of these borrowers in making decisions as to whether they shall continue to carry the securities on bank-credit or dispose of them in the long-term markets."

very low, not only does this attraction disappear, but another motive enters in, namely, a fear lest the institution may be unable to maintain its established level of income, any serious falling off in which would be injurious to its reputation. A point comes, therefore, when they hasten to move into long-dated securities ; the movement itself sends up the price of the latter ; and this movement seems to confirm the wisdom of those who were recommending the policy of the change-over. Thus, unless there is a serious reason in the minds of the majority of those controlling funds for positively fearing long-term securities at their existing price-level, this price will tend to rise a little, and the initial small price will tend to become a bigger one through its increasing the general anxiety amongst those who cannot afford to see their income from running yield suffer a serious fall, lest they miss the bus.

This is particularly the case with the banks themselves. I believe it would be found, both in Great Britain and in the United States, that the purchase and sale of securities by the banks for their own account have been the dominating factor in determining the turning-points in the price-level of bonds. For they hold a very large volume of such securities—in the United States of the order of $10,000,000,000, in Great Britain of the order of £250,000,000, so that any considerable change-over on their part between short-term assets and long-term assets has an important effect on the price of the latter.

Now banks above all prefer short-term assets, if they can afford to hold them. But when their yield falls below a certain point, they cannot afford to hold them. This may be illustrated as follows from the results of the Member Banks in the Boston Federal Reserve District in 1929. Worked out as a percentage of their earning assets, *i.e.* their loans, discounts and investments, the interest they earned was nearly 6 per cent, the interest they paid out was nearly $2\frac{1}{2}$ per

cent, and their other expenses were a little more than
2 per cent, so that their profits were about $1\frac{1}{2}$ per cent.
It is evident, therefore, that there is not room for much
fall in their average interest earnings without a serious
reaction on their profits.   There are no such detailed
figures available for Great Britain, but London banks
probably do not make a net profit of much more than
1 per cent of their deposits (they publish a smaller
profit than this).   If we set off changes in the rate they
earn on advances against changes in the rate they pay
on deposits, we are left with their other short-term
assets (bills and call-money) and their longer-term
securities, the former being round 25 per cent of their
deposits and the latter round 15 per cent (these are, of
course, fluctuating figures).   Thus a drop of 2 per cent
in the yield on their bills and call-money will reduce
their aggregate profits by an amount equal to $\frac{1}{2}$ per
cent on their deposits, *i.e.* will reduce their profits by
somewhere near a half.   Thus the motive for a shift
from short-term assets to long-term assets when the
yield from the former falls sharply is obviously a
strong one—a conclusion which is corroborated by the
statistics.[1]

(c) How far the motives which I have been attri-
buting above to the market are strictly rational, I
leave it to others to judge.   They are best regarded, I
think, as an example of how sensitive—over-sensitive
if you like—to the near future, about which we may
think that we know a little, even the best-informed
must be, because, in truth, we know almost nothing
about the more remote future.   And the exaggerations
of this same tendency, to which we now come, also
play a part.

---

[1] Mr. Riefler's very detailed figures for the United States bear this out
in a most striking way.   " Through their own purchases and sales of investments," he concludes (*op. cit.* p. 119), " commercial banks have exercised a
marked pressure on the market for bonds and contributed to a considerable
extent to the agreement in relative movements between bond yields and
short-term money rates."

For part of the explanation which we are seeking is to be found in a psychological phenomenon which appears even more strikingly in the current market valuation of ordinary shares. The value of a company's shares, and even of its bonds, will be found to be sensitive to a degree, which a rational observer from outside might consider quite absurd, to short-period fluctuations in its known or anticipated profits. The shares of a railway company will be highly sensitive to its weekly traffic returns, even if it be well known that these are influenced by necessarily transient factors, such as an exceptionally good or bad harvest in the country concerned, or a strike in the district served by the railway, or even an international exhibition. Such events will often cause the capital value of the shares to fluctuate by an amount which far exceeds any possible change in its profits due to the event in question. These are extreme cases, perhaps ; but it must be well known to anyone who follows the prices of ordinary shares that their market valuation shows a strong bias towards the assumption that whatever conditions and results have been characteristic of the present and the recent past, and even more those which are expected to be characteristic of the near future, will be lasting and permanent. And the Bond Market is not exempt from the same weakness.

Nor need we be surprised. The ignorance of even the best-informed investor about the more remote future is much greater than his knowledge, and he cannot but be influenced to a degree which would seem wildly disproportionate to anyone who really knew the future, by the little which he knows for certain, or almost for certain, about the recent past and the near future, and be forced to seek a clue mainly here to trends further ahead. But if this is true of the best-informed, the vast majority of those who are concerned with the buying and selling of securities know almost nothing whatever about what they are doing. They do not possess even the rudiments of what is required for a valid judgment, and are the prey of hopes and fears easily aroused by transient events and as easily dispelled. This is one of the odd characteristics of the Capitalist System under which we live, which, when we are dealing with the real world, is not to be overlooked.

But there is also a further reason why it may often profit the wisest to anticipate mob psychology rather than the real trend of events, and to ape unreason proleptically. For the value of a security is determined, not by the terms on which one could expect to purchase the whole block of the outstanding interest, but by the small fringe which is the subject of actual dealing ;—just as current new investment is only a small fringe on the edge of the totality of existing investments. Now this fringe is largely dealt in by professional financiers—speculators you may call them—who have no intention of holding the securities long enough for the influence of distant events to have its effect ;—their object is to re-sell to the mob after a few weeks or at most a few months. It is natural, therefore, that they should be influenced by the cost of borrowing, and still more by their expectations on the basis of past experience of the trend of mob psychology. Thus, so long as the crowd can be relied on to act in a certain way, even if it be misguided, it will be to the advantage of the better informed professional to act in the same way—a short period ahead. Apart, moreover, from calculations of greater or less ignorance, most people are too timid and too greedy, too impatient and too nervous about their investments, the fluctuations in the paper value of which can so easily obliterate the results of so much honest effort, to take long views or to place even as much reliance as they reasonably might on the dubieties of the long period;—the apparent certainties of the short period, however deceptive we may suspect them to be, are much more attractive.

Nor is it so precarious as might be supposed to depend upon these psychological characteristics of the market. It is a case, indeed, of a homœopathic cure. For it is just these half-unreasonable characteristics of the market which are the source of many of the troubles which it is the object of management to remedy. If investors were capable of taking longer views, the fluctuations in the natural-rate of interest would not be so great as they are. The real prospects do not suffer such large and quick changes as does the spirit of enterprise. The willingness to invest is stimulated and depressed by the immediate prospects. It is not unreasonable, therefore, to depend on short-period influences for counteracting a violent, and perhaps unreasoning, change in sentiment.

We may carry away, therefore, to the next section of our argument the conclusion that short-term rates influence long-term rates more than the reader might expect, and that it is not difficult to find sufficient explanations for this observed fact.

(iii.) Can the Banking System control the Rate of Investment ?

We have not, as yet, made more than a very little progress towards answering this question in the affirmative. We have shown that the long-term market-rate of interest can be influenced to a certain extent in the desired direction by movements of the short-term rate. But even if the market-rate changes a little, the natural-rate may be changing much faster. For our conclusion to hold, it is necessary, therefore, that we should raise a presumption of an ability on the part of the Banking System to cause the market-rate of interest to move as much and as quickly as the natural-rate is likely to move in any ordinary circumstances.

We shall not be able to prove this by an appeal to statistics. For the mere occurrence of a Credit Cycle is in itself a demonstration of the fact that the Banking System has failed to change the market-rate so as to keep pace with changes in the natural-rate. It is certain, therefore, that hitherto the Banking System has not succeeded in controlling the Rate of Investment with sufficient success to avoid serious instability.

Thus we cannot do more at present than marshal the various means at the disposal of the Banking System. Only the future can show for certain whether the conscious and well-directed use of all these means, confidently employed in the right degree and at the right time, is capable of solving the problem.

(a) The Direct Influence of Changes in the Short-term Rate of Interest

Apart from international complications which we are putting on one side for the present, there is no reason to doubt the ability of a Central Bank to make its short-term rate of interest effective in the market. These changes in themselves must have *some* effect in the desired direction ; for they at least determine the interest-cost of the revolving fund of working capital and of carrying liquid stocks. I do not believe, however—for reasons already given in Book VI.—that the volume of investment either in working capital or in liquid capital is sensitive to changes in the short-term rate of interest by itself and unless these changes create an expectation of changes in prices. Fluctuations in the volume of investment in working and liquid capital play a large part, of course, in the accentuation of booms and depressions ; but I doubt if they can be either caused or avoided merely by changes of bank-rate. They generally represent a belated response to changes in the price-level which have been brought about by an unbalanced volume of investment in fixed capital.

Such effects as can be produced directly on the willingness to invest in working and liquid capital are attributable, I think, rather to the greater or less degree in which the fringe of " unsatisfied " borrowers, as I shall call them in (b) below, is satisfied than to the cheapness or dearness of money in itself.

On the other hand, the direct effects of cheap money operating through changes, even small ones, in the bond market, as described in Section (ii.) of this chapter, on the volume of new investment is probably of more importance. Willingness to invest more or less in manufacturing plant is not likely to be very sensitive to small changes in bond-rate. But the quantity of new fixed capital required by industry is relatively trifling even at the best times, and is not a big factor in the situation. Almost the whole of the fixed capital of the world is represented by buildings, transport and public utilities; and the sensitiveness of these activities even to small changes in the long-term rate of interest, though with an appreciable time-lag, is surely considerable.

(b) The Fringe of Unsatisfied Borrowers

The relaxation or contraction of credit by the Banking System does not operate, however, merely through a change in the rate charged to borrowers; it also functions through a change in the abundance of credit. If the supply of credit were distributed in an absolutely free competitive market, these two conditions—quantity and price—would be uniquely correlated with one another and we should not need to consider them separately. But in practice there is the contingency to be considered that the conditions of a free competitive market for bank-loans are imperfectly fulfilled. For it is not in fact the case— at least not in Great Britain, I believe that the market in the United States is much more freely

competitive—that anyone offering security can borrow
as much as he likes from the British banking system
merely by offering a rate of interest high enough
to outbid other borrowers. There is, that is to say,
in Great Britain an habitual system of rationing in
the attitude of banks to borrowers—the amount lent
to any individual being governed not solely by the
security and the rate of interest offered, but also by
reference to the borrower's purposes and his standing
with the bank as a valuable or influential client. Thus
there is normally a fringe of unsatisfied borrowers who
are not considered to have the first claims on a bank's
favours, but to whom the bank would be quite ready
to lend if it were to find itself in a position to lend
more.

The existence of this unsatisfied fringe and of
a variability in the banks' standards of eligibility of
borrowers in respects other than the rate of interest,
allows the Banking System a means of influencing the
rate of investment supplementary to mere changes
in the short-term rate of interest. The process of
stimulating investment in this way cannot be continued beyond the point at which there is no longer
any unsatisfied fringe ; nor can the reverse process
be continued beyond the point at which the unsatisfied fringe begins to include borrowers so influential that they can find ways round, *e.g.* by creating
bills of first-class quality or by borrowing direct from
the banks' depositors. But within these limits the
banks can produce effects on the rate of investment
out of proportion to what properly corresponds to the
changes, if any, in the short-term rate of interest
which are taking place at the same time.

That is to say, the Bank of England does not fix
bank-rate and leave the quantity of bank-money to
find its own level ; nor does it fix the quantity of
bank-money and leave bank-rate to find its own level.
It fixes *both*—and fixes them, to a certain extent,

independently. It then—in effect—invites the member banks and the money-market to co-operate in keeping the bank-rate, thus fixed, effective on the basis of the quantity of bank-money also thus fixed.

Its weapons for securing this co-operation are terror, agreement and convention. The Bank can influence the situation *per terrorem*, because in the last resort it always lies within its power to make its bank-rate effective by altering the quantity of bank-money ; so that it is not safe, when the official bank-rate is ineffective, to enter into transactions which are based on the assumption that it will remain so for some little time. Thus the latent threat to alter the quantity of bank-money if necessary may, in the appropriate conditions, have much the same effect on money-rates as an actual alteration.

The element of agreement comes in because the Clearing Banks have agreed to pay interest to their fixed depositors in London at a rate bearing a defined relationship to the official bank-rate—formerly $1\frac{1}{2}$ per cent less and now 2 per cent less. This reacts—psychologically, perhaps, rather than rationally—on the rates at which the banks are disposed to lend, in particular on the rates at which they will lend money at call to the money-market, which rates have also been subject from time to time to an agreed minimum settled amongst themselves by the Clearing Banks. And in addition to these matters of agreement, there are a number of customs and conventions by which the rate of interest charged for bank-loans bears a more or less fixed relationship to the official bank-rate; for example loans to the Stock Exchange, and the innumerable standing arrangements for overdrafts and advances, the rate for which is agreed beforehand at a figure fixed relatively to the official bank-rate and is not lightly altered. Accordingly when, for example, the official rate is raised, the rate for many bank-loans goes up automatically by the same amount. If some previous borrowers no longer care to borrow at the higher rate, then more of the unsatisfied fringe gets the accommodation for which it has been asking. This power of the Bank of England to fix independently—within limits—the bank-rate and the quantity of bank-money is of particular importance when international complications are requiring a level of bank-rate which may interfere with the equilibrium rate of home investment.

The above analysis relates primarily to London, where the course of events cannot be understood without it. In the United States the influence on a Member Bank of the amount of its indebtedness to its Reserve Bank has acquired an almost analogous importance, especially in the last few years. The most marked change in the practical operation of the Federal Reserve System since the Boom and Slump of 1920–22 has been the gradual evolution of a conventional unwillingness on the part of Member Banks to be continuously indebted to the Reserve Banks. Thus it makes a great difference to the practical help which the Member Banks accord to projects for new investment whether the volume of federal reserve credit existing at the moment is based on member-bank discounting or on gold and open-market operations by the Reserve Banks themselves. In the former case the Member Banks will be struggling to lend less and to fob off borrowers of marginal eligibility ; in the latter case they will be eagerly seeking an outlet for their funds. Which of these two situations prevails at any given time, it lies within the power of the Federal Reserve Banks to determine.

(c) The Position of Issue Houses and
Underwriters

In the modern world the volume of long-term borrowing for purposes of new investment depends most directly on the attitude of the leading Issue Houses and Underwriters, who act as middlemen between the ultimate borrowers and lenders. The system in its present phase is a somewhat peculiar one, a full and accurate account of which is not yet to be found in print, nor indeed a history of the evolution of the underwriting system,—which is less than fifty years old.

Now Issue Houses on a large scale are few in number and often act in accord with one another. They are also subject to the influence of the Central Bank, without whose goodwill their operations would become unduly risky. They are very much concerned with their reputation and with the "success" of their issues from the point of those who have purchased them. Thus if the price of bonds is a slowly rising one, so that recent previous issues show a profit on their issue price rather than a loss, the Issue Houses will tend to facilitate further borrowing, and to restrain it, on the other hand, if there is a falling tendency ;—for in the latter case they will try to "protect" the market for their previous issues by restricting the output of new ones. Here again—in effect—there is an unsatisfied fringe of would-be borrowers at the existing market-rate, and the market is not an entirely free one.

Thus easy credit conditions and an atmosphere in which the Central Bank is encouraging Issue Houses to operate may make an immense difference to the rate at which new investment can get itself financed, as compared with the opposite state of affairs in which the Central Bank is frowning on new issues,—a difference which may be quite out of proportion to the change, which may be slight, in the quoted price of bonds.[1]

---

[1] Cf. Riefler (*op. cit.* p. 121) : " When the market for bonds is under pressure and bond prices are falling, the full current demand for long-term loans is subject to a measure of restraint. During these periods, for example,

This is another illustration of the sensitiveness of long-term operations to short-term considerations, and how much the Central Authority can do to retard or stimulate the rate of investment over the short period merely by creating an atmosphere and without any sensational change in the rate charged for loans.

(d) OPEN-MARKET OPERATIONS TO THE POINT OF SATURATION

So far we have been dealing with the normal and orthodox methods by which a Central Bank can use its powers for easing (or stiffening) the credit situation to stimulate (or retard) the rate of new investment. If these measures are applied in the right degree and *at the right time*, I doubt whether it would often be necessary to go beyond them or to apply the extra-ordinary methods next to be considered. It is only, that is to say, if the milder remedies have not been applied in time, so that conditions of acute slump or boom have been allowed to develop, that more extreme measures will have to be invoked and that

---

the volume of new bond flotations usually shrinks to small proportions. In part this reflects the fact that borrowers are unwilling to pay current rates, but it is also affected by the fact that investment houses are loath to add further to the pressure that is already apparent in the market. Even borrowers who are willing to pay current rates, consequently are apt to find it difficult to obtain the accommodation they desire. Some may be rejected entirely when they undertake negotiations with investment houses for new loans, or possibly advised to wait. Others may be temporarily accommodated with bank loans or issues of short-term notes, which banks are willing to buy. . . .

" At times when bond prices are rising, on the other hand, and bond yields are falling in response to an increase in the volume of investment funds, the full effect of this increase in supply of funds may not be wholly reflected in . . . a decline in bond yields. Some portion of the funds, instead, may be absorbed in the rapid increase in new security issues which almost always appears at such times. . . . Demands originating in sources which under other conditions would not have been exploited are permitted to enter the market. . . . Some of this increase in flotations represents a stimulation of demand arising out of lower interest charges, but much of it represents in addition the release of a partially controlled demand which enters the market mainly when other conditions as well as rates are favourable."

doubts may be reasonably entertained whether even these more extreme measures will be wholly efficacious.

These extra-ordinary methods are, in fact, no more than an intensification of the normal procedure of open-market operations. I do not know of any case in which the method of open-market operations has been carried out *à outrance*. Central Banks have always been too nervous hitherto—partly, perhaps, under the influence of crude versions of the Quantity Theory—of taking measures which would have the effect of causing the total volume of bank-money to depart widely from its normal volume, whether in excess or in defect. But this attitude of mind neglects, I think, the part which the " bullishness " or " bearishness " of the public plays in the demand for bank-money ; it forgets the financial circulation in its concern for the industrial circulation, and overlooks the statistical fact that the former may be quite as large as the latter and much more capable of sharp variation.

I suggest, therefore, that bolder measures are sometimes advisable, and that they are quite free from serious danger whenever there has developed on the part of the capitalist public an obstinate " bullishness " or " bearishness " towards securities. On such occasions the Central Bank should carry its open-market operations to the point of satisfying to saturation the desire of the public to hold savings-deposits, or of exhausting the supply of such deposits in the contrary case.

The risk of bringing to bear too rapidly and severely on the industrial circulation, when it is the financial circulation which is being aimed at, is greater I think in the case of a contraction of credit than in the case of an expansion. But, on the other hand, it is less likely to be necessary to resort to extreme measures to check a boom than to check a slump. Booms, I suspect, are almost always due to tardy or inadequate action by the banking system such as should be avoid-

able ;—there is much more foundation for the view
that it is slumps which may sometimes get out of hand
and defy all normal methods of control.   It will be,
therefore, on the problem of checking a slump that we
shall now concentrate our attention.

My remedy in the event of the obstinate persistence
of a slump would consist, therefore, in the purchase of
securities by the Central Bank until the long-term
market-rate of interest has been brought down to the
limiting point, which we shall have to admit a few
paragraphs further on.   It should not be beyond the
power of a Central Bank (international complications
apart) to bring down the long-term market-rate of
interest to any figure at which it is itself prepared to
buy long-term securities.   For the bearishness of the
capitalist public is never *very* obstinate, and when the
rate of interest on savings-deposits is next door to
nothing the saturation point can fairly soon be reached.
If the Central Bank supplies the member banks with
more funds than they can lend at short-term, in the
first place the short-term rate of interest will decline
towards zero, and in the second place the member
banks will soon begin, if only to maintain their profits,
to second the efforts of the Central Bank by themselves
buying securities.   This means that the price of bonds
will rise unless there are many persons to be found
who, as they see the prices of long-term bonds rising,
prefer to sell them and hold the proceeds liquid at a
very low rate of interest.   If (*e.g.*) the long-term rate is
3 per cent per annum above the short-term rate, this
means that the mathematical expectation for bond
prices in the minds of such persons is for a fall of 3 per
cent per annum ; and at a time when bond prices are
in fact rising and the Central Bank is accentuating the
cheapness of money, there is not likely to be a large
volume of such selling—unless the price of bonds has
been driven to a level which is generally believed to be
quite excessive from the long-period point of view, a

contingency and a limiting factor to the consideration of which we will return shortly. If the effect of such measures is to raise the price of " equities " (*e.g.* ordinary shares) more than the price of bonds, no harm *in a time of slump* will result from this ; for investment can be stimulated by its being unusually easy to raise resources by the sale of ordinary shares as well as by high bond-prices. Moreover, a very excessive price for equities is not likely to occur at a time of depression and business losses.

Thus I see small reason to doubt that the Central Bank can produce a large effect on the cost of raising new resources for long-term investment, if it is prepared to persist with its open-market policy far enough. What, however, are in practice the factors limiting the degree in which it can push such a policy home ?

There is, first of all, the question of the sufficiency of its " ammunition ", *i.e.* of its power to go on buying or selling in adequate quantity securities of a suitable kind. The lack of suitable ammunition is more likely to hamper a Central Bank when it is seeking to contract the volume of bank-money than when it is seeking to expand it, since its stock of securities at the commencement of its contraction policy is necessarily limited. But it also operates, in a sense, against an expansionist policy, since a Central Bank is generally limited in the type of securities which it purchases, so that, if it continues such purchases beyond a certain point, it may create an entirely artificial position in them relatively to other securities. It is to provide against the contingency of insufficient ammunition for the carrying on of open-market operations *à outrance*, that I have suggested above (p. 77) that the Central Bank should have power to vary within limits the reserve requirements of its member banks.

In the second place, circumstances can arise when, for a time, the natural-rate of interest falls so low that there is a very wide and quite unusual gap between the ideas of borrowers and of lenders in the market on long-term. When prices are falling, profits low, the future uncertain and financial sentiment depressed and alarmed, the natural-rate of interest may fall, for a short period, almost to nothing. But it is precisely at such a time as this that lenders are most exigent and least inclined to embark their resources on long-term unless it be on the most unexceptionable security; so that the bond-rate, far from falling towards nothing, may be expected—apart from the operations of the Central Bank—to be higher than normal. How is it possible in such circumstances, we may reasonably ask, to keep the market-rate and the natural-rate of long-term interest at an equality with one another, *unless we impose on the Central Bank the duty of purchasing bonds up to a price far beyond what it considers to be the long-period norm.* Yet, if its instincts as to the long-period norm are correct, this will mean that these purchases, when in due course they have to be reversed by sales at a later date, may show a serious financial loss. This contingency—the reader should notice—can only arise as the result of inaccurate forecasting by the capitalist public and of a difference of opinion between the Central Bank and long-term borrowers as to the prospective rate of returns.

We might perhaps expect the Central Bank, as representing the public interest, to be ready to run the risks of future prospects when private interests reckon these risks to be unusually high. But the choice may conceivably lie between assuming the burden of a prospective loss, allowing the slump to continue, and socialistic action by which some official body steps into the shoes which the feet of the entrepreneurs are too cold to occupy.

I would repeat, however, that these extreme situations are not likely to arise except as the result of some previous mistake which has prevented the slumping tendency from being remedied at an earlier stage before so complete a lack of confidence had sapped the spirits and the energies of enterprise.

The third limiting factor arises out of the presence of international complications which we have been excluding so far from our purview but to which we must now attend.

(e) INTERNATIONAL COMPLICATIONS

We come finally to what is in the world of to-day the insuperable limitation on the power of skilled monetary management to avoid booms and depressions,—a limitation which it would be foolish to overlook or to minimise. No national Central Bank which is a member of an international system, not even the Federal Reserve System of the United States, can expect to preserve the stability of its price-level, if it is acting in isolation and is not assisted by corresponding action on the part of the other Central Banks. Moreover, whilst the broad interests of the various Central Banks are likely to be concordant, we cannot rely on their being so in detail and at all times. For the reasons which we have explained above in dealing with the problem whether the standard of value should be international in character, the immediate interests of different countries may be divergent, and action calculated to preserve the stability of employment in one of them may not necessarily have the same result in another.

Against the international complications which at present prevent any successful attempt at managing our Standard of Value scientifically and preserving investment equilibrium throughout the world, the only adequate remedy could be found in a system of supernational management such as we shall outline very briefly in the next chapter.

Meanwhile the only courses capable of mitigating

the evils of the rule of Hap-hazard, which is so firmly riveted on our shoulders, seem to be the following.

In the first place, one need not exaggerate the importance of international dependence. A country can do a great deal by sound internal management to keep its employment and its business life on a level keel. If international trade and international lending make up a comparatively small proportion of its economic life, the extent to which it will be compelled to share in international disturbances will be correspondingly limited.[1] Moreover, any country can at least prevent itself from being a storm-centre of trouble and the initiator of disequilibrium elsewhere and can contribute its quota of stability, for what it is worth, to the general situation.

In the second place, one need not exaggerate the degree of the divergence of interest between different countries. When it is a question of a major disturbance, everyone is in the same boat. For example, in 1929 it was plausible to suppose that the interests of the United States were divergent from those of the rest of the world ; but by acting on this assumption the authorities of that country were in fact making certain the bursting in 1930 of the storm—which was already incipient for causes for which Great Britain was perhaps primarily responsible—which has affected them at least as severely as anyone else. Broadly speaking, therefore, co-operation, rightly understood, is in everyone's interests.

Now it is the action of the lending countries of the world which mainly determines the market-rate of interest and the volume of investment everywhere. Thus, if the chief lending countries would co-operate, they might do much to avoid the major investment

---

[1] The problem of maintaining internal stability in the United States is for this reason a much simpler one than the corresponding problem in Great Britain. Foreign investment, for example, absorbs, say, 5 per cent of the national savings in the United States but perhaps (in equilibrium) more nearly 40 per cent in Great Britain.

disequilibria ;—that is to say, Great Britain, the United States and France. And if France prefers to live in a gilded grotto, Great Britain and the United States acting together could usually dominate the position.

Finally, there remains in reserve a weapon by which a country can partially rescue itself when its international disequilibrium is involving it in severe unemployment. In such an event open-market operations by the Central Bank intended to bring down the market-rate of interest and stimulate investment may, by misadventure, stimulate foreign lending instead and so provoke an outward flow of gold on a larger scale than it can afford. In such a case it is not sufficient for the Central Authority to stand ready to lend—for the money may flow into the wrong hands ; —it must also stand ready to borrow. In other words, the Government must itself promote a programme of domestic investment. It may be a choice betweeen employing labour to create capital wealth, which will yield less than the market-rate of interest, or not employing it at all. If this is the position, the national interest, both immediate and prospective, will be promoted by choosing the first alternative. But if foreign borrowers are ready and eager, it will be impossible in a competitive open market to bring the rate down to the level appropriate to domestic investment. Thus the desired result can only be obtained through some method by which, in effect, the Government subsidises approved types of domestic investment or itself directs domestic schemes of capital development.

About the application of this method to the position of Great Britain in 1929–30 I have written much elsewhere, and need not enlarge on it here. Assuming that it was not practicable, at least for a time, to bring costs down relatively to costs abroad sufficiently to increase the foreign balance by a large amount, then a policy of subsidising home investment by promoting (say) 3 per cent schemes of national development was a valid means of increasing both employment to-day and the national wealth hereafter.   The only alternative remedy of immediate applicability, in such circumstances, was to subsidise foreign investment by the exclusion of foreign imports, so that the failure of increased exports to raise the foreign balance to the equilibrium level might be made good by diminishing the volume of imports.

(iv.) THE SLUMP OF 1930

I am writing these concluding lines in the midst of the world-wide slump of 1930.   The wholesale Indexes have fallen by 20 per cent in a year.   The prices of a large group of the world's most important staple commodities—wheat, oats, barley, sugar, coffee ; cotton, wool, jute, silk ; copper, tin, spelter ; rubber—stood a year ago 50 per cent higher in price than they do now. The American Index of Production has receded by more than 20 per cent.   In Great Britain, Germany and the United States at least 10,000,000 workers stand unemployed.   One cannot but be moved by a feeling of the importance of diagnosing correctly the scientific causes of these misfortunes.   Was the catastrophe avoidable ?   Can it be remedied ?

Thus I am lured on to the rash course of giving an opinion on contemporary events which are too near to be visible distinctly ; namely, my view of the root causes of what has happened, which is as follows.

The most striking change in the investment factors of the post-war world compared with the pre-war world is to be found in the high level of the market-rate of interest.   As a rough generalisation one may say that the long-term rate of interest is nearly 50 per cent higher to-day than twenty years ago.   Yet the population of the industrial countries is not increasing as fast as formerly, and is a good deal better equipped per head than it was with housing, transport and machines. On the other hand, the volume of lending to the less advanced parts of the world is not markedly large—indeed the contrary, since Russia, China and India, which include within their borders a substantial proportion of the population of the world, are able, for one reason or another, to borrow next to nothing on the international markets ; whilst the United States has converted itself from a borrowing to a lending country. Why, then, should the rate of interest be so high ?

The answer is, I suggest, that for some years after the war sundry causes, to be enumerated, interposed to maintain the natural-rate of interest at a high level ; that these, more recently, have ceased to operate ; that sundry other causes have nevertheless maintained the market-rate of interest ; and that, consequently, there has now developed, somewhat suddenly, an unusually wide gap between the ideas of borrowers and those of lenders, that is, between the natural-rate of interest and the market-rate.

For a few years after the war there were obvious reasons why the natural-rate of interest should stand for a time above its long-period norm. In particular, a large volume of investment was required to restore the revolving fund of working capital for peace-time production. Then there was war damage to be made good, arrears of housing, etc., to be made up. Perhaps this phase was coming to an end in 1924-25. Meanwhile, certain new industries were leading to large-scale investment, especially in the United States— public utilities based on the use of electricity (and also natural gas), the motor industry and roads [1] to serve motorists, the cinema and radio industries. These operated to maintain the natural-rate of interest to

[1] In 1904 expenditure on roads and bridges in the United States was $59,500,000, and in 1914 $240,000,000. By 1928 the figure had risen to nearly $1,660,000,000 (cf. *Planning and Control of Public Works*, p. 127).

some extent. But, looking back, I am inclined to think
that the seeds of the recent collapse were already being
sown so long ago as 1925. By that date the natural-
rate of interest, outside the United States, was probably due for a fall. But round about that date—some
of them beginning rather earlier, others rather later—
there supervened two sets of events, not wholly dis-
connected, which served to maintain the market-rate
of interest somewhat regardless of the underlying
realities of the natural-rate—namely, the general return to the Gold Standard, and the settlement of
Reparations and the War Debts.

For these events, though they had no bearing whatever on the real yield of new investment, were a
powerful influence on the market-rate of interest.
Those Central Banks which had entered upon the new
responsibility of maintaining gold parity, were naturally nervous and disposed to take no risks—some of
them because they had but just emerged from currency
catastrophes attended by a total loss of credit, others
(especially Great Britain) because they had returned
to the Gold Standard at a dangerously high parity
probably inconsistent with their existing domestic
equilibrium. This nervousness inevitably tended in
the direction of credit restriction, which was not in the
least called for by the real underlying economic facts,
throughout Europe and, sympathetically, in many
other quarters. Great Britain played a leading part
in tightening the hold on credit and in urging a hurried
all-round return back to gold. The inadequacy of free
gold supplies (*i.e.* gold in the hands of ready sellers
of the metal) much aggravated the position. At this
stage, indeed, only the United States was entirely
exempt from some measure of credit restriction.

Whilst this tendency towards restriction was
tightening the terms of lending and stiffening the
attitude of the purchasers of securities, another aspect
of the same set of events was providing a supply of

borrowers who were prepared to pay terms which were not based on any calculation of the probable yield of actual new investment. These borrowers were of two types. The first were the "distress" borrowers—as they are conveniently called—chiefly governments, who were borrowing, not for investment in productive enterprise, but to meet their urgent liabilities, to satisfy their creditors, and to comply with their treaty obligations. The terms which such borrowers will pay have but little to do with the prospective returns of current investment and are dictated by the borrowers. The second class were the "banking" borrowers—sometimes governments and sometimes banks—who were borrowing, again not for investment in productive enterprise, but to build up liquid reserves, partly gold and partly foreign balances, with which to protect their newly restored currencies. We had the extraordinary situation in 1927–28 of the United States lending on long-term at high rates of interest, largely to Europe, amounts several times greater than her favourable balance, and being able to do so because these borrowers at once re-deposited with her on short-term the major part of what they had just borrowed on long-term at rates nearly double, perhaps, those which they could obtain on short-term for their re-deposits. In two or three years some £500,000,000 was thus borrowed on long-term and re-deposited on short-term—which naturally had a tendency to upset the normal relation between short-term and long-term rates of interest, such as these would be, if they were mainly determined, as in the long run they must be, by the ideas of those who are borrowing for actual investment.

Finally, in 1928–29 these "artificial" borrowers on long-term—if we may so designate borrowers who are not influenced by the return on actual current investment—were reinforced by a third class of "artificial" borrowers, this time on short-term, namely, the "speculative" borrowers, who, once more, were borrowing not for investment in new productive enterprise, but in order to participate in the feverish " bull " movement in " equities " (mostly of a semi-monopolistic character which could not easily be duplicated), which was occurring most sensationally in the United States but also in varying degrees on most of the Stock Exchanges of the world. Moreover, the anxiety of conservative banking opinion to bring this speculative fever somehow to an end provided a new motive for credit restriction by the Central Banks.

By the middle of 1929 "genuine" borrowers—if we may so designate borrowers for purposes of actual new investment which they deem profitable on the terms offering—whose activities were already, in my judgment, below par in most countries other than the United States, were becoming squeezed out. The more urgent needs of post-war reconstruction and of the new types of industry having been satisfied, it simply was not worth their while to borrow on a scale equal to the volume of savings at the high market-rate of interest, which was being maintained partly by the " artificial " borrowers and partly by the credit policy of the Central Banks.

The divergence thus arising between the market-rate of interest and the natural-rate was, therefore, the primary cause of the sagging price-level. But once this had proceeded far enough to generate " slump " psychology in the minds of entrepreneurs, it was, of course, reinforced, as usual, by other, and perhaps quantitatively greater, influences.

For I should not suppose that—taking the world as a whole—the deficiency of current investment relatively to saving, which initially engendered the slump, would be responsible by itself for a fall in the price-level of much more than 5 per cent. But as soon as the losses thus caused have become sufficiently patent to entrepreneurs to lead them to curtail output, there

is at once developed a far greater deficiency in net
investment, due to the reduction in the volume of
working capital corresponding to the lower level of
production. Thus each curtailment of production by
further reducing net investment causes a further fall
of prices, which increases the losses of those entrepreneurs who are still carrying on and thus tends to
reproduce itself in the shape of a still further curtailment.   In Chapter 30 (vii.) we have estimated the
influence of this factor in respect of the working
capital of the United States.

During the earliest phase of the slump this reduction in working capital was probably partly offset by
an increase in liquid capital as a result of the accumulation in stocks.   In the second phase, stocks usually
begin to fall, and this prolongs the period during which
the aggregate deficiency of net investment exceeds the
deficiency of fixed investment.   But in the end a point
comes—because firms cannot keep together their organisation and their connections if they cut output
any further, even though they are making a loss, or
because the expectations of the business world change,
or because stocks are at a minimum, or, if for no other
reason prior in time, because the general impoverish-
ment of the community reduces saving—when neither
working capital nor liquid capital are falling any
further ; and when this point is reached the slump
touches bottom.

For the dis-investment in working capital, which so
greatly aggravates the deficiency of investment in fixed
capital, only proceeds so long as production is in the
act of slumping.   When production has got down to a
low level and remains there, the reduction of working
capital ceases ; for the latter is a function, not of a
low level of output, but of a declining level of output.
Thus, as soon as the Index of Production ceases to fall
further, the deficiency of net investment is immediately decreased, which by itself tends in the direction

of raising prices and diminishing losses ; for the low
level reached by prices is one which is only possible so
long as output is declining, and when output ceases
to decline prices must necessarily take a kick upwards
again. Not only so—as soon as the Index of Production is rising again, increased investment in working capital will be necessary to balance the previous
dis-investment. During the time that this is going on,
the re-investment in working capital may balance,
partly or wholly, the deficiency of investment in fixed
capital, and the natural-rate of interest will temporarily catch up the market-rate. But as soon as the
Index of Production ceases to rise, then, if the excess
of the long-term market-rate of interest over the long-
term natural-rate has not been remedied by a decrease
of the former or an increase of the latter, again a kick-
back of prices will be started. In this way, as a result
of these self-generating secondary oscillations, an intermediate revival of quite impressive dimensions
might be staged in spite of the basic conditions being
unfavourable to a lasting recovery.

A partial recovery, therefore, is to be anticipated
merely through the elapse of time and without the
application of purposeful remedies. But if my dia-
gnosis is correct, we cannot hope for a complete or
lasting recovery until there has been a very great fall
in the long-term market-rate of interest throughout
the world towards something nearer pre-war levels.
Failing this, there will be a steady pressure towards
profit deflation and a sagging price-level. Yet the fall
in the rate of interest is likely to be a long and a tedious
process, unless it is accelerated by deliberate policy.
For the slump itself produces a new queue of " distress " borrowers who have to raise money on the
best terms available to meet their losses, particularly
governments of countries whose international equilibrium has been upset by the fall in the price of
their exports,—Australia and Brazil being notable

examples.   The thing will never cure itself by the lack
of borrowers forcing down the rate ; *for it absorbs just
as much savings to finance losses as to finance investment.*
In the second place, lenders have now been long accustomed to high rates of interest.   The war, the post-
war reconstruction, the epoch of " artificial " borrowing have kept rates up for fifteen years to a level
which would have seemed a generation ago quite
beyond reasonable probability.   Consequently a first-
class bond yielding $4\frac{1}{2}$ to 5 per cent, at a time when
the short-term rate is not much above 2 per cent, does
not strike the modern financier as the outstanding
bargain that it would have seemed to his father.   For
there are very few people whose test of the normal and
the permanent is not mainly fixed by the actual experience of the last fifteen years.

Yet who can reasonably doubt the ultimate outcome—unless the obstinate maintenance of misguided
monetary policies is going to continue to sap the
foundations of capitalist society ?   In the leading
financial countries savings are high enough, when
they are being embodied in investment and are not
being spilt in the financing of losses, to cause capital
to increase five times faster than population.   Unless
we spill our savings, how are we to go on year after
year finding an outlet for them in projects which will
yield anything approaching the present long-term rate
of interest ?   I am bold to predict, therefore, that to
the economic historians of the future the slump of
1930 may present itself as the death struggle of the
war-rates of interest and the re-emergence of the pre-
war rates.

Now, at long last, this will doubtless come by itself.
In Great Britain, perhaps £1,000,000,000, and in the
United States, perhaps £4,000,000,000 of investment
resources, not required as cash, are being held on
short-term.   Until quite lately these funds have
earned a handsome rate of interest.   In these difficult

and dangerous days their holders may be slow and reluctant to move them. But in time they will. It will bore them in time to be earning 2 per cent or 1 per cent or nothing, when they might be earning 6 per cent or 5 per cent or 4 per cent. In time the multitude will move ; and then it will suddenly be found that the supply of bonds at the present rate of interest is very strictly limited.

If, then, these are the causes, was the slump avoidable ? And is it remediable ? The causes to which we have assigned it were the outcome of policy; and in a sense, therefore, it was avoidable. Yet it is evident that the policy could not have been radically different, unless the mentality and ideas of our rulers had also been greatly changed. That is to say, what has occurred is not exactly an accident ; it has been deeply rooted in our general way of doing things.

But, granted that the past belongs to the past, need we be fatalistic about the future also ? If we leave matters to cure themselves, the results may be disastrous. Prices may continue below the cost of production for a sufficiently long time for entrepreneurs to feel that they have no recourse except an assault on the money-incomes of the factors of production. This is a dangerous enterprise in a society which is both capitalist and democratic. It would be foolish of us to come to grief at a time when the pace of technical improvements is so great that we might, if we choose, be raising our standard of life by a measurable percentage every year. It has been my rôle for the last eleven years to play the part of Cassandra, first on the Economic Consequences of the Peace and next on those of the Return to Gold ;—I hope that it may not be so on this occasion.

The level at which prices will ultimately settle down will depend on whether a fall in the rate of interest or a successful assault on the earnings of the factors of production comes first ; for, in so far as the latter comes first and an income deflation is accomplished, the equilibrium price-level, after profit deflation has come to an end, will be correspondingly lower. The risk ahead of us is, as I have suggested in Chapter 30 (viii.), lest we are to experience the operation of the " Gibson Paradox ", that is to say, of a market-rate of interest which is falling but never fast enough to catch up the natural-rate of interest, so that there is a recurrent profit deflation leading to a recurrent income deflation and a sagging price-level. If this occurs, our present régime of capitalistic individualism will assuredly be replaced by a far-reaching socialism.

The remedy should come, I suggest, from a general recognition that the rate of investment need not be beyond our control, if we are prepared to use our banking systems to effect a proper adjustment of the market-rate of interest. It might be sufficient merely to produce a general belief in the long continuance of a very low rate of short-term interest. The change, once it has begun, will feed on itself.

Of specific remedies the argument of this chapter suggests two as appropriate to the occasion. The Bank of England and the Federal Reserve Board might put pressure on their member banks to do what would be to the private advantage of these banks if they were all to act together, namely, to reduce the rate of interest which they allow to depositors to a very low figure, say $\frac{1}{2}$ per cent. At the same time these two central institutions should pursue bank-rate policy and open-market operations *à outrance*, having first agreed amongst themselves that they will take steps to prevent difficulties due to international gold movements from interfering with this. That is to say, they should combine to maintain a very low level of the short-term rate of interest, and buy long-dated securities either against an expansion of Central Bank money or against the sale of short-dated securities until the short-term market is saturated. It happens

that this is an occasion when, if I am right, one of the
conditions limiting open-market operations *à outrance*
does not exist ; for it is not an occasion—at least not
yet—when bonds are standing at a price above reasonable expectations as to their long-term normal, so that
they can still be purchased without the prospect of a
loss.

Not until deliberate and vigorous action has been
taken along such lines as these and has failed, need
we, in the light of the argument of this Treatise, admit
that the Banking System can *not*, on this occasion,
control the rate of investment and, therefore, the level
of prices.

CHAPTER 38

PROBLEMS OF SUPERNATIONAL MANAGEMENT

In Chapter 36 we have reached the tentative conclusion that, subject to certain safeguards and compromises for securing a reasonable measure of domestic autonomy, the ideal currency of the immediate future should probably conform to an international standard.

If this be granted, then there are great and obvious advantages in retaining gold as our international standard, provided, as we have previously expressed it, that we can retain the metal as a constitutional monarch, wholly subject to the will of a cabinet of Central Banks who would hold the sovereign power. For by this means we shall—though at some expense, measured by the annual cost of mining monetary gold—give confidence to the timid and perhaps accelerate the adoption of scientific methods by several decades.

The ultimate problem before us is, therefore, the evolution of a means of managing the value of gold itself through the agency of some kind of supernational institution.

In an earlier draft of this chapter, prepared in June 1929, I had written that, if the falling tendency of wholesale Index-Numbers were to be continued much further, the evil would reach the dimensions of a catastrophe. It is horrible, I continued, to contemplate the waste of wealth and retardation of progress which it is fair to attribute already to the muddle, confusion and division of purpose with which the Central Banks of the world have conducted their common affairs in the years which have passed since the Resolutions of the Genoa Conference of 1922 voiced the reasonable fears and wise counsels of the most prudent opinion in Europe. The international gold standard cannot, surely, last for long, unless the Central Banks develop and practise a measure of the public spirit of which the Bank of England (however mistaken it may have been in some things) has given, under the leadership of Mr. Montagu Norman, a shining example.

Since I wrote these lines the further fall in the price-level which I then feared has taken place. For that reason, perhaps, the public opinion of the world may be getting readier to consider with a friendly eye proposals for radical change, than it was in 1925.

(i.) The Dual Problem of Supernational Management

The management of the long-period trend of the international value of gold and the avoidance of short-period fluctuations on either side of this trend are two distinct problems. At least, they are distinct in the sense that methods which secured its long-period stability would not necessarily avoid the oscillations of the Credit Cycle ; though the two are sometimes connected in that a long-period trend, which requires induced changes in the price-level to bring it about, is one of the possible causes of short-period fluctuations, because it can only realise itself by setting up a series of oscillations round the long-period trend.

We must, therefore, distinguish sharply between these two objectives of Supernational Management. If our primary purpose is to make our present economic machine work as efficiently as possible for the production of wealth, the aim of avoiding investment disequilibria is the more important of the two. This is a reason why it might be expedient to choose for our long-period trend that type of movement which was least likely to require induced changes, and therefore least likely to interfere with the task of maintaining equality between saving and investment. But since some money-contracts are necessarily of longer duration or more resistant to induced changes than others, the question of the long-period trend also raises some problems of its own affecting expediency and equity in the distribution of incomes. With what criteria, therefore, can we furnish our Supernational Authority to guide it in the long run, over and above the daily task, with which we shall also charge it, of maintaining as close a balance as it can between Saving and Investment the world over? We shall best answer this question by gathering together the results of various discussions scattered through this Treatise.

It is much more important that the long-period movements in price-levels should be slow and steady, than that any one of the various plausible claimants to the throne should be chosen rather than another. It is a case, therefore, where, for my own part, I should be ready to bow to the majority and accept that choice which could command the largest body of support. As soon, however, as we have decided that our standard is to be international in character, the number of plausible claimants is, I think, very much reduced.

For, having settled this point, we must, it seems to me, discard all those standards of value which aim at preserving the stability of the money-value of a unit of human effort, *e.g.* at stabilising hourly-earnings rather than efficiency-earnings or earnings per unit of output. It is reasonable that an international standard should relate to the money-value of some international aggregate or collectivity of objects. But since the efficiency of human effort varies widely in different parts of the world and changes in different degrees in different places between one decade and another, there is no one standard of this type which is capable of an international application. Those who feel strongly in favour of stabilising the Earnings Standard (cf. Vol. i. p. 63) must, therefore, be advocates of a national or local standard, and not of an international standard.

The same argument serves also to dismiss any detailed or accurate version of the Consumption Standard or Purchasing Power of Money as our international standard. For this also will vary from locality to locality ; and, again, we have to admit that there is no standard of this type which is capable of an international application.

We are driven back, therefore, on some more rough-and-ready international aggregate of objects. I do not think we can do better than take (say) sixty of the standardised foods and raw materials of world-wide importance, and combine them into a weighted index-number, the aggregate importance of each article being determined by the money-value of the world output of it calculated in the producing countries, and its price by the weighted average of its f.o.b. price in these countries, each year being compared with the next by the chain-method or link relatives.

I am proposing, that is to say, that the long-period trend in the value of gold should be so managed as to conform to a somewhat crude international Tabular Standard. In the Production Index of the Economic and Financial Section of the League of Nations sixty-two commodities are taken into consideration.[1] These, with the addition perhaps of sea-freights, provide a rough indication of the broad

[1] *Memorandum on Production and Trade, 1923 to 1928-29.*

character of the sort of Tabular Standard which I have in mind. The list of commodities is as follows :

Wheat.
Rye.
Barley.
Oats.
Maize.
Rice.
Potatoes.
Beet-sugar.
Cane-sugar.
Beef and veal.
Pork.
Mutton and lamb.
Coffee.
Cocoa.
Tea.
Hops.
Tobacco.
Cotton-seed.
Linseed.
Rape-seed.
Hemp-seed.
Sesame-seed.
Soya beans.
Ground-nuts.
Copra.
Palm and palm-kernel oil (raw).
Olive oil (raw).
Cotton.
Flax.
Hemp.
Manila hemp.
Jute.

Wool.
Raw silk.
Artificial silk.
Raw rubber.
Mechanical pulp.
Chemical pulp.
Cement.
Coal.
Lignite.
Petroleum.
Pig-iron and ferro-alloys.
Steel (ingots and castings).
Copper.
Lead.
Zinc.
Tin.
Aluminium.
Nickel.
Silver.
Natural phosphates.
Potash.
Sulphur.
Natural guano.
Chilian nitrate of soda.
Nitrate of lime (Norwegian and ammoniated).
Cyanamide of calcium.
Sulphate of ammonia.
Superphosphates of lime.
Basic slag.
Sulphate of copper.

It may be interesting to add that the figures given in the League of Nations' Memorandum indicate that the value of this Tabular Standard in terms of gold fell about 7 per cent between 1926 and 1928.

The Tabular Standard would measure with accuracy neither the Consumption Standard nor the Earnings Standard, i.e. neither the Purchasing Power of

Money nor its Labour Power. But apart from its simplicity and its international character, it has, I think, three other features to recommend it.

As we have seen in Book II., the prices of commodities are likely, with the progress of technical discovery, to fall relatively to the price of services, and the wholesale standard is likely to fall relatively to the retail standard, because the latter includes a larger proportion of services of a kind not likely to be much affected by technical improvements. Consequently, stability of the Tabular Standard will mean a tendency of the Consumption Standard to rise, and, besides, the Earnings Standard will rise more than the Consumption Standard ; *i.e.* money-incomes will increase and the cost of living will tend upwards, but not as much as money-incomes. I say that this is a recommendation of the Tabular Standard, because such movements are likely on the whole to fit in with the " spontaneous " tendency of earnings, and, if so, will help to avoid the necessity of " induced " changes to counteract the " spontaneous " tendency and the short - period disequilibrium associated with such changes. For human nature is such that the urge towards higher money incomes, left to itself, will tend to be ahead of the equilibrium position.

The second reason for favouring a downward, rather than an upward, tendency of the Purchasing Power of Money and of the Labour Power of Money appeals to me, but not so much, possibly, to those who value more highly than I do the vested interest of the past. I think it desirable that obligations arising out of past borrowing, of which National Debts are the most important, should, as time goes on, gradually command less and less of human effort and of the results of human effort ; that progress should loosen the grip of the dead hand ; that the dead hand should not be allowed to grasp the fruits of improvements made long after the live body which once directed it has passed away. Thus the divergence between the Tabular Standard and the other standards will be beneficial in the long run, whilst over short periods it is not likely to be considerable. Even if the movement were fully foreseen and fully allowed for in the rate of interest obtained by lenders, no harm would be done ;—it would merely mean that the current yield on long-term securities would include a small element of sinking fund to pay off the capital sum.[1]

The third attraction which I find in the Tabular Standard lies in the way in which the aim of stabilising this standard over long periods fits in with the aim of avoiding investment disequilibria over short periods. For the wholesale index, which the International Tabular Standard would closely resemble, is the most sensitive and responds most quickly to investment disequilibria ; so that a managing authority which has its eye on the Tabular Standard as its long-period norm will be the less likely to overlook its parallel short-period responsibilities.

For the task of abolishing the Credit Cycle must be the preponderating responsibility of our Supernational Authority, and—in the present state of knowledge and opinion throughout the world—its most difficult, perhaps its too difficult, problem. This is a task in which it must collaborate with, and aid the individual efforts of, its adherent Central Banks. It can do little or nothing without them ; and how much it can do with them will depend on their collective wisdom and public spirit. Some suggestions as to the machinery which might be employed are made in the next section.

---

[1] I believe that it might be a sound principle of finance that all loans at a fixed rate of interest for a term exceeding (say) ten years should be compelled by law to take on the character of terminable annuities for a term not exceeding (say) fifty years, so that nothing would be repayable at the end of the term.

(ii.) Methods of Supernational Management

Is the system of supernational Currency Management of the future to be born ready-made or gradually evolved? Probably the latter. Nevertheless, sitting down to outline the ideal system, one naturally imagines something complete. I will, therefore, first describe what appears to me to be the minimum degree of management which would be useful, and then proceed to a more complete system. Since there is at the present time an unquestionable downward trend of gold prices, we shall primarily assume in what follows that the immediate object is to economise gold. Nevertheless, the opposite contingency might easily arise at some future time—more probably through a revolutionary discovery in the metallurgy of gold than through an abundance of new gold mines.

1. *The Minimum.*—A conference of Central Banks, convened in accordance with the long-ago recommendation of the Genoa Conference, might be asked to agree to the following broad principles of common action:

(1) All countries must agree not to admit gold (or gold certificates) into their active circulations and to retain it solely as reserve-money for Central Banks.

We have already seen (p. 297 above) that gold has been largely withdrawn from the active circulation throughout the world, more than 90 per cent of monetary gold being now held by Governments and Central Banks.[1] In the United States gold coin is still admitted to the active circulation, and gold certificates amount to practically the same thing.[2] In

---

[1] This includes U.S. Gold Certificates in the total of "held by Governments." If we reckon Gold Certificates in the active circulation as the equivalent—which they are—of gold coins, the above "ninety per cent" becomes "eighty per cent."

[2] Recently there have been circulating in the United States outside the reserves of the Federal Reserve Banks about $375,000,000 in gold coin and $950,000,000 in Gold Certificates, or a total of (say) £265,000,000, which exceeds by more than 50 per cent the gold reserves of the Bank of England.

the new French Currency law there is a dangerous clause permitting the introduction of gold into the active circulation by decree, but it has not yet been acted upon. In other quarters there is in this respect little or nothing to alter.

(2) All Central Banks must agree to accept some substitute for gold as a part of their own reserve-money, reducing—or at least varying in accordance with circumstances—the quantity of gold which they think it necessary to hold in their own vaults as a backing for a given quantity of the Central Bank-money which they create. Just as Current Money gradually became representative during the nineteenth century, so Reserve Money must gradually become representative during the twentieth.

The use of something other than gold as a part of Central Bank Reserve-money has been beginning to creep in through the employment of Exchange Standards and Exchange Management.[1] We have already discussed in Chapter 33 (pp. 262 et seq.) the part which foreign balances are allowed to play in the legal reserves of Central Banks. It is not possible, however, to give an exact statement of the part which they actually play in the total reserves of these Banks, inasmuch as they are not in every case separately stated. For example, the Bank of England does not, if and when it holds foreign bills or balances, state the amount of them, and the " Reserves in foreign exchange " published in the weekly statements of the Reichsbank do not represent the whole amount. The following figures, however—to which there would have been nothing comparable before the war—will illustrate the magnitude of the part now played by " bills and balances abroad."

In June 1929[2] the Central Banks of Europe published holdings of "bills and balances abroad" amount-

[1] Cf. Vol. i. pp. 350 et seq., and Vol. ii. pp. 316 et seq.
[2] The amounts were not materially changed a year later.

ing to about £400,000,000, of which the major items
were the following :

		£1,000,000
Bank of France		208
Bank of Italy		53
Reichsbank		18
Austrian National Bank . . .		16
Bank of Greece		15
Bank of Belgium		13
Bank of Poland		12
Swiss National Bank		11
Bank of Czechoslovakia		11

It might appear, therefore, that there is already a
decided evolutionary trend in the desired direction.
But I am afraid, nevertheless, that this appearance
is a little deceptive. Partly for the reasons given in
Chapter 21 (Vol. i. pp. 350 *et seq.*), the popularity of
methods of Gold Exchange management seem to be
waning. Partly, also, this may be due to the feeling
that the use of these methods is a sign of weakness
or is characteristic of countries which do not aspire to
be financial centres on their own account. In order,
therefore, to set a standard and a fashion it is desirable
that *all* Central Banks should be expressly allowed a
discretion to hold up to at least a half of their legal
reserve-requirements in the shape of balances with
other Central Banks or, preferably, with the Bank of
International Settlements.

(3) The legal reserve-requirements of all Central
Banks should be subject to variation by an amount
not exceeding 20 per cent of the normal upwards or
downwards on the recommendation of a Committee of
the Central Banks.

Some provision of this kind would be of great importance as providing a means by which the collectivity of Central Banks could increase or decrease,
when necessary, the effective supply of gold.

(4) In all countries the margin between the Central
Bank's minimum buying price and its maximum sell-

ing price for gold should be widened to 2 per cent. The usefulness of this provision has been already explained in Chapter 36 above.

None of these provisions, with the exception of the first, which does not depart materially from existing practice, *compels* any Central Bank to alter its behaviour. They would not be forced to keep a part of their reserves in foreign balances; there is no limitation on the excess reserves which they might keep in practice; and there is nothing to prevent them from announcing their readiness for the time being to buy and sell gold at closer prices. The object is, rather, to free Central Banks from a compulsory conformity to rigid rules, the strict observance of which is neither in their own interest nor in the common interest. A joint recommendation of general rules on the above lines, as being something which conforms to the requirements of safety, respectability and public spirit, might serve to allay the timidity or nervousness which a single bank acting in isolation might feel in adopting them, even if it was convinced in its own mind that the direction was a right one.

Such rules would not prevent individual banks from making the situation difficult for their neighbours by absorbing and hoarding more than their reasonable share of the world's supply of gold; I see no way of doing that. But they would set up certain standards the adoption of which would at least render major fluctuations in the purchasing power of gold less probable and diminish the likelihood of an instability of credit. For the first three rules would make possible so great an economy of gold as to remove the risk of a shortage for many years to come; whilst the fourth rule would allow Central Banks sufficient latitude of action—which they have not got at present—to handle their short-period domestic credit situations, when these domestic situations were not of a uniform character the world over.

2. *The Maximum.*—A satisfactory system of supernational management of the value of gold would need, however, to go much further than this—especially if we are to find any effective remedy against the Credit Cycle. The ideal arrangement would surely be to set up a Supernational Bank to which the Central Banks of the world would stand in much the same relation as their own member banks stand to them. It is a waste of time to draw up an elaborate paper constitution for such a Bank long in advance of its entering the field of practical politics. But an outline constitution may be the best way of indicating the kind of thing that is desirable:

(1) I see no necessity for the Bank to have any initial capital, but its liabilities should be guaranteed by the adherent Central Banks.

(2) It should do no business except with Central Banks. Its assets should consist of gold, securities and advances to Central Banks, and its liabilities of deposits by Central Banks. Such deposits we will call Supernational Bank-money (or S.B.M. for short).

(3) S.B.M. should be purchasable for gold and encashable for gold at fixed prices differing from one another by 2 per cent.

(4) The amount of the Bank's gold reserve should be determined at its own discretion and should not be compelled to exceed any fixed minimum percentage of its liabilities.

(5) The national moneys of all Central Banks adhering to the Supernational Bank should be compulsorily purchasable and encashable in terms of S.B.M. on the same terms as gold, *i.e.* at a difference of 2 per cent between the buying and the selling price. Furthermore, it would be very desirable that national moneys should *only* be encashable in terms of S.B.M. ; so that S.B.M. would become the international standard of first instance, with gold, into which S.B.M. would be itself encashable, as the ultimate standard.

(6) S.B.M. would reckon equally with gold for the purposes of the legal reserves of the adherent Central Banks.

(7) The adherent banks would be expected at the start to set up an account with the Supernational Bank by the deposit of a substantial amount of gold ; thereafter their holdings of S.B.M. would be replenished by further deposits of gold, by transfer of S.B.M. from other Central Banks, and by borrowing from the Supernational Bank.

(8) The Supernational Bank would establish a Bank-rate at which the adherent Central Banks could borrow from it for periods not exceeding three months at a time. The extent to which any adherent Bank would be allowed to avail itself of these discount facilities might be determined by reference to the amount of that Bank's average deposits with the Supernational Bank over (say) the previous three years, and initially by the amount of gold which it had deposited. For example, Banks might be entitled to discount initially up to an amount equal to that of their initial gold deposit, and after three years to the amount of their average deposits over the previous three years. But the maximum permissible proportion should, just like the Bank-rate, be re-fixed from time to time, according to the need of increasing or diminishing the total quantity of S.B.M. in the interests of the stability in its value. Thus the Supernational Bank would control the terms of credit to Central Banks in two directions—that of the Bank-rate and that of the Discount Quota, as we may call it. It would be desirable that the adherent Central Banks should normally be borrowers from the Supernational Bank and not only in emergency.

(9) The Supernational Bank should also have a discretionary power to conduct open-market operations, by the purchase or sale on its own initiative either of long-term or short-term securities, with the

assent, in the case of a purchase though not necessarily in the case of a sale, of the adherent Central
Bank in whose national money the securities in
question are payable. There would, however, be
nothing to prevent the issue of international loans in
terms of S.B.M., and this might tend to become more
usual as time went on. Then the Supernational Bank
would be free to buy or sell entirely at its own discretion.

(10) The Constitution of the Bank is a matter of
detail which need not be entered upon here. But
presumably the management should be independent,
and have a high degree of authority and discretion
in daily management, subject to the ultimate control
of a Board of Supervision consisting of representatives
of the adherent Banks.

(11) The profits of the Bank might be divided into
two parts, one of which would be placed to reserve,
and the other distributed to the adherent Banks in
proportion to their average deposits.

(12) So far I have said nothing as to the objectives
of the Bank's management. I should prefer to leave
this a matter of general directions rather than of
specific obligation. The principal directions would be
two in number. It would be the first duty of the
management of the Supernational Bank to maintain,
so far as possible, the stability of the value of gold (or
S.B.M.) in terms of a Tabular Standard based on the
principal articles of international commerce, as proposed above. Its second duty should be the avoidance, so far as possible, of general Profit Inflations and
Deflations of an international character. Its methods
of attaining these ends would be partly by means of its
Bank-rate, its Discount Quota and its open-market
policy, but largely by consultation and joint action
with and between its adherent Central Banks, who
would be expected to discuss their own credit policies
at monthly meetings of the Board of the Supernational

Bank and to act, so far as possible, on lines jointly agreed.

It is plain that one can ensure nothing by the terms of a paper constitution. The desirable objectives can only be attained through the exercise of daily wisdom by the monetary authorities of the world. But if something on the lines of the above were to be instituted, the Central Banks of the world would, I think, have an instrument to their hands with which the major objectives could be attained if they chose, and knew how, to use it.

(iii.) THE BANK OF INTERNATIONAL SETTLEMENTS

The Report on German Reparations by the experts assembled in Paris early in 1929, under the chairmanship of Mr. Owen Young, included an Annex outlining the scope and organisation of a proposed " Bank for International Settlements ". A Bank along the lines proposed has since been set up, and is in its initial months of operation as these pages go to press.

The primary purpose of this Bank is to facilitate the payment and transfer of Inter-governmental Debts arising out of the war—German Reparations, inter-allied Debts, and payments due from European Governments to the Government of the United States. But it is evidently intended—Sir Josiah Stamp, one of its progenitors, has publicly said as much—to be capable of exercising wider functions, and perhaps to fulfil the same rôle as that which I have indicated above in relation to the Supernational Management of Money. It is therefore relevant to examine its structure from this point of view.

The Annex outlining the Bank and the Statutes establishing it are long and complicated.[1] But the salient points can be summarised shortly :

---

[1] The details are conveniently set forth in Einzig's *The Bank for International Settlements*.

(1) " The objects of the Bank are to promote the co-operation of Central Banks and to provide additional facilities for international financial operations ; and to act as Trustee or Agent in regard to international financial settlements entrusted to it under agreements with the parties concerned."

(2) " The operations of the Bank shall be in conformity with the monetary policy of the central banks of the countries concerned."

(3) " The entire administrative control of the bank shall be vested in the Board of Directors ", who shall also have power by a two-thirds majority to alter certain of its statutes and the remaining statutes if " sanctioned by a law supplementing the charter of the Bank ".[1]

(4) The Directors shall consist of, or be nominated by, the Governors of the Central Banks of Great Britain, France, Belgium, Italy, Japan, Germany and the United States, which shall have two members each, except that Germany and France shall have an additional representative, and about a third of the Board shall be selected from a panel proposed by the Central Banks of certain other countries.

(5) The Bank may accept deposits from Central Banks on current account or on deposit account, may make advances to Central Banks, and shall be free to buy and sell gold, foreign exchange, bills and securities.   But no financial operation shall be carried out (except the withdrawal of funds to the introduction of which no objection had been raised) if the Central Bank concerned disapproves.

(6) The Bank is not limited in its transactions to dealing with Central Banks, provided that the Central Bank with whose nationals the transactions are made does not object.

(7) The Bank may not (a) issue notes, (b) accept bills, (c) make advances to governments (but it may

---

[1] It is not stated who or what the law-making body is for this purpose.

buy their Treasury Bills and Securities) or open current accounts in their name, (d) acquire a predominant interest in any business concern or own real property, not required for its own business, except temporarily.

(8) " The Bank shall be administered with particular regard to maintaining its liquidity ", but it is not required to hold any specified proportion of gold or bills.

(9) The Bank has a subscribed capital, and the profits are divided in prescribed proportions between its reserves, its shareholders, Central Banks which maintain long-period time-deposits with it, and the German Reparation account.

It is evident that the clauses have been drafted in wide terms, and that they would be consistent with the Bank's evolving into an organ of Supernational Monetary Management on the lines suggested above. But in this case there is a certain difficulty arising out of its constitution. The preponderant representation given to the Reparation Powers is quite out of place in a truly international institution ; yet the constitution is such that it might not be easy to alter this later on.

Criticism might also be directed against the powers allowed to the Bank to do general financial business not limited to Central Bank customers. It would be better, I think, that the Bank should be strictly confined, so far as deposits and discounts are concerned, to doing business with Central Banks and should not enter into direct relations with any other parties ; just as it is probably better that a Central Bank should be confined, apart from open-market operations, to doing business with its own Member Banks and other Central Banks. If the International Bank enters into the field of general financial business, competitive jealousies will be uselessly provoked.

We may hope, nevertheless, that we have here the

nucleus out of which a Supernational Bank for monetary management may be eventually evolved. At the
least, it provides a meeting-place where the governors
of the Central Banks of the world can acquire habits
of confidential discussion and familiarity with one
another's methods and ideas, out of which collabora-
tion and joint action may gradually grow. The future
usefulness of the Bank of International Settlements
must, however, largely depend—like that of several
other immature international institutions—on the support it receives from the United States. So long as the
American Administration feels it necessary to clear
itself before its domestic public opinion of the slightest
suggestion of unselfish action, progress must be slow.
But we may expect Americans to grow out of an attitude which is not really due to selfishness—quite the
opposite ; but to a sort of suspicion towards the older
centres of civilisation.

(iv.) CONCLUSION

In recent years most people have become dissatis-
fied with the way in which the world manages its
monetary affairs. Yet they distrust the remedies
which are suggested. We do badly ; but we do not
know how to do better. I do not think that practical
bankers are primarily blameworthy for this. There is
a famous passage by Bagehot where, after complain-
ing that the directors of the Bank of England were
not acquainted with right principles, he continues :
" They could not be expected themselves to discover
such principles. The abstract thinking of the world
is never to be expected from persons in high places ;
the administration of first-rate current transactions is
a most engrossing business, and those charged with
them are usually but little inclined to think on points
of theory, even when such thinking most nearly concerns those transactions." Yet when we turn to the

work of economists, whose proper business is " the abstract thinking of the world ", it is noticeable how little serious writing on monetary theory there is to be found anywhere, prior to the stirrings of the last few years. The events of recent years have—it is true—stirred up much thinking on these matters, which will yield its fruit in due time. But it is characteristic of economics that valuable and interesting work may be performed and steady progress made for many years, and yet that the results will be almost useless for practical purposes until a certain degree of exactness and perfection has been reached. Half-baked theory is not of much value in practice, though it may be half-way towards final perfection. Thus it would not be true to say that there has been sound instruction available, the conclusions of which practical men have neglected.

Is monetary theory now ready to take the critical leap forward which will bring it into effective contact with the real world ? I believe that the atmosphere in which active economists are now working in Great Britain, the United States, Scandinavia, Germany and Austria, is favourable to such a result. And not only in monetary theory. Marshall's *Principles of Economics* was published forty years ago, and most of the thinking in it was done more than fifty years ago. For thirty years after its publication the progress of economic theory was very slight. By 1920 Marshall's theory of economic equilibrium had been absorbed but not materially improved. Unfortunately Marshall, in his anxiety to push economic theory on to the point where it regains contact with the real world, was a little disposed sometimes to camouflage the essentially static character of his equilibrium theory with many wise and penetrating *obiter dicta* on dynamical problems. The distinction between the long period and the short period is a first step towards the theory of a moving system. But now at last we are, I think,

on the eve of a new step forward, which, if it is made
successfully, will enormously increase the applicability
of theory to practice ;—namely, an advance to an
understanding of the detailed behaviour of an economic system which is not in static equilibrium.   This
Treatise, in contrast to most older work on monetary
theory, is intended to be a contribution to this new
phase of economic science.

But before we can either perfect our theory or
apply it with safety to practical issues, there is another
kind of knowledge which we need to increase;—namely,
exact quantitative information concerning contemporary economic transactions.   In this respect—in
Great Britain at least—the practical bankers are open
to much more blame.   All the pioneer work—and in
the last five years much of it of the highest quality—
has been done in the United States, under the auspices
sometimes of the Federal Reserve Board (directed by
Dr. Stewart, Dr. Goldenweiser and others) and sometimes of semi-private bodies such as the National
Bureau of Economic Research, the Harvard Bureau
of Business Research and the Harvard Economic
Society.   The collection and arrangement of comprehensive statistics is of vast importance " in order to
eliminate impressionism", as Dr. Miller of the Federal
Reserve Board has expressed it.[1]   In Great Britain,
on the other hand, our banks—the Bank of England
and the Big Five alike—have, until recently, looked
on the economic inquirer as though he were the
policeman in the pantomime who warns the fellow
under arrest that " everything he says will be taken
down, altered and used in evidence against him ".

---

[1] " Impressions ", he went on to say, giving evidence before the Committee on Stabilisation (U.S. Congress, 1927), p. 700, " inevitably play a
very large rôle in human affairs, but in my judgment they play too big a
rôle in some of our administrative proceedings in America.   And it is desirable for everyone concerned with the business of administration who can
set up competent scientific apparatus, to do so, in order to be relieved of
guess-work."   Impressions, I would add, play a still greater rôle in every
other country.

Or I would liken them to doctors refusing to collect or supply statistics of birth and of mortality and of the incidence of health and of disease, partly on the ground that to disclose such information would be a breach of confidence towards their patients, and partly lest use might be made of the information to assist their competitors or to reflect on their professional competence. They have not merely maintained a reasonable reserve towards the fluctuating conclusions of an imperfect and undeveloped science; they have —until recently—done little or nothing to facilitate its improvement. Elsewhere, at Geneva, the Economic and Financial Section of the League of Nations and the International Labour Office have made brave efforts, but they have been limited by their dependence on what figures happen to have been collected by authorities other than themselves; whilst in Whitehall the statistical departments of the Board of Trade and the Ministry of Labour have been hampered by inadequate staff and resources.

In the case of monetary science there is a special reason why statistics are of fundamental importance to suggest theories, to test them and to make them convincing. Monetary Theory, when all is said and done, is little more than a vast elaboration of the truth that " it all comes out in the wash ". But to show this to us and to make it convincing, we must have a complete inventory. That the amount of money taken by the shops over the counter is equal, in the aggregate, to the amount of money spent by their customers; that the expenditure of the public is equal, in the aggregate, to the amount of their incomes *minus* what they have put on one side :—these simple truths and the like are those, apparently, the bearing and significance of which it is most difficult to comprehend.

INDEX

Printed in Great Britain by R. & R. CLARK, LIMITED, *Edinburgh.*